LOSING TRACK

BY JOHN NELSON

AN INSIDER'S STORY OF BRITAIN'S RAILWAY TRANSFORMATION FROM BRITISH RAIL TO THE PRESENT DAY 1968 TO 2019

Published by New Generation Publishing in 2019

Copyright © John Nelson 2019

First Edition

The author asserts the moral right under the Copyright, Designs and Patents Act 1988 to be identified as the author of this work.

All Rights reserved. No part of this publication may be reproduced, stored in a retrieval system or transmitted, in any form or by any means without the prior consent of the author, nor be otherwise circulated in any form of binding or cover other than that which it is published and without a similar condition being imposed on the subsequent purchaser.

ISBN: 978-1-78955-667-4

www.newgeneration-publishing.com
New Generation Publishing

CONTENTS

INTRODUCTION 1

ACKNOWLEDGEMENTS 5

CHAPTER ONE: 1968-81: A good grounding: Working on the front Line... 7

An autobiographical account of early years at British Rail

CHAPTER TWO: 1981-97: The Advent of the Commercial Railway: my part in its creation 28

An autobiographical account of BR's move to Business Sectors and privatisation

CHAPTER THREE: The Railways after BR: I go 'private' 49

An autobiographical account of life in the private sector

CHAPTER FOUR: 1981 – 1992: The Commercialisation of British Rail... 63

The battle for the creation of Business Sectors in British Rail

CHAPTER FIVE: To Vertical Integration and Back 93

The creation of vertically integrated businesses and their abolition as British Rail is privatised

CHAPTER SIX: Letting the first franchises.................. 125

The inside story of the competition for the first franchises

CHAPTER SEVEN: Franchises get off the ground – some fly, some crash, one burns.. 177

How the first franchises fared

CHAPTER EIGHT: The death of privatisation?........... 212

The collapse of Railtrack and increasing Government control of franchises

CHAPTER NINE: It's Not Going Well: Let's Have a Review 240

How various crises prompted reviews to reform the industry's structure and how they failed.

CHAPTER TEN: What Next? 280

What could and should be done to improve the industry's structure

ABOUT THE AUTHOR 294

INTRODUCTION

This book describes how Britain's passenger railways have evolved over the last 50 years; and does so from the perspective of someone who has been centrally involved. It plots the story of how and why they developed from being a traditional post-war nationalised industry that was hierarchically-structured and monolithic, to the diverse and fragmented public private partnerships that exist today. It provides an insider's view of how a fundamentally production led railway evolved to become one that by the time of its privatisation in 1997 was commercial and market based. It describes what it was like to be involved in the process of privatisation itself and tracks the industry's development to the present day. Along the way it discusses franchising and the various models adopted to manage the rail infrastructure. It considers what has worked and what hasn't.

The narrative is semi-autobiographical in that it describes events in the context of my own railway career, which spans one of the most exciting and controversial periods in railway history: one in which I have had the good fortune to be centrally involved. However, in defining the views expressed in these pages I have also taken on board the opinions and experiences of many of the other key players who have been involved and with whom I have had the pleasure of working over the years. I am immensely grateful to them for their time and openness in helping me determine the book's account of events and personalities; and of its conclusions. Ultimately the opinions expressed in these pages are mine.

The book does not seek to prove the value of private over public ownership or the opposite, although at a time when this remains a central theme of British politics there are certainly some aspects that the author would wish the politicians to take note of in developing their own policies. One of my personal disappointments has been the extent to which they have not taken on board the professional views of railway people in developing their own preferred industry models. This needs to change although I live in the hope rather than the expectation that it will.

Ownership and Government control remain hotly contested political issues with outcomes often determined by political preference rather than practicality. Consequently 'nationalisation' is as controversial a proposition now as 'privatisation' was in the 1990s. It often seems that the way the railway is run is made to fit whatever ownership model is preferred politically. This does not always make for an effective railway, especially when its effectiveness is not judged simply by whether the trains run on time but by whether it meets the social, environmental and economic demands of the country. These are changing rapidly and must also take account of the regions and nations of this country too. The concept of the public interest is much more nuanced than it was 50 years ago.

I make no apology for starting with three short autobiographical chapters. In one sense the experiences, events and personalities described in these early chapters justify my own credentials for what follows. In describing the career of one railwayman, I hope that the autobiographical narrative provides a vivid picture of how the railway that I joined in 1968 has changed and sets the scene for a description of the more critical events that have occurred. Because I have been fortunate enough to work alongside many of the key game changers in the industry and to have managed many of the major changes myself, I hope that my personal experience over the last 50 years can contribute something to the reader's understanding of events.

After a period of getting to know the railways when I joined from university in 1968 and then operating at the grass roots for 10 years, I subsequently worked for Sir Robert Reid in the 1980s when he was forging great change in the industry. In the 1980s and 1990s I ran large sections of the railways whilst further major changes were taking place, and then in the mid-1990s I was responsible for turning the railway's largest organisation, Network South East, into the multi-company, multi-franchise industry matrix that came to represent the privatised railway in 1997. In the process I chaired 13 train operating companies and, after these were franchised, as a consultant I was centrally involved in advising the Strategic Rail Authority (and its predecessor OPRAF), the Department for Transport, the Office of Rail Regulation, Transport Scotland, Transport for London and other public bodies on many aspects of railway organisation and structure. The consulting company I set up at that time managed franchise bidding on behalf of a number of private sector clients, including providing strategic advice on UK market entry to several foreign state owned railway companies. I also served on the Board of Sir Roy McNulty's Value for Money Study of the railways, his report being published in 2011.

As a Non-Executive Director of Laing Rail for 10 years after privatisation I saw first-hand at Chiltern Railways what could be achieved on a franchised railway; conversely, in a similar capacity on South Eastern Trains following the sacking of French-owned Connex, I was able to observe how franchising could also go badly wrong. Along the way I was deeply involved at Hull Trains in establishing the first open access passenger train company in Britain enabling me to understand the profile of running an entirely risk based private company without recourse to public subsidy. The impact of the Hatfield, Potters Bar, and Great Heck tragedies all affected this company's operations directly, demonstrating clearly that the risks were real and not theoretical. All of these experiences also provided a valuable insight into the operator/infrastructure interface with Railtrack and Network Rail as well as the dynamics of on-rail competition.

At the time of publication I am still involved in various advisory roles in the industry and remain as interested in it as ever. I hope the reader will find this book of interest too; but beyond that, in the context of the latest review of railway structure ordered by the Secretary of State, I hope it can also be seen as a contribution. The reader will not have to be too discerning to notice that the history of the last half century is full of cautionary tales.

ACKNOWLEDGEMENTS

I am especially grateful to James Dark, until recently Associate Editor of "Passenger Transport Magazine" and a former Editor of "Transit Magazine", for his assistance with the writing and editing of the book; and for undertaking several aspects of the research.

I am also immensely grateful to Janet Reid, daughter of Sir Robert, who provided me with material from his personal archive as well as her own personal reminiscences of her father.

Others who were kind enough either to allow me to interview them at length or who otherwise contribute thoughts included Neil Atkins, Cyril Bleasdale, Ian Buchan, the late Brian Burdsall, Euan Cameron, John Edmonds, Dick Fearn, Giles Fearnley, Robin Gisby, Richard Goldson, Chris Green, Terence Jenner, Mike Jones, Jeremy Long, Nick Newton, John Palmer, Frank Paterson, Gordon Pettitt, Adrian Shooter, Martin Shrubsole, Anthony Smith, Chris Stokes, and Peter Trewin.

CHAPTER ONE

1968-81: A good grounding: Working on the front Line

I joined British Rail as a graduate management trainee in 1968, a year in which to many the railways appeared to be in terminal decline. At 9%, the passenger railway's market share was about half the level it had been only 16 years earlier. The network had been reduced by roundly a third over the preceding decade and in the coming years there would be talk of further cutbacks and, in one extreme case, of turning the main lines into roads. These were the days of carefree motoring. Motorways were in their infancy with massive expansion imminent and by the 1980s railways were not being seen as an asset that could fulfil an expanding societal and environmental role but as a drain on national resources. As a nationalised industry BR was prey to the Government's regulation of the economy. Funding could rise when there was a perceived need to stimulate economic growth but at other times, and increasingly from 1970 to the mid-90s, cutting public spending was a constant theme of Government policy.

Despite the prevailing climate, railways continued to bump along at more or less the same level of market share for a number of years. Only in 1982, a year when BR suffered a series of industrial disputes, did it dip lower. Notwithstanding the musings of the more extreme economists and the politicians' tendency to view them as a problem rather than a potential solution, railways stubbornly maintained their position in the transport firmament – and to an important extent, the affection of the public.

Not that there was unanimity about the nature of the "problem". In contrast to a greater consensus that was to emerge in the late 1990s there were distinctly different political attitudes displayed by the main parties in the period that preceded it. Labour, the Party mostly in Government during the 1960s and 70s, attempted to define the railways in a social and wider economic context. Barbara Castle's 1968 Transport Act encapsulated values which encouraged me as an undergraduate looking for a job with a social purpose to apply to join BR's Management Training Scheme. The establishment of Passenger Transport Authorities in the major conurbations was a progressive move that can be seen to have been immensely successful for integrated public transport in general and railways in particular. They continue to be so.

In the 1970s Labour Governments put in place valuable funding structures around the railways, notably one that came to be known by the acronym PSO. The Public Service Obligation was a grant; the first real attempt to recognise the social role of railways where they remained unprofitable in simple financial terms. By implication the rest of the railway was now seen as more 'commercial', in competition with other modes of transport. However, the creation of a financially ring-fenced 'social railway' meant that strict financial disciplines could be applied there too. There began a process that was to accelerate in subsequent years; of considering the various constituent parts of the railway in terms of their direct costs and revenues.

None of this was remotely obvious to me on the morning of 16th September 1968 when I travelled down the Great Western Main Line to Bristol to meet my new employers for the first time. On a misty autumn day the platform signs on arrival at the first station en route advertised my emergence into the time warp that was Swindon. Surely here was a place that in the late 1960s encapsulated the declining railway more than anywhere else; one that had changed little in physical form from the railway Brunel himself had created yet one that was now under threat. The vista of the dismal station buildings was followed by my first view of the vast GWR locomotive works on the Bristol side of the town offering images of a railway just as it had been over a century ago. As my train edged westwards slowly and with reluctance it was soon greeted by another major physical manifestation from the age of Brunel. As we entered the Box Tunnel I recalled that my great grandfather had started work on this railway in the 1880s and that his great grandfather had moved from Scotland to apply his skills as a stone mason in the construction of this feat of Victorian engineering. I reflected on the railway's incongruity in the otherwise modernising era of the 1960s. Yet here too was a reminder of its history, its traditions; even of its permanence.

The range and extent of railway activities remained vast and all-embracing and the two year management training programme that I entered covered all the bases. Apart from the absence of steam locomotives, which had finally been withdrawn the year before, this was a railway my forefathers would have recognised. From parcels and freight depots with their weighbridges, trolleys and tow trucks, to marshalling yards and isolated Devonian milk sidings, this railway hadn't really changed. Even the Scillonian ferry remained under the wing of what one of my later colleagues would refer to as "the mother railway". The captain of that vessel would sometimes break his journey at my lodgings in Exeter, half way between London and his home station of Penzance.

Neither had this nationalised railway forgotten its private sector company roots and traditions. The Area Manager's organisation at Exeter to which I was attached covered the most splendid part of South Devon and had recently been remapped to combine the Great Western Main Line and part of the old Southern Railway routes from Waterloo to Devon and Cornwall. Although this epitomised the geographical, functional approach to BR's operations in those days, there remained intense rivalry amongst those who had worked for the two private companies. When the Southern part was 'acquired' by the Western Region many files and records at Exeter Central were burned to prevent them "falling into the wrong hands". At the same time, a visible reminder of the dramatic technical changes taking place existed in the form of a graveyard of recently retired steam locomotives at Exmouth Junction, a stark contrast to the usually double headed main line trains hauled by the spanking new Hymek diesel hydraulic locomotives that operated between Paddington and the West of England. *Western Zulu* was a particular favourite of mine.

Historically significant traffic flows acted as a reminder of the important place that the railway continued to play. The problem was that they were declining. Before the days of package holidays to the Costas, overnight trains would arrive from towns and cities in the North and Midlands with passengers seated in standard coaches en route to resorts in Devon and Cornwall. These would start arriving at Exeter during the small hours of the morning and would be interspersed with what were known as "brute trains"[1] conveying parcels from mail order companies in Bradford and Sunderland destined for homes in the small towns and villages of south Devon.

Even in the wake of Beeching, several country branch lines remained active and isolated groups of staff could be found at signal boxes and milk sidings dotted about the Devon countryside. In my first week I acted as 'shotgun' accompanying a manager distributing pay packets in a way that was reminiscent of an ancient barter system as he traded eggs, honey and chickens, and delivered them in turn to other members of staff elsewhere on the round. The

---

[1] BRUTE was the acronym for British Rail Universal Trolley Equipment, a clunky method of conveying parcels in bulk on trains and for distribution to road vehicles for delivery to people's homes.

signalmen at Exeter Riverside trapped otters and the skins were hung up on redundant parts of the lever frame to dry out. Practically all the railway staff had other occupations; bed and breakfast accommodation or smallholdings in the main. They were friendly, welcoming people and I fell in love with the railway family straight away.

It was quickly apparent that the underlying management preoccupation was the financial pressure created by declining industries on which the railway had relied; and by the decreasing dependence folk had on public transport. There was heavy emphasis on the need to reduce costs which was often seen simplistically as the need to rationalise the infrastructure. This was exemplified by two situations I encountered, the first being a proposal to withdraw passenger services between Exeter and Okehampton because revenues did not cover the costs of operation. The calculations, based on Government approved costing systems, allocated all costs to this service despite the fact that the line remained open for the supply of railway ballast from Meldon Quarry which lay beyond Okehampton in the lee of Dartmoor. Decades later services were restored when more sensible costing rules were applied.

Secondly, I was charged with evaluating the feasibility of closing the signal box at Exeter Riverside Yard, it being thought that declining freight traffic could be handled just as easily by shunting staff operating a simplified form of signalling controlled by point levers and a ground frame. I was able to demonstrate feasibility and furthermore that the layout could be simplified to facilitate operations and reduce infrastructure costs. Those who suggest that the railways then were overburdened by tradition and tolerated inefficiency are not entirely right. Certainly they had to deal with the legacy of traditional traffic but it is wide of the mark to assert that inefficiency was always tolerated. It is forgotten that the railway was by law a 'common carrier'. It could not pick and choose from the profitable and loss making traffics. It was Barbara Castle who put a stop to this.

Nevertheless BR's acceptance of rules for negotiating productivity changes meant they could not always be implemented without opposition from the trade unions. BR was not unique in this respect and in fact had inherited many of these traditions from the former private railway companies. Neither were its practices much different from other large industries, whether nationalised or privately owned. 'Restrictive practices' were endemic in British industry at this time and in 1969 I had an early taste of what they meant.

The same 1968 Transport Act that had attracted me to the industry separated parts of BR's goods traffic and placed substantial elements in the ownership of a new, largely road based, National Freight Corporation in acknowledgement of the changing profile of freight logistics. The NFC had a parcels or 'sundries' division called National Carriers (NCL) which was given control of the road vehicles that collected and delivered all parcels – including those that continued to be transported by BR passenger train. It was suspected that NCL was prioritising its parcels in preference to BR's and I was remitted to find out. My project involved visiting West of England depots to observe the way traffic was handled following the arrival of the respective BR and NCL parcels trains. The suspicions proved to be right. At depot after depot the procedure was the same. Road delivery vehicles were loaded up with both traffics but in such a way that NCL's got priority. In rural areas this meant that BR parcels arriving in the early hours that could have been delivered from about 9am the same day (effectively an overnight delivery from London, for example) were left for up to three days until the next delivery to that area. My report formed the basis of a new contract between BR and NCL in which a fairer arrangement was agreed but the situation exemplified the drag effect that restrictive operating practices had on the quality of service experienced by the customer, not to mention efficient operation of the service. This practice was inherent in the split company structure but there were also shades of restrictive labour practices. Many jobs were tied up in this inefficient methodology and the unions had a strong grip on certain railway departments, particularly at the larger locations. I was specifically instructed not to observe operations at the Western Region's two most militant depots – Paddington and Bristol – for fear that the unions would think I was undertaking a time and motion efficiency study and call strike action.

Other developments were more positive and in retrospect it can be fairly said that the late 1960s were a period when the role of railways was being reconsidered in the context of transport as a whole. The 1968 Act was not just about railways; it also had a focus on road transport including new licensing standards for lorries. New Testing and Plating Regulations imposed more exacting safety standards on road hauliers who saw them as detrimental to their business. Yet at the same time motorway construction was underway everywhere, including the M4 and M5, making road haulage much quicker than rail. Another project I was given was to assess the likely impact of these developments on the West of England Division's freight business. Obviously the construction of the motorways was an adverse factor for railways but the new plating regulations worked in their favour. This was the first time I had been able to undertake a project that was both interesting and intellectually demanding. It involved visiting all kinds of freight customers from Mr Kiplings Cakes to Bowyers Sausages. The report did influence BR's approach to road competition. The point to register though is that railway management was alive to commercial forces and concerned to react to them.

In another project I recommended that spare engineering components for the Bath Road locomotive maintenance depot at Bristol could be more efficiently delivered by road and the traditional practice of sending them by rail was cancelled. This was further evidence of an open minded approach to management and a willingness to eliminate inefficiency.

In 1970 the West of England Division initiated the railway's first attempt at what became known as market pricing, pitching fares according to demand and competition. I was involved in reviewing the competitive context for railway fares and the outcome was that these moved away from being simply mileage based. Financial and competitive pressures encouraged a more innovative approach to generating revenue, at the same time starting to move BR towards being a more commercial, market orientated business. Since then market pricing has spread across the whole rail network. Although today this is seen by critics as unnecessarily complex (and perhaps it is), it does go some way to explaining why the railway has been able to boost passenger numbers. Many fares on offer are now much cheaper than might otherwise be the case.

The railway then was in transition and doing much to face up to its challenges through a combination of cost and marketing initiatives. I consider myself fortunate to have been exposed to these issues and it speaks well of BR that it was prepared to set challenging projects to young graduates that placed a great deal of confidence in their ability to tackle them and which were clearly trying to address the financial and commercial realities of the time in innovative ways. The breadth and depth of training given at that time was of an order that provided a comprehensive appreciation of the railway as a total system, a perspective which in the years after privatisation became so diminished that it detracted from the overall efficient functioning of the industry. It still does. Given the fragmented industry that was established by the Railways Act 1993 an overall rail industry training scheme would have been worth its weight in gold. Sadly a lack of perceived demand (in itself a poor reflection of the value system then in play) meant that it didn't happen.

Safety was another aspect of railways that was imbued in the management culture from the very start and which featured strongly in training programmes. It was re-enforced on me not just by classes and examinations but also by the experience of two serious train accidents that occurred whilst I was in the West of England. The first of these was between Bristol and Gloucester on 8th March 1969 when part of a freight train (the 0750 from Washwood Heath to Stoke Gifford) derailed at Ashchurch travelling at excessive speed and ploughed into the 1040 Bristol-Newcastle express, killing two passengers and injuring another 30. I attended the public inquiry in Cheltenham. Such inquiries always started with a minute's silence to remember the accident victims, something that brought home in a very poignant way the reality of the risks inherent in railway operations. The second inquiry followed an accident that had occurred before I joined the railways, on 13th June 1967. In this case a passenger train derailment was caused by the buckling in heat of a continuously welded rail at Somerton on the main Berks and Hants line near Taunton. Continuous welding of railway tracks was a relatively new innovation and replaced the age old practice of expansion joints between rails. It was decided that as management trainees we would benefit from attendance at the public inquiry which was held at Ilminster, Somerset. I felt privileged to be exposed to such an experience at a very early stage in my career. Following a tragic accident at Cowden (Kent) in which people were killed much later in my career when I was Managing Director of Network South East, I experienced myself the stress of being the principal BR witness at a public inquiry.

For someone who as an undergraduate less than two years earlier had been oblivious to their complexities these experiences and exposures were invaluable means of acquiring an early appreciation of the railways as a system. The interaction of the various component parts was clear. The methods and processes applied to make them work together would become central management themes during the whole of my railway career. They remain so today.

In 1970 I received my first management appointments, seen then as an extension of training and designed to induce practical experience of the railway and provide a test bed to develop management skills. Initially I found myself at Slough. My posting as Assistant Area Manager (Commercial) meant that I was nominally in charge of all commercial activities in this fairly small area. I say "nominally" because my experience was very limited. The idea was that I should learn. I knew Slough well as I had taken my A Levels at its Grammar School five years earlier. The Area extended from West Drayton to Maidenhead and included a freight branch to Colnbrook (more recently canvassed as a possible link to Heathrow Airport) and the intermediate stations of Iver, Langley, Burnham, Taplow and Maidenhead where there was a branch line to Marlow via Bourne End. Slough, the biggest station, also had a branch line connection, to Windsor & Eton Central.

At the time I was too busily occupied in the daily routines to reflect much on whether or not the way things were organised made sense. The form of organisation remained geographical, essentially covering a discrete section of railway controlled from a single signal box at Slough. In those days, most BR Areas were established on a similar basis – fundamentally a geography that coincided with railway operations in a defined signalling control area. Everything that happened in the Area was prioritised operationally. Commercial activity was of secondary importance. There was no marketing role and no focus on any individual commercial sector. Mine was essentially a customer service role and extended to all businesses though the principal focus was on the passenger services operating through the Area – commuter trains to Paddington with occasional long distance expresses serving the towns and cities of the West Country, the Cotswolds and South Wales.

There was also significant freight activity in the Area which included a Ford van factory at Langley, a goods depot at Slough and a Fife's banana warehouse at Taplow. These activities had little in common. The Ford's traffic was distributed by transporter train on a daily basis, bananas arrived in individual van loads having started their UK journey at Southampton Docks and which on arrival required shunting into a small private siding for transfer to a local road distribution system. Whilst the Ford traffic was handled in a patently modern and efficient way, the banana operation reflected the vestiges of an inefficient and costly system of distribution entailing the retention of marshalling yards where whole trainloads were broken down for onward distribution in individual wagons, often requiring the deployment of under-employed but expensive locomotives.

Infrastructure and fleet maintenance were not part of the Area Manager's responsibilities, sustaining a separation of the railway's essential operating elements that was to continue for another 20 years. The managements responsible for the various functions appeared to have no formal meetings and it often seemed that they were working to separate agendas. Although the railway was still production rather than commercially driven, there was a further separation between the production functions themselves that was additionally inefficient. This was not what I would call a vertically integrated railway, even though it was all part and parcel of a single BR entity.

Nevertheless this was a period in which several marketing and commercial initiatives were beginning to take place, mostly initiated by the British Railways Board's

(BRB) central passenger marketing directorate, several of whom were recruited for their private sector expertise. Amongst the initiatives were the development of fares such as the Britrail Pass to attract foreign tourists and the launch of Golden Rail Holidays. I was for a short while seconded to help develop the pricing structures for both of these products. Golden Rail holidays were to become very popular and my job was to calculate the discounted rail element of the total price to be negotiated with a tour operator (Sidney De Haan), an entrepreneur based at Folkestone where he had recently established Saga, a company promoting holidays for senior citizens. This company was to develop into one of the largest in Britain and made Sidney and his son Roger multi-millionaires. The scheme worked very well for many years, generating substantial additional passenger revenues for BR.

I was soon sent down the line to Didcot as Assistant Manager in another Area that was responsible for multiple operational and commercial activities. During this period I undertook the decimalisation training of all the staff that needed to understand the new currency system when the country switched from pounds, shillings and pence. There were commuter stations at Didcot and in the Thames Valley at Pangbourne, Goring & Streatley, Cholsey & Moulsford, Appleford, Culham and Radley. There was a short freight line from Cholsey to Wallingford with a one train a day operation, and a large marshalling yard at Didcot which came into its own at Christmas as a redistribution point for parcels and mail vans destined for depots all over the country. Didcot was also home to a coal fired power station that received several merry-go-round train loads of coal from northern pits each day. Consequently it was a significant operations centre for several activities and special in the sense that it boasted a busy and complicated set of railway junctions connecting the Great Western Main Line on either side of Didcot station to Oxford, the central marshalling yards, and the power station. The points would sometimes fail and my first experience of having to hand crank and screw padlock points was at Foxall Junction. A detail too far? Not really because these multiple experiences offered valuable insights into many different aspects of railway operations and enabled me to understand more than I would otherwise have got to know if I had been working with a much narrower focus.

In 1970 I started a new job in the Western Region Chief Passenger Manager's Office at Paddington. The Chief was Geoffrey Huskisson, a remote and haughty man descended from a Nineteenth Century politician, William Huskisson, the President of the Board of Trade who was killed by Stephenson's Rocket at the Rainhill Speed Trials in 1830. My job involved planning the timetable from a commercial as opposed to operational point of view in an organisation that had been set up to recognise that the traditional operating department control of the timetable did not necessarily reflect market or customer requirements. In retrospect this can be seen as an important evolutionary development in which the railway started to move away from its traditional production led culture towards one which within a few years was to become commercially driven. A major point of interest was the responsibility we had for planning the introduction of the very first High Speed Train (HST) sets in Britain, later to be known as the InterCity 125. These were allocated to the Western Region because of the capability of the infrastructure built by Brunel, initially on the broad gauge which had required a track layout that minimised curves. The fact that as I write this book these same trains are still operating is a testimony to BR's innovation half a century ago. A number of them have even been refurbished recently to provide a brand new InterCity service in Scotland, a firm reminder of the longevity of railway assets.

Three years into my railway career the dynamics of management were increasingly focused on commercial opportunities as much as they were in handling the impact on the railway's infrastructure and economics of the declining freight and parcels traffics that were being exposed to more and more road competition. Meanwhile passenger volumes were up about 10% compared with 1968, although market share overall fell to 8% as car ownership grew at a faster rate.

In 1971 I was appointed Assistant Station Manager (Commercial) at London's Liverpool Street station, one of the country's busiest. There I became increasingly aware of some of the important human factors that were at play in running the railway. Sadly some of these reflected every bit as badly on management as they did on the trade unions. The manager in overall charge of commercial activities on what is known today as Greater Anglia kept 'gentleman's hours' which seemed to be 10 to 4 each day with two hours for lunch. He saw himself as "something in the City", a member of one of the City of London Livery Companies which in reality meant that each day he spent a long and liquid lunch at the Great Eastern Hotel with his cronies probably under the self-deception that he was furthering the interests of the railway. Meanwhile the operations function was beset with a similar drinking culture, a serious problem amongst all manner of management and staff on the railways at this time. One senior manager was notorious for his heavy drinking. Someone told me that "he was poured into his car by his chauffeur every night". The same man was responsible for implementing important changes to driver management following a serious accident that occurred when an excursion train returning to London from the Kent coast was derailed because the train took a curve in the line at excessive speed [2]. The driver had been intoxicated.

In the early 1970s there was deep suspicion and antipathy between the management and unions which I experienced at first hand. BR had recently decided to introduce a new devolved form of management known as the Field Re-organisation. The railway was to be divided into a number of new, empowered, locally-accountable entities (in this case the whole of East Anglia) in which a far more integrated approach would apply to the co-ordination of all its activities. One aspect involved the transfer of driver management to the Area Managers and away from the train depots where it had lain alongside responsibility for train maintenance since the days of steam. Using the arcane practices of the Negotiation and Consultation Machinery, the drivers' union, ASLEF, had successfully delayed implementation and in fact eventually thwarted the reorganisation, though at Area Management level it was put into effect. The whole process was accompanied by the drivers adopting a work to rule approach to disrupt the service.

About this time I was remitted to assess staff productivity at Tilbury Riverside, an exercise which again illustrated the effects of weak management and protective trade unionism. Not that the railways were unique because this was a period when the whole country seemed to be in the grip of industrial unrest. Riverside station was aptly named as the station concourse sat on stilts above the lapping waters of the Thames. It had been built for the use of TransAtlantic Ocean Liners and in the age before aeroplanes must have been a sight to behold. Along with Southampton and Liverpool, Tilbury was one of the main ports of embarkation having an enormous baggage handling hall and massive ramps that had been built to enable

---

[2] The accident occurred at Eltham Well Hall in South East London on 1st June 1972

luggage to be trolleyed up to and down from the liners' decks in all tides. The infrastructure was impressive but the station was still staffed as if liners were docking on a daily basis when the only ships at the time were occasional Mediterranean or Baltic cruisers of Soviet ownership. My report recommended a substantial reduction in staff.

Such restrictive practices were not confined to the railways. One day I discovered that a taxi company was operating a scam that involved selling on, at a grossly inflated price, the right (acquired from BR) for individual owner-drivers to ply for hire at one of the stations in my patch. Consequently I took a unilateral commercial decision to massively increase the rates. I proceeded to follow this up at other stations on the line. This action created a huge protest from the taxi companies in the area and after howls of protest reached the Divisional Office I was forced to compromise on the rates enabling the big firms to continue to profiteer at the expense of the railways and individual, largely self-employed taxi drivers.

In 1975 I attended a six week residential middle management course at the Derby School of Transport. The letter from the Principal informed me that "the course has been devised to enable you to study the elements and skills of management and their application to the Railway and its subsidiaries". It added ominously: "I am also enclosing a short guide to the technique of Discounted Cash Flow. I shall be grateful if you will read this carefully and endeavour to grasp the main principles, so that you will be able to take part in a simple exercise during the course." Intimidating and patronising at the same time! I was allocated to Syndicate Group D along with eight other people including a press officer, a computer manager, an accountant from the Shipping Division, two locomotive maintenance controllers, a headquarters passenger commercial expert, a Signal & Telecommunications Projects Engineer, and someone from Central Supplies.

Course members as a whole covered the whole gamut of railway activities, adding yet another dimension to my understanding of the interconnectivity between the various elements of the industry.

Coursework was interspersed with visits to private companies including the chemical giant ICI's Runcorn site. ICI had recently introduced a form of 'workers participation', something not much in fashion then or since, although when Theresa May became Prime Minister in 2016 she briefly advocated the concept of 'worker directors' before quickly diluting the proposals in the face of business objections. At Runcorn the only visible manifestation of 'equality' was a canteen which provided self-service meals to all directors, managers and staff. At the time BR's own catering arrangements were heavily stratified including traditional military style messes for different management grades. During this period at BRB HQ, for example, there were six levels of catering, each of them exclusive to particular grades of personnel.

Following my attendance at the Derby course I started to apply for promotions and in 1977 was appointed to another commercial post, Divisional Passenger Sales Officer in Leeds. This role was emblematic of the commercial approach then being adopted by BR embracing the marketing of passenger services throughout North and West Yorkshire as well as providing the key interface with the recently established West Yorkshire Passenger Transport Executive (PTE). During this period the earliest plans were laid for the expansion of the local rail network in West Yorkshire whilst BR itself began the introduction of the HST on the East Coast Main Line, a precursor to the electrification that was to occur 10 years later. This was the first time that I had held a budget responsibility for revenue and some devolved responsibility for setting local fares. In retrospect it is clear that BR was rapidly developing a much more dynamic approach to marketing but it is also plain that it was a one dimensional approach. There was no bottom line accounting associated with the revenue line. Cost management was a largely separate activity divided amongst several different operating and engineering functions, none of which were brought together at any meaningful level where they could be assessed against one another; even less against revenue. It also became increasingly apparent that vigorous but disconnected cost management could adversely affect revenues.

The overall management of the railways at this time remained firmly in the grip of the production functions, unsurprising in as much as BR as a whole was seen to be a massively costly organisation demanding large amounts of public money at a time when the country was in a fairly parlous financial state. All the financial pressure was being felt by the production functions, mostly under the wing of BR's five Regional General Managers – Scotland, London Midland, Eastern, Western, and Southern. Although most of the occupants of these positions and their immediate functional chiefs were in themselves well qualified, able people, the very structure of organisation encouraged a turf mentality whereby geography rather than markets ruled the thinking.

This hit me between the eyes when in 1979 I moved to Sheffield to take up the role of Divisional Passenger Manager. The Division was one of seven on the Eastern Region and abutted the London Midland Region to the south and to the west. Its Eastern Region status was as a result of its massive freight traffics which made it the largest by tonnage of any on BR. It was, however, one of the smallest Divisions geographically and its passenger activity was not substantial. Passenger services to London were routed to St. Pancras whereas the East Coast Main Line with its new compliment of High Speed Trains to and from Kings Cross was the jewel in the crown. Sheffield's Midland Main Line services including its prestige business service, The Master Cutler, comprised of hand me down stock incapable of achieving the East Coast journey times. This very quickly came to dominate my time at Sheffield where an 'unholy alliance' was at work made up of Sheffield Chamber of Commerce, Sheffield City Council, and the South Yorkshire Metropolitan County Council (then also the Passenger Transport Authority) which rejoiced in its appellation of The People's Republic of South Yorkshire.

Pressure for High Speed Trains to operate on the Midland Main Line became intense but was met with total resistance from the Eastern Region. The prevailing argument was that the Midland Main Line's curvature meant High Speed Trains could not realise their potential, which was better achieved on the East Coast. At the time the BRB under the Chairmanship of Sir Peter Parker was propounding a policy of electrification of the Midland coupled with the deployment of the tilting Advanced Passenger Train which, it was argued, could achieve the journey time improvements being sought. The difficulty was that there was no imminent prospect of electrification and at the time of writing this book that situation remains. Meanwhile many South Yorkshire passengers were taking their custom to nearby Doncaster bolstering East Coast revenues whilst depressing those on the Midland Line, further worsening the case for investment. The high point of farce was reached in 1980 when the combined alliance of local authorities offered to pay BR to convert the Master Cutler to an HST service. BR declined. It was classical territorial production led turf management and paid no regard to commercial justification.

The other major issue in Sheffield was the refusal of the South and West Yorkshire PTEs to provide financial support for the cross-boundary local services that ran between Sheffield and Huddersfield via Penistone. BR's view was that under the 1968 Transport Act the PTEs were obliged to fund these local services through a so called Section 20 Agreement; if not they would be withdrawn. However, BR's position was compromised by its contemporaneous decision to close the freight route between Sheffield and Manchester, a proposal that was progressing in the teeth of trade union and local political opposition. The Penistone-Sheffield passenger service ran over the southern section of this route, the so-called MSW (Manchester, Sheffield, Wath), and the proposal to withdraw it put the South Yorkshire politicians in a difficult position. Failure to provide financial support could be seen as contributing to the closure of local railway depots, notably at Wath-upon-Dearne, once a major centre for the distribution of coal to power stations in Lancashire, but by then a shadow of its former self. The worst problem was the high subsidy which neither PTE was prepared to pay, unsurprising given the financial pressures they themselves were facing from central Government. BR brought matters to a head with a proposal to divert trains via Barnsley, a less direct route but one that enabled an improved service frequency between the South Yorkshire town, then its County town, and Sheffield, the largest city. This was a tactic that put South Yorkshire politicians on the spot. BR thought that it would be too difficult a solution for them to resist and simultaneously put forward a proposal to withdraw services between Penistone and Sheffield via the direct route. In those days the closure procedures for passenger services required notice to be given in sufficient time for the organisations representing passengers (then known as Regional Users Consultative Committees) to determine whether to hold a public inquiry before making a recommendation to the Secretary of State for Transport, who incidentally, was free to ignore the advice if he or she saw fit.

Penistone proved to be the most controversial closure case that had ever been made. The number of objections ran into several hundred with people writing in from all parts of the country. Public hearings were inevitable and took place over four or five days in the opulent surroundings of Huddersfield Town Hall and the Royal Victoria Hotel, Sheffield, the former city terminus of the defunct Great Central Railway. Both events were well attended and it was my job to represent BR's case. The outcome was that a re-routed service from Penistone via Barnsley would after all be funded by the PTEs. When this was introduced it proved to be popular and substantially increased the number of people using the line, especially after the local pits closed making it necessary for people to travel to surrounding towns and cities for employment. However, local sentiment for the direct line to Penistone never went away and there remains a strong lobby for its reopening as a local transport artery into the city centre to this day.

Nearly 40 years on and with controversy continuing to rage about the lack of fast connections between the cities of the North there is no doubt in my mind that, had these links remained, they would have formed the basis of the rapid passenger services between Sheffield and Manchester that are so necessary. Perhaps as the mounting costs of the much vaunted High Speed Line to the North become too great for Government to bear, they could still do so.

CHAPTER TWO

1981-97: The Advent of the Commercial Railway: my part in its creation

My job in South Yorkshire was soon done and it was time to move on. It was the back end of 1981, a year that in retrospect can be seen as pivotal to the direction the whole railway would take over the next decade. It would start with the creation of BR's business Sectors and end with privatisation, developments which I describe fully in Chapters 4 to 6. I didn't know then that I would spend the rest of my time in BR centrally involved with these events, working at its most senior levels.

Looking back it is clear that the early 1980s were a period when the struggle between the production led railway and the commercial usurper began. It took 10 years for BR to resolve and then it was broken asunder soon afterwards by the form of privatisation chosen in 1993. Despite this it is possible to trace the rail industry structure that emerged then, and which has remained fundamentally intact ever since, to the decisions taken by BR in 1980/81 to move decisively to a commercially driven railway.

When these decisions were being taken I was lucky enough to be at the centre of power within BR as Personal Assistant to the Chief Executive (Railways), Bob Reid (later Sir Robert), and was a close observer of Sectorisation. This would turn the production led railway on its head, in effect making the Regions and engineering functions suppliers to the new business Sectors. I was privy to his thinking on implementation and my subsequent postings right up to the time of privatisation were involved with its refinement, entrenchment and subsequent transformation into what came to be known as vertical integration, or sometimes as

Organising for Quality (OfQ) when the Regions, engineering functions and Sectors were merged. After the 1993 Railways Act was passed it was my job to dismantle these same integrated railway organisations on half of the entire rail network and re-arrange them into the component parts of the privatised railway.

There were several reasons for the changes that began in the early 1980s. The first was politics. There had been a change of Government in 1979 when Margaret Thatcher's Conservatives were returned. Adopting a stance towards the public sector that was essentially sceptical (hostile even) and another towards public spending that was tight, there was pressure on BR to up its game. This it did when its Labour supporting Chairman, Sir Peter Parker, (an appointee of the previous Government but with a background himself in business) pushed moves to commercialise BR much further. He had a ready ally in Bob Reid who had himself pursued a largely commercial career in the industry and who was highly critical of its production functions, many of which he had done battle with, often unsuccessfully, over the years. His knowledge of the people and power structures within BR made him the ideal man to apply the principles of commercialisation. After all he had himself held a series of posts that gave him the necessary insight into how the regional power bases worked. As a Divisional Manager (at Doncaster), Regional Deputy General Manager (Eastern Region) and General Manager (Southern) he had managed substantial and complex parts of the railway. He also knew well the principal personalities who might be expected to support or seek to undermine him.

The second impetus to Sectorisation was funding. There was huge pressure from the Thatcher Government, not just to control public spending but to reduce it very significantly. This was to lead to the wholesale privatisation of most of the country's utilities whilst in others public spending cuts were to bite hard. Reid reckoned that Sector Management would lead to both revenue expansion and cost reduction. He gave the emerging business Sectors responsibility for underwriting and approving production budgets and, although this created management conflict, it did deliver a more cost effective railway.

Parker's business background made him a natural proponent of commercial company norms and using Reid's know-how he was able to implement them. Reid frequently complained that the only point in the vast monolith that was BR where revenues and costs generated a bottom line was at his desk. Breaking these down to create bottom lines for BR's various passenger, freight and parcels businesses was achieved quickly and with increasing precision and accuracy over the next 10 years.

Not content with taking on the whole BR management hierarchy in pushing through Sectorisation – daunting enough in itself – Reid determined at the same time to implement a series of productivity changes in the teeth of trade union opposition. Although these generated a number of strikes in 1981 and 1982 his resolve saw to it that driver only operation and flexible rostering of drivers were both implemented. So although 1982 was a watershed year it was nonetheless one in which BR's finances suffered as a result of the industrial unrest. In that year passenger kilometres fell to 31 billion in what proved to be the low water mark for Britain's railways. Subsequently a combination of real terms fares increases and a significant recession in the early 1990s combined to ensure that volumes and market share remained flat during the remainder of BR's tenure. Nonetheless its reliance on Government subsidy was massively reduced.

Following my stint working directly for Bob Reid I moved into one of the new Sector roles created by his innovations. The job in question, Southern Region Parcels Manager which I took up towards the end of 1982, exemplified precisely the internal tensions then at work within BR's management structures as the reforms were introduced. There had not previously been such a post on the Region and I was given bottom line responsibility for all its related activities – Red Star parcels, Royal Mail letters and parcels post, and the distribution of newspapers. However, the job was set up as a half-way house, typical of the muddled thinking of the time so that although it had all the operational and commercial responsibilities associated with the parcels business it also had reporting lines that made no sense. I reported to the Region's Operations Manager for all station personnel and train movements but to its Freight Manager for the marketing of Red Star. This reflected a power-struggle and was a messy compromise. Commercially there was no synergy between parcels and freight and operationally parcels activities were pretty well free-standing from the generality of train working on what was primarily a commuter railway. The Region's General Manager was deemed far too important to take direct responsibility for the despised and undervalued parcels business so span breakers had to be found. Despite this, from my office redoubt in the Victory Arch at Waterloo station I was able to plot many a skirmish and campaign with my small army of excellent soldiers, operators and sales people alike, thrown together in the cause of Bob Reid's Sector Crusade.

Protecting the business from shooting itself in the foot became a prime task. In those transitional days between Regional and Sector direction of the railway, the Regional Operations Manager had control of the staff budget through three Divisional Managers[3]. Faced with target cuts to make across the board, the then powerful Divisions came up with proposals to withdraw afternoon staff at scores of stations. These would have meant that most Red Star offices would

---

[3] South Eastern with its HQ at Beckenham; South Central with its HQ at Croydon; and South Western with its HQ at Wimbledon

close at around 3pm, just before the peak hours for dispatching parcels. Such decisions would have devastated my business and I set out to stop them. What happened then was symbolic of the changes that were taking place within the industry. Divisional Managers were God-like creatures, unaccustomed to being challenged, certainly not by pip-squeaks like me; but I made my case that if these cuts went ahead they would damage the revenue much more than the savings made. The Regional Operations Manager, Alec Bath, was a shrewd operator in every sense. The fact that he ruled in my favour said that he understood the mood music in the industry was changing and within months I had also broken free of the span breakers' shackles and became a direct report of the General Manager.

In 1984 I was appointed to a new post of Business Manager (Red Star) taking bottom line responsibility for parcels nationally. My plan was to grow it through a major marketing and sales effort whilst keeping a handle on costs and resources, which my experience at Waterloo and on other Regions had shown was under threat from the operating side of management. Over a period of three and a half years Red Star's business turnover grew from around £20m to reach £80m. Profitability increased too reinforcing my experience that there was tremendous commercial management capability within the railways if only it could be released. This is what Sector Management unlocked.

I was given complete freedom to develop the business and working with the private sector deployed several notable innovations that underpinned its growth. A nationwide network of collection and delivery agents was established using the National Private Hire Association[4]. Red Star took the first 0345 telephone contact number ever issued in the UK, using it as our collection number and stimulating parcels volumes to soon reach the hundreds and thousands. A nationwide sales team of 80 was set up with

---

[4] It involved the creation of a company called Road Express

the first incentive scheme introduced anywhere on the railways. Telesales were established through a contractor and a major rebranding exercise was established to promote products which included international dispatches through a contract with DHL, a US based company.

Then in 1987 things took a very different turn for me when I was appointed General Manager of BR's Eastern Region, a profound change from anything I had ever done before. In this job I had huge operational and safety responsibilities leading a team of experienced functional managers, a mix of operators and engineers, some of whom were highly innovative in their approach whilst others were fundamentally conservative having reached the pinnacle of their careers and were deeply suspicious of changes that might affect them personally. There is no doubt that I was regarded with a high degree of scepticism not least because of my arrival from Red Star, very far from being considered a main stream operational role out in the 'real railway'. Bob Reid had by then succeeded Peter Parker as BR's Chairman in 1983, and my appointment by him was intended to make a statement. Because of the success of Red Star and the manner in which it had been achieved the appointment was symbolic of the ascendancy of the commercial over the operational railway; on a Region furthermore that had a reputation for being amongst the most traditional.

My task was not eased by the fact that Bob Reid had also decided to break up the geographical integrity of the Eastern Region by creating a separate Anglia Region from it, restoring a structure that had existed in the mid-1960s. The new Anglia General Manager was to be John Edmonds, a man who had a reputation amongst railway engineers akin to that of King Herod amongst two year olds. He and I were jointly given the remit to create a new framework and in the eyes of some York-based colleagues this became a test of my ability to resist unpopular changes. However, as with most things in life I discovered that amongst my York team there were far more people with a positive approach than a negative one.

I found the engineers especially responsive to the idea that they would thrive on the basis of their ability to meet the demands of the various railway businesses then operating within the Region. I was able to demonstrate that far from being antagonistic towards engineers I wanted to release them into a more commercial environment in which they could make an even greater contribution. Consequently this was the first part of the railway to establish engineering organisations as 'profit centres' trading as internal suppliers to other departments including the Sectors. This worked so well that similar initiatives were developed in other parts of the Region. We went on to develop internal customer facing production organisations at local level that were for the first time aligned not just geographically but commercially. The Area Manager Kings Cross was aligned with the commuting business of the Great Northern Division in Network South East as well as with InterCity East Coast, whilst the Doncaster Area Manager's organisation was split into InterCity and Yorkshire Freight. Further north, Leeds and Sheffield became Areas that were aligned with Regional Railways services whilst the Newcastle and Middlesbrough Areas became passenger and freight respectively, to add to the North East Coal organisation that had already been established at Sunderland. Elsewhere Immingham became a freight only Area with local passenger operations transferring to Sheffield. The infrastructure engineering organisations were restructured on a line of route basis. I also brought the infrastructure departments together under the leadership of the most senior engineer, who I made my deputy, so that best practice and productivity could be driven faster, heralding future more radical changes that would take place in the early 1990s.

During the same period the electrification of the East Coast Main Line was taking place and although there was a well-established project management team set up reporting to the Managing Director, InterCity, it was my role to ensure that the appropriate co-operation and resources from within the Region were given to what was then the largest single investment made in the railways since the Second World War. This worked well and looking back it is remarkable not only that the project was completed to time and budget but that a full train service was operated throughout some of the largest re-signalling programmes the railway had ever witnessed. York and Newcastle were both re-signalled during the period 1989-91, yet trains ran throughout. The methods used then would not be permitted in the safety culture that subsequently came to prevail yet these programmes were undertaken with the utmost professionalism and without incident at the time.

Experiences such as these reconfirmed my view that railway production managers were accomplished, innovative and thrived in a business focused environment. Based on a lifetime's experience of their trade it is tragic how this valuable human asset was so dissipated during the subsequent privatisation of the railways and the approaches then adopted by Railtrack[5]. More recently Network Rail and the Conservative Government have promoted the idea of closer working between the infrastructure organisation and train operating companies. The East Coast electrification exemplified the sort of intercompany co-operation that can deliver projects efficiently. Nothing has worked as well as this in the privatisation period.

Meanwhile on Anglia John Edmonds controversially set about establishing a very much leaner organisation, one which would be reflected later with the principles he applied when he was appointed Chief Executive of Railtrack at the time of privatisation.

During this period I was also at the forefront of the quality programme adopted by the railways. Entitled

---

[5] Much of this is described in Chapter 8

Quality through People, I was heavily involved in what was a major education programme in the techniques of total quality management (TQM) pioneered by Japanese and American gurus such as Deming. Based on the same systems of measurement associated with scientific and production processes, this approach targeted continuous improvement in delivering customer needs. 'Quality' was defined as "meeting the needs and expectations of customers". This became a passion of mine and I spent a great deal of time speaking at seminars and establishing Quality Fairs aimed at promoting the concepts. A vast amount of management energy was focused on the approach and we began to see some major innovations and improvements in the way the railway was performing, the most obvious of which were associated with punctuality.

This was an initiative that I look back on with a great sense of achievement because what we did then would become the standard means of managing railway service performance right up to and beyond privatisation. We did it by creating a data capture system that enabled us to allocate every minute's delay to a location, a cause and an accountable manager or supervisor. We were able to establish a performance budget akin to a financial one and to use it as the basis for a focus on continuous improvement. In recent years the railway has struggled to replicate the effectiveness of this type of approach, hampered by the separation of responsibilities amongst different companies.

The Quality programme was also fun. On one occasion we hired Doncaster Race Course exhibition hall for work groups to showcase their projects and ideas. On another we initiated a Hollywood Oscars evening (the first at York Race Course, the second at the Royal York Hotel), at which awards were presented to winning teams the length and breadth of InterCity East Coast from Aberdeen to Kings Cross. These were the first such events ever held on the railways in a tradition that has continued, morphing into National Award ceremonies in the privatised railway.

In the light of the changes I had adopted on the Eastern Region, BR's Chief Executive, David Kirby, asked me to review the interaction of production interfaces with the Sectors across the railway as a whole. I recommended the redefinition of the production functions as suppliers to the various business Sectors. The approach secured widespread support from colleagues in the Sectors and most Regions but it wasn't until John Edmonds was promoted to the British Railways Board in 1989 that positive moves were made. If anything his reforms were more radical opting as he did for vertical integration whereby the production functions were subsumed within business Subsectors.

As the politicians today look at ways to better align train companies with infrastructure management, both the fully integrated and the customer-supplier models should be revisited.

The period 1990/91 was consumed by restructuring for vertical integration. Reflecting the emphasis placed at the time on the Quality Through People initiative, the project was badged Organising for Quality (OfQ). The Eastern Region was quickly out of the starting blocks and by April 1991 the job was done. To all intents and purposes the Region was abolished and replaced by new businesses. In the process I had made myself redundant as General Manager and was appointed the first Managing Director of InterCity East Coast. The completion of electrification and its inauguration by Her Majesty the Queen coincided with the change.

In November 1991 I was appointed Managing Director Network South East (NSE), one of the three newly integrated passenger Sectors established by Organising for Quality. Previously it had existed as a marketing, planning and business development Sector since the early 1980s but with the introduction of vertical integration, NSE also took on total responsibility for all operations and infrastructure engineering including safety, as well as the associated costs and revenues. I was thrilled to move away from an environment of constructive tension between production and business to become responsible for everything on a Sector that had by far the biggest bottom line responsibility on the railways.

When I started my new job after the Christmas break I had no idea how eventful this period of my working life was to become as for the next five years not only was I to play a central role in several major initiatives but I was also to become heavily involved in privatisation. Sadly this was also a period when the operation of the railway in and around London was interrupted on an almost daily basis by IRA Bomb threats.

I succeeded Chris Green, a legend for getting things done and a person who had left a mark wherever he had been. He had been at NSE for about five years and in that time had, in conjunction with Regional General Managers, transformed it from a rag-bag of operating divisions within those former Regions into a brand that had high recognition throughout the London area and beyond. His first act had been the symbolic one of painting all the station lamp posts red and to initiate a process of total route modernisation starting with the most archaic parts of the railway. This meant modernising every aspect of the railway on a line of route basis. However, his role as a Sector Director before OfQ was not to implement these changes but to sponsor and fund them. The Regions did the implementation. When I went to NSE it was to a very different job. As the Managing Director of an integrated railway organisation I was to be both sponsor and implementer. Disappointingly the money ran out at about the same time!

The approach to running NSE that I adopted would best be described as "devolution with accountability". Route based Divisions were established as profit centres, each self-sustaining but accountable to me. Accountability was achieved through monthly review meetings supported by the use of key performance measures to monitor progress and encourage improvement in all aspects of running the railway. The Divisions became much more mature (and therefore responsible) whilst several HQ functions became good commercial suppliers. Although it had not been done with privatisation in mind, when this occurred a couple of years later the changes enabled many more people to survive the experience than would otherwise have been the case.

My period in London lasted from January 1992 to April 1997 and was dominated by two things: lack of money, and privatisation; reflecting the key thrusts of the John Major Government's policy towards the railways. These seemed to epitomise a dislike of the public sector. The biggest issue to deal with was cuts in Treasury payments to the railways which bizarrely the politicians managed to portray as "record investment". They got away with this because the money they gave to the railways as a whole did actually go up slightly but the major capital outlay within it was committed to the Channel Tunnel Rail Link between Folkestone and Waterloo. This project absorbed huge expenditure and meant that the amount of money available to go into the existing railway was less; and in the case of Network South East a whole lot less.

Initially I had been optimistic and entertained hopes of persuading the Government to put more investment into NSE. A business plan submission was produced that would form the basis for a subsidy level that would improve the safety and performance of the railway. Building on work initiated by Chris Green, we produced a do-nothing scenario, a base case and an enhanced railway option. I commissioned a condition survey of all railway assets. These were prioritised on a safety first basis and informed the production of plans which were then submitted to the

Department of Transport. Our hope was to influence the public spending round and the approach did at least get us to the point where I made a direct presentation to the Treasury officials who determined the budgets that we received. It was a fruitless endeavour. In my first full year in charge the money available was cut by £600m visiting major damage to our strategies. I was given only a day's notice of the settlement, which was even made after the financial year had begun. Such were the vagaries of Government as funding overlord – a warning to anyone contemplating future funding models for the railways. Treasury mandarins appeared to believe that the best way to get innovation was to starve the railway of cash and to some extent we helped this argument through the efficiency results that we achieved. By this time it was overwhelmingly clear that the Government was in no mood to provide additional funding to an industry it had decided to privatise. That was to happen afterwards.

Despite these cuts the Government wanted to see significant improvements in the punctuality of services which was to be done under the umbrella of the Citizens' Charter[6]. In the case of NSE we devised a series of line of route punctuality and cancellation reduction targets which were marketed under the strap line Track Record. Each service group had to achieve a percentage target of operating to within five minutes of the scheduled arrival times of trains. In the following years by using strict quality control and monitoring methods we succeeded in bringing about a very substantial improvement in train service performance coupled with a noticeable and sustained improvement in passenger perceptions as measured by surveys undertaken independently. Fares were changed upward or downward in relation to the performance results achieved on each line. We sensibly set individual route

---

[6] Aimed at improving service quality in the public sector through publishing clear targets for levels of service.

targets that were stretching but achievable, allowing for continuous improvement, a cornerstone principle of Total Quality Management. This was unlike the position in the InterCity companies[7] which were all set the same 90% objective (within 10 minutes in their case). Too often organisations and Governments have gone in for simple targets without a delivery strategy underpinning them; leading to failure, cynicism, and bad headlines.

The Government demand for reduced subsidy was rendered even more difficult than it would have been by the fact that between 1992 and 1995 London and the South East experienced a major recession when 25% of jobs in central London were lost. This affected the numbers of commuters and the finances of the business were put under even greater pressure. Being a business with high fixed and low variable costs the impact was disproportionate and the upshot was that we had to develop rapid cost reduction strategies and re-prioritise investment on a safety-first basis. Schemes were risk assessed in terms of their impact on safety which brought various re-signalling schemes to the top of the list displacing others (notably fleet replacement) which on a comparable risk assessment ranked lower. Total route modernisation, in which all aspects of a route were re-invested at the same time, was abandoned: it was unwelcome but inevitable in the circumstances. Despite this re-prioritisation the reduction in subsidy was so great that some previously committed safety based schemes fell in the rankings. Subsequently there was a terrible train crash on a single line at Cowden in Kent[8] which might have been prevented had a cab secure radio system been introduced. It had been deferred in favour of other more highly rated safety critical schemes and at the subsequent public inquiry

---

[7] These were East Coast Main Line, West Coast Main Line, Great Western, Midland Main Line, Cross Country, Anglia, and Gatwick Express

[8] 15th October 1994

into Cowden I was required to explain in great detail why cab secure radio had not been introduced by the time of the crash.

Some high profile schemes were implemented, the most important being the London, Tilbury and Southend line re-signalling[9]. Others were delayed through lack of cash. One of the most concerning was the Dartford line re-signalling, the need for which I witnessed at first hand on a site visit. Notwithstanding the financial pressures I ordered the immediate development of a replacement system and initiated a project to finance a new signalling system through a Private Finance Initiative (PFI). Treasury approval was received although it was necessary for sufficient risk transfer to the private sector to be demonstrated. The scheme was still under development when Railtrack was created in 1994 and I was dismayed to discover that this and similar schemes were either delayed or cancelled. Another PFI would have involved transferring the whole of the decrepit Southern Region third rail power system, badly in need of replacement, to a private investor (probably an electrical generating or distribution company) on a 100-year lease. This was not progressed by Railtrack either.

Despite funding constraints we were able to complete two major investment projects during my time at NSE, both initiated by Chris Green in better financial times. The first was the modernisation of the Thames and Chiltern lines into Paddington and Marylebone respectively. The second was the Networker project that involved the replacement of the entire inner suburban fleet in South East London. The Networker project sat alongside the modernisation of the East Coast Main Line as the most expensive project on BR since nationalisation. It too was completed to budget and on time, something the subsequent railway structures have had difficulty in emulating.

---

[9] A route control and signalling centre was established at Upminster

Another success was a major change in the approach to marketing. Network South East had contented itself with being a commuter railway yet at off-peak times trains carried massive empty capacity at minimal marginal cost. The strategy was therefore to raise awareness of services for leisure travel and the result was the biggest increase in off-peak business that the Sector had ever seen. This laid the foundations on which privatised companies were able to build in later years.

And then there was militant Irish Republicanism. My period at NSE coincided with the IRA's last major bombing campaign in London; continuous throughout the five years I was there. Even now it would be difficult to exaggerate the extent to which this affected the running of railways at the time. The strangest press interview I ever did occurred early one morning when an IRA bomb went off at a London station shortly after I got to work. There was no-one else in the office and when I heard the news I went round to the press desk to discover it was unmanned. The phones were ringing continuously and I picked one up to find I was speaking to Dick Murray, transport correspondent of the *London Evening Standard*. He asked me what I thought of the bombing and I made an off-the cuff kind of reply as you do when on autopilot. The lunchtime edition of the paper then appeared with the headline "We will not let them win", under which was printed the interview I had given.

My first holiday (February half term 1992) was interrupted by a bomb that went off in the gents lavatories on platform 4 at London Bridge Station. It happened at about 8am in the rush hour and resulted in the death of one man. The biggest bombing of all, however, had no casualties. This occurred at Liverpool Street station and blew most of the glass panels out of the roof creating a hazard of falling shards onto the concourse below. That Saturday morning I travelled to London to view the scene, ascending onto the station roof to see the effects. Bob

Breakwell, the Divisional Director, and I were determined to get the station open again for commuters on the Monday morning but to do so needed to have all the dangerous shards removed from the roof to eliminate the sword of Damocles effect on the concourse below. It was a tremendous tribute to the roof contractors and Bob's team that the station did open for the Monday morning rush hour.

Thereafter there was a series of bombings around London to which the railways reacted by developing regular station searches which enabled staff in conjunction with the British Transport Police[10] to determine whether a bomb warning was a hoax or probable. This had an immediate benefit in that many more stations remained open in the face of bomb callers' efforts to disrupt the railway. It was so successful that the IRA changed the target from stations to the trackside. Sevenoaks Tunnel was a favourite choice for such attacks but although these continued to cause some disruption to services it was by no means as bad as it had been. Eventually the IRA mainland bombing campaign ceased. I am certain that part of the rise in rail travel after 1996 was attributable to this ceasefire. It also seems probable to me that part of the explanation for more depressed demand in the period after 2017 was the return of terrorism 'inspired' by Islamic extremists.

NSE was a melting pot for major initiatives during this period. Not only did my team have to deal with the whole privatisation implementation and a cash crisis of huge proportions but we also had to confront the need to improve punctuality and reliability which had fallen to low levels at the time I arrived there in January 1992. The reputation of the railways had reached a (then) low point following a particularly bad autumn and winter season. Leaves on the line became something of a media running joke which was compounded following a period of very wintry weather during which a number of relatively new trains broke down

---

[10] A railway based, specialist police force

due to sucking snow into the engines causing them to short out. Terry Worrall[11], a colleague with every good intention, telephoned the radio broadcaster Jonathan Dimbleby following his *Any Questions* programme one Saturday to explain the effect of a particularly light type of snow on the traction motors of these new trains. The next day the papers were full of headlines heralding "the wrong kind of snow".

When I arrived at NSE I discovered that performance management techniques were not very effective and proceeded to implement the same systems that had proved successful on the Eastern Region in my previous job. The benefits were immediate and by the time NSE was restructured to take on the shape of the privatised railway to be, punctuality had reached its highest recorded level of over 90% for the whole London and South East area. Passenger approval ratings also reached high levels, including a value for money score of 80%. More recently this figure had fallen to 44%[12].

Another business priority during this immensely busy period was to ensure that major strategic projects that enhanced the capacity of the South East rail network were progressed. However, because we were short of funds to run the day-to-day railway it was difficult to justify putting money into projects like CrossRail and Thameslink 2000. CrossRail was a project that was jointly sponsored by NSE and London Underground under the auspices of London Transport. A high powered steering group on which I sat included the Chairmen of British Railways and London Transport; and the MD of London Underground. This group was seeking to promote the construction of a tunnel connecting Paddington and Liverpool Street stations so that local services from the east and west of London could be connected with a spur line running to Heathrow Airport.

---

[11] British Rail Director of Operations at the time
[12] National Rail Passenger Survey, London and South East companies, Spring 2019

The Project Director was Don Heath with whom I had worked at York when he performed the same role for the East Coast Main Line Modernisation. CrossRail was making some progress and we promoted a Bill to the House of Commons seeking powers to build it. Unfortunately the project was not without its critics and the Special Committee of MPs appointed to consider the proposition comprised four renegade politicians of both Right and Left. Opponents included groups who feared the undermining of their central London homes and clubs – especially around several famous London squares that were to be used as access points for the tunnel and for waste disposal. Interest groups also engaged some bright consultants to oppose the plans. The Bill was defeated and CrossRail stopped in its tracks. The Government then withdrew significant development funding and much of the project team had to be made redundant. When Network South East was finally broken up and privatised I succeeded in keeping the core part of the BR team going by transferring it to London Underground where it lived to fight another day. It took another 10 years for a Parliamentary Bill to succeed and for Gordon Brown[13] to give the project his approval. Work got underway in 2011.

I confess that at the time I was involved I had greater belief in another project. Although not opposed to CrossRail if I had been forced to make a choice I would have opted for Thameslink 2000. I believed too that as a vertically integrated railway this project could have been financed and engineered at little or no cost to the Treasury because of the commercial returns it was possible to make. These did not include the even greater property development value that would be released by the project, especially in the Farringdon/Smithfield area of London. Although we failed to get Government to back this concept, I did play a strong part in getting the project back on the agenda after it had

---

[13] Chancellor of the Exchequer (1997-2007); Prime Minister (2007-2010)

lost Government support altogether. NSE was instrumental in establishing a Thameslink 2000 support group of local authorities that acted as a lobby to Government and when Railtrack was privatised I was delighted that it chose to float with a commitment to fund the project. Subsequently this commitment was diluted but at least the scheme made progress, albeit much later than the year 2000 when it was first meant to open. It was eventually completed in 2018.

Privatisation was the other major theme of my years at Network South East and being in charge of a big chunk of the railway at the time meant I came to play a pivotal role in implementing the policy that was adopted. From autumn 1992, when the Government announced its intentions through a series of White Papers, until March 1997, when the last part of the railway was privatised, my job was central to the privatisation process. This is described fully in Chapter 6.

Media interviews were already a regular feature of my work at NSE but the political controversy surrounding privatisation added further intensity. Interviews were normally undertaken for London and South East TV News but as privatisation became the key political issue of the day, so I began to be asked to do more controversial interviews for main news channels as well as national newspapers. I was interviewed on *The World at One* lunchtime radio news programme with John MacGregor, the Secretary of State, and took part in a *Panorama* TV special for which I was interviewed in a dilapidated signal box at Fenchurch Street, selected to highlight the dire investment problems faced by the railway at that time. Memorably, I appeared on the *Frost Report* for Thames Television where I witnessed a political punch-up between John Prescott (then Shadow Transport Minister – later Deputy Prime Minister) and Steven Norris (Minister for Transport in London and subsequently twice mayoral candidate for London in the Conservative cause). In the run up to the

1992 General Election, when railway privatisation had been promised in the Conservative Party manifesto, I took part in a live broadcast on an afternoon consumer programme where I was the sole representative of the railways on a panel that included the front bench spokesmen on rail from all three major parties. I marvelled at their ignorance and felt that I put in a strong performance setting out facts. When I got back to the office I was cheered all the way back to my desk for my defence of BR. It turned out that everyone had watched the programme live on the TV set in the press office.

In the end the Government's privatisation plans were successfully implemented, thanks to the efforts of the whole management team. Of course there were no actual thanks in it but it had proved to be one of the most fascinating periods of my career.

CHAPTER THREE

The Railways after BR: I go 'private'

During the course of 1997 and 1998 I laid the foundations for what would become a portfolio career, still rooted in the railway, though not so bound up in it that I was not able to pursue other interests. These included a five year spell as chairman of two NHS Ambulance Trusts in Yorkshire[14] and writing a book (published in 2015) on the history of Parliamentary Constituencies in Greater London[15]. Along the way I established a publishing company (First Class Insight), a management consultancy (First Class Partnerships, or FCP), and two open access train companies (Hull Trains and Wrexham & Shropshire). I also served on the Boards of two other train company holding groups (Laing Rail and South Eastern Trains); an AIM listed plc (Tracsis); and collaborated in establishing a magazine (*Passenger Transport*). Having joined BR with public service aspirations I ended up rather unexpectedly as a railway entrepreneur. My career has been broadly split between the public and private sectors.

I was made redundant when my job at BR disappeared in April 1997. I was coming up to my fiftieth birthday and took an early decision not to take a high level post in the new industry structure. By then I was familiar with running large parts of an integrated railway and was not attracted by the prospect of running smaller, separated units. Neither was I keen on 'working for someone else'. I was also convinced that my long term health prospects would be improved if I avoided stressful executive positions. So it

---

[14] The North Yorkshire Ambulance Service; then the Tees, East & North Yorkshire Ambulance service
[15] "Voters' Limits"

was going against these principles when I agreed to submit myself for interview when approached by Railtrack Chief Executive John Edmonds to undertake such a job. Having been promised the role of Commercial Director by both John and the company's Chairman Bob Horton, only then to have it withdrawn by the Non-Executive Directors, I grew cynical. The mood music of an interview with the Remuneration Committee was typified by two questions: "Do you not think there are already too many railwaymen on the Board of Railtrack?" and "Do you think that the next Chief Executive of Railtrack should be a railwayman?" This flavour of hostility towards anyone with a BR background was unendearing yet it appeared to be central to the company's ethos at that time. Its failure to then deliver on promises made to me by its top two executives seemed to typify the somewhat dysfunctional house style and arrogant reputation that the company was already acquiring amongst the vast majority of railway managers. It would take another 20 years for a rounded railwayman to be appointed to head up the railway's infrastructure operator[16].

I quickly came to regard this as a lucky escape; one that served to reconfirm my instinct that I should pursue a more varied form of second career. So I embarked on a series of ventures in the private sector instead. First Class Insight was an early such venture; a vehicle for me to publish my own assessment of the bids of all the successful franchise companies. In Chapter 7 I describe the process by which the first 25 franchises were offered, in part drawing on a report that I published in 1998. In fact its publication led to my becoming a Non-Executive Director of M40 Trains, owner of the Chiltern Railways franchise. Following an early morning appearance on the BBC *Breakfast Business* programme to talk about my report I got a call from Adrian Shooter, Chiltern's Managing Director, asking if I might be

---

[16] Andrew Haines, a former railway management trainee, was appointed Chief Executive of Network Rail in 2018

interested in the role. I joined the Board in May 1998, serving until June 2006 by which time the company had been wholly acquired by John Laing plc.

Then as a management consultant trading as First Class Partnerships (FCP), I got my first assignment following a phone call in the autumn of 1997 from John Prideaux, former Managing Director of BR's InterCity Sector, who was by now Chairman of the Angel Trains rolling stock leasing company. John went on to make a reported £10m from the sale of the company a couple of years later. He had spotted that when they were sold off the rolling stock leasing companies were seriously underpriced and made a killing along with others who found themselves sitting in similar positions. One man made £8m having occupied a job for a matter of only about six months after privatisation simply because BR was desperate to find a qualified engineer to sit on the company's Board. At the time I considered this to be gut wrenchingly obscene and one of the worst examples of what can happen when state concerns are privatised. To favour this sort of thing happening you really do have to take a long, strategic view and not be overly concerned by what happens in the short term. My Tory voting friends tell me that the reason the rolling stock companies were underpriced was that the Labour Party had made noises whilst in opposition about re-nationalisation. Whether this is post-event rationalisation or not others will have to decide. I was sceptical at the time but it is true that the companies were all sold on for much higher prices than the original privatisation demonstrating that they had been sold cheap in the first place.

The piece of consultancy work John commissioned me to undertake was to forecast the future demand for rolling stock based on the franchise bid analysis in my First Class Insight report. Very soon consultancy work of immense interest and significance was beginning to come my way. I led a feasibility study for the Eurostar Consortium to advise whether or not Eurostar train sets that were built for an aborted project to operate to provincial centres in the UK could instead be deployed between Paris/Brussels and Heathrow Airport. After these skirmishes in the world of consulting it was clear that in the privatised railway there was considerable interest in an informed, professional management consultancy offering practical expertise. I decided to invite a number of very capable former colleagues representing all railway disciplines to join me and within a matter of months I was approached by Sir Alistair Morton, Chairman of the Strategic Rail Authority (SRA), who appointed the company "operator of last resort"[17]. In this capacity, First Class Partnerships stood ready to run any failed franchise on behalf of the Government, and took a lead role when the decision was taken to remove Connex from the South Eastern franchise. This is described in detail in Chapter 7.

FCP soon established itself as an adviser to public authorities and private companies alike, securing consultancy work in all five continents as well as with the vast majority of train companies and infrastructure bodies in the UK. It supported several companies' franchise bids whilst I myself provided mentoring support to various bodies across the industry including the new SRA Board when this was established to replace OPRAF in 2000. Shortly afterwards, in 2001, I facilitated a series of workshops for its new Chairman and Chief Executive Richard Bowker and other Board members, aimed at clarifying the organisation's strategic objectives. Later on when the SRA itself faced abolition following a change of Government in 2010 I ran similar workshops to help the Board develop an approach to handling its demise.

---

[17] Operator of last resort would be deployed by Government to run a franchise in the event that the private company running it was either dismissed or itself took the decision to opt out.

When in 2002 the Labour Government decided that Railtrack's time was up, I interviewed industry stakeholders with a view to advising the Government and Chairman of the SRA on how the successor organisation, Network Rail, should work with the rest of the rail industry. I also supported the joint Boards of London Underground and Railtrack in developing a memorandum of understanding to improve their working relationships; and in 2009 was engaged by the Office of Rail Regulation to evaluate the effectiveness of the process of its 2008 Periodic Review of Network Rail's Outputs and Funding, making recommendations for improving its approach to the 2013 Review. In 2010 I was appointed to the Advisory Board established by Sir Roy McNulty to make recommendations to Government concerning the rail industry's value for money, a report that was published in 2011.

In the meantime FCP had worked on several continents advising on how best to structure the railways where reforms were being considered. We provided advice in countries that were considering dipping a toe in the water of UK privatisation. I even visited Washington at the request of the Department for Trade and Industry to do a presentation to a joint committee of the US Congress on the benefits and pitfalls of rail restructuring in Britain.

Alongside my consulting work, from 1998 I was active in developing open access train companies [18] through Renaissance Trains which I jointly owned with Mike Jones, someone I knew from earlier in my career when we had been BR management trainees. Mike had been a very active Young Conservative and when the privatisation of the railways came on the agenda he became an influential figure. He was a party member in Huntingdon, the very constituency represented in the House of Commons by the

---

[18] Privatisation allowed for new entrants to bid for space on the railway to run new ventures and were distinct from the services franchised by Government.

Prime Minister. He knew John Major personally and was well connected within the Party in whose councils he had been active for many years. His views on railways were listened to with respect because he worked in them. He favoured freer access to the railway infrastructure including the idea of open access to enable new markets to be exploited by new operators. He was four square behind the idea of separating the track from the trains and of lowering the barriers to entry for freight and new passenger operators alike.

An initial idea to operate trains from Kings Cross to Nottingham via Grantham evolved into a substantive proposition to create the Hull Trains company. Facing opposition from Railtrack's East Coast management team, Mike and I persisted and created a joint venture company with GB Railways, an AIM-listed business which had been established to bid for rail franchises during the privatisation process. We then set about the crucial task of putting our case to the Rail Regulator's office where we did battle with Railtrack, WAGN[19] and GNER[20] for the right to run trains on the East Coast Main Line. I took the major role for Renaissance Trains in putting together the business case and with Mike was Hull Trains' spokesman at the hearing which was opened by the Regulator, Tom Winsor. During the course of the inquiry we were able to debunk the opposition to what we were seeking to achieve and were armed with a massive body of support from stakeholders in Hull and East Yorkshire. Consent was given for a 10-year access agreement provided we invested in new 125mph rolling stock within five years of starting the operation. This was to ensure compatibility with other operators' services and to optimise use of capacity on the route.

---

[19] West Anglia Great Northern Railway operating mainly local franchised services from Kings Cross and Liverpool Street to commuter destinations in Hertfordshire and Cambridgeshire; and to North West Norfolk

[20] Operator of the East Coast Inter City franchise

We had won a stunning victory, becoming the first new passenger operator on main line railways since the creation of the Great Central Railway in 1899. Hull Trains began operating in September 2000, but within a matter of weeks was hit by one of the most notorious incidents in the history of the privatised railway; an event that was to trigger a series of further events that would lead to the abolition of Railtrack. A GNER train was derailed and several passengers were killed at Hatfield on the East Coast Main Line. The accident was found to have been caused by a track failure (gauge corner cracking) as a result of which Railtrack immediately undertook tests all over the national network. The company concluded that the same condition potentially existed at other sites and placed an enormous number of speed restrictions on the railway. The consequence was the disruption of the timetable nationally in a process that Sir Alistair Morton (Chairman of the SRA) described as "a collective nervous breakdown" in the industry. The disruption affected Hull Trains directly as Hatfield was on the East Coast Main Line. Journey times were massively increased and the aftermath had a drastic effect on the new service which had to be re-launched nine months later when the effects of the disaster began to wear off. The service was then hit by two other serious accidents involving GNER trains, one at Potters Bar where defective points caused a derailment; and another at Great Heck near Selby where the driver of a car fell asleep at the wheel allowing his vehicle to career off the M62 onto the railway. That same winter unprecedented flooding of rivers in the Vale of York brought further chaos.

Despite these early setbacks Hull Trains started to grow; it was successful in securing more train paths, firstly at weekends, then on weekdays. Subsequently these were increased again to five, six and then seven in each direction. In 2005 the company launched brand new 125mph diesel multiple unit Pathfinder trains (Class 222s) and the business went into overdrive. Passenger numbers reached ever higher numbers, passing the half million mark in 2006 and moving into profit. In the meantime, the owners of GB Railways' had sold their company to FirstGroup which acquired all its businesses including Hull Trains in 2004. During this early period in its development Hull Trains won several awards for the excellence of its customer service and engineering and won praise from local authorities, politicians, businesses and newspapers alike. Its operating performance was the best of any long distance train company and when the first customer satisfaction survey was undertaken it revealed an 87% satisfaction level, with the remainder believing that the service actually exceeded their expectations. National passenger surveys continued to place the company at or near the top of the satisfaction table and in 2016 it was awarded Passenger Operator of the Year at the Public Transport Awards.

Looking back over this and other experiences in the privatised railway it is striking how often franchise owners operating on lucrative Government contracts resorted to the law to protect their quasi-monopoly market positions. Mike Jones and I were to experience this again in a subsequent open access venture and I formed the view that competition was the last thing private sector franchise operators wanted to see and that monopoly was the preferred modus operandi. Despite this, an injunction brought by GNER that threatened the very existence of Hull Trains was defeated in 2006, meaning that open access remained a key, if still relatively minor, element in the make-up of the liberalised railway.

The success of the Hull operation had already caused us to consider the development of further open access opportunities and the Judicial Review's verdict was grist to the mill. We talked about operating a service between Nottingham and Glasgow but we didn't progress things much beyond the bright idea stage because initial desk research concluded that the business case probably required a degree of public funding to make it work. A possible Glasgow-Liverpool service revealed similar characteristics and because we both held to the view that public subsidy and free enterprise were not proper bed fellows we turned our attentions to a feasibility study for a brand new train service from Shrewsbury to London using the Marylebone route operated by Chiltern Railways. The prospects looked attractive and a new joint venture company was established, this time with Laing Rail which had decided to opt out of the franchising round taking place at that time due to the expense of bidding. Eventually our plans settled on a proposition to run five trains a day each way from the North East Wales town of Wrexham calling at Shrewsbury, Telford and Wolverhampton en route to Marylebone. WSMR[21] was born in February 2006 followed by a public announcement to stakeholders and news media throughout the areas to be served.

Between February and November 2006 action occurred on many fronts and at the end of the period WSMR was in a position to make a formal application to the Office of Rail Regulation (ORR) to support our Track Access Agreement with Network Rail; but whilst we were finalising the arrangements for the company's start up John Laing plc made a decision to divest all its rail interests. These were acquired by DB Regio, a subsidiary of the German State Railway (DB), a company with deep pockets, although we were very nervous about their management methods, which we thought might be centralising and slow moving. We were to be proved right on all these essential points despite DB assuring us at the time that it would run a devolved operation with decisions taken in the UK. Instead we found simple decisions being referred back to Berlin; often to the Chairman of DB.

---

[21] Wrexham, Shropshire & Marylebone Railway

As it turned out the transfer to DB did not work out well for WSMR and in the end it was closed down, the principal reason being the company's failure to obtain the journey times on which the revenue projections were based. Management optimism that everything would be alright on the night was in stark contrast to the reality of Network Rail's approach to timetable planning which favoured the franchised operators and was possibly illegal. Secondly the company failed to secure the rolling stock on which the business case was based. Finally, a highly anti competitive clause in the Track Access Agreement[22] of West Coast Trains (a franchise run by Virgin and Stagecoach) prevented WSMR from conveying passengers between Wolverhampton and London. Whilst this was bound to be overturned in time, ORR said it was legally unable to allow us to compete. Although we substituted the planned call at Wolverhampton with a stop at nearby Tame Bridge Parkway, it never developed in the way we expected. It was galling a year or two later to hear from within ORR that its determination in favour of Virgin and against WSMR was probably one of its worst decisions.

The way the industry operated was basically hostile to small, independent operators. Although our appeals to the Industry Timetable Disputes Committee and subsequently to the Regulator about unfair treatment in the timetable planning process were upheld, neither was prepared to reverse the decision. As far as the rolling stock was concerned, Angel Trains reneged on a verbal commitment to lease the Class 170 units that WSMR had planned to use. Angel's directors told us privately that they could not go against the Department for Transport which had indicated that it wished to deploy the sets on local services in the West Midlands instead. Angel was free to offer us the trains but chose not to rather than risk its position with Government. Despite these setbacks, train services began

---

[22] An agreement between a train company and the infrastructure operator

operating in April 2008 but it was soon apparent that the money needed to bank roll operations would be more than originally agreed. After a number of abortive negotiations DB took the decision in Berlin that WSMR should cease trading in January 2011. Meanwhile passengers had voted Wrexham & Shropshire the most popular railway service in the country with a customer satisfaction rating of 97%, the highest ever recorded for any train company at that stage. So our efforts had not been entirely unsuccessful after all. From the facts that I was able to glean from a number of sources after the event, DB's decision to close the company down was motivated as much by a desire to re-deploy the high specification rolling stock onto the Chiltern franchise as to any other factor. I also learned that DB Regio's UK directors were on a bonus scheme that incentivised them to maximise short term profits. WSMR stood as an obstacle in their way despite the fact that the company would probably have approached break even within two years. It was also despite the considerable marketing advantage (which I doubt DB even considered) of owning a company with the highest passenger approval rating of any. Given the relatively small losses set against DB's UK and global turnover the WSMR position would have been dwarfed by the overall marketing spend of the group. But I don't think DB thought in these terms.

Bizarrely, after DB subsequently acquired the Arriva transport group, it embarked on an ambitious open access operation through Arriva's Grand Central subsidiary which at the time was losing vastly more money than WSMR ever did. Then in 2012/13 it acquired Alliance Rail which promoted a range of eye catching open access services on the East Coast Main Line in competition with franchised operators. In the light of these developments the decision to close down WSMR seems even more puzzling, though the change in thinking was possibly a reflection of a change of approach amongst UK rail authorities to the idea of competition on long distance routes.[23]

In 2012 Mike and I discussed the future of Hull Trains. We concluded that the best prospect for a longer term Track Access Agreement lay in a plan to invest more heavily in the operation and that a privately funded electrification was the best solution. The line from Kings Cross to Temple Hirst Junction near Selby, where our trains left the main line, was already electrified but the rest of the route to Hull was not. Electrification would reduce operating costs and was expected to improve reliability as well. Our chosen joint venture partner was Amey, a large multi-functional engineering company. Meetings were held with Network Rail, whose own electrification plans for the route had not met required benefit to cost ratios, and Amey produced a proposal to undertake the work at a guaranteed price substantially lower than that which Network Rail had used in its own evaluation.

I led discussions with Network Rail, Amey, FirstGroup and with the Rail Regulator. Our initial proposal was for an entirely privately owned infrastructure with charges for use being paid by train operators. The problem was that the majority of operators[24] were three rail franchises and were therefore of interest to the Department for Transport. Access charges would be higher under a privately funded scheme than if Network Rail had undertaken the work itself because the cost of finance was higher and the payback period shorter. Consequently it was deemed unlikely that the DfT would require the franchised operators to use the facility. This meant that the model didn't work as a business case. We looked instead to a model whereby the joint venture would promote, design, build and transfer the scheme to Network Rail. This had two beneficial effects.

---

[23] The short history of Wrexham & Shropshire is told in a book of that name published by Adelstrop Press

[24] Northern, TransPennine Express, and East Coast (now LNER)

The first was to reduce the ongoing access charges annually to operators (including Hull Trains) because Network Rail would depreciate the asset over 60 years. The second was that an early transfer to Network Rail would allow us to borrow money at a cheaper rate of interest. Such a scheme required the support of Government because ultimately the Treasury underwrote Network Rail's infrastructure asset base and I took the lead in meeting DfT officials. In February 2014 I made a presentation to the Secretary of State for Transport himself (Patrick McLaughlin). The meeting went well and we awaited a positive outcome which we hoped might be part of the Chancellor of the Exchequer's Budget announcement in March 2014. On 20th March a letter was sent from McLaughlin to Alan Johnson MP (Hull West) which confirmed that he was "making available up to £2.5m to Network Rail to enable further development studies for the electrification of the route to Hull to be progressed". He said he wanted the work to be undertaken "as soon as possible". Sadly the scheme became delayed by Network Rail's wider industry problems that were beginning to beset electrification elsewhere. In the light of Network Rail's reluctance to engage, FirstGroup decided instead to invest in new bi-mode rolling stock that would enable trains to operate off the East Coast Main Line without overhead wires. The downside for the wider railway was that it left unresolved the prospect of an electrification of the whole TransPennine route to Hull[25].

In August 2014, Mike and I sold our shares in Hull Trains to FirstGroup which became the sole owner. Two years later I also sold my final interest in FCP. The company continues to trade with a high reputation all over the world and 70% of its business is now said to be outside the UK. In the 18 years of my involvement with the company since starting it up in the early years after

---

[25] The TransPennine Route in question runs from Liverpool to Hull via Manchester, Huddersfield and Leeds

privatisation, its activities had become wide ranging in both scope and geography. In Britain FCP worked with all the major public sector transport bodies (all the PTEs, the DfT, Transport Scotland, Northern Ireland Railways, OPRAF, the SRA, ORR, TfL, and LUL). In addition it had worked with all bar one or two UK rail companies, and with overseas railway organisations in France, Denmark, the Republic of Ireland, Georgia, Poland, Portugal, Mongolia, Mozambique, Argentina, South Africa, and Nigeria.

My remaining rail activities became centred on my membership (since 2007) of the Board of Tracsis plc[26] and *Passenger Transport Magazine*, a fortnightly publication. I retired from the Tracsis Board in October 2018 but accepted the Chairmanship of another transport consulting business, Flash Forward, which is active in the UK, Ireland, and increasingly internationally, in both rail and bus sectors. These activities keep me current with industry developments and in contact with a number of senior people in the sector, enabling me to look forward as well reflect back on past events. With a continuous involvement and interest in the railways going back over 50 years I finally decided to write an opinionated account of the way in which the industry has developed over that period of time. Since much of the narrative is about industry structure, I am also publishing this book in part as a contribution to the Government's rail review led by Keith Williams.

The story starts with a decision to make British Rail a more commercial organisation

---

[26] Tracsis specialises in solving a variety of data capture, reporting and resource optimisation problems with products and services used to increase efficiency, reduce cost and improve the operational performance and decision making capabilities for clients and customers.

CHAPTER FOUR

1981 – 1992: The Commercialisation of British Rail

More eminent students of the rail industry than me have described the history of British Rail and it is not my intention to contest what is already on record. Gourvish remains a thoroughly reliable source for those who want to delve deep into the events and facts that underpinned BR's evolution in the 1970s and 1980s. So in discussing these developments I am more concerned to consider why and how the commercialisation of BR occurred during this period and its relevance to the railway today.

The personalities interest me too and there is none greater to begin with than Bob (later Sir Robert) Reid who I was privileged to know and work for between 1981 and 1990, initially as his Personal Assistant when he was the Chief Executive (Railways), and later when he was Chairman and I was a Regional General Manager. I and practically all my contemporaries agree that he was probably the greatest railwayman of modern times. He became Chief Executive when BR was at a low ebb and through his implementation of Sector Management transformed the railway's culture and finances, setting it on a course for growth and innovation. In retrospect we can see that the changes he introduced were on the flight path to privatisation even if this was a prospect he did little to encourage himself. The extent to which his reforms facilitated the privatisation proposals that finally passed into law just after he died remains a matter of conjecture but what can be asserted with certainty is that his guiding principle at every stage in his career was serving and developing the market. He viewed the railway through a commercial prism.

Reid (or simply RBR as he was widely known in the industry) was the son of a senior civil servant in India whose postings included Governor of Assam and acting Governor of Bengal. Public service and a respect for the civil service were in the genes. He was educated privately and studied PPE[27] at Brasenose College, Oxford, and after war service, which included a period as a prisoner in Italy, he applied to join the railways, becoming a traffic apprentice in 1947 with the London and North Eastern Railway. This was just before nationalisation. Subsequently his career in BR was almost entirely in the commercial, customer facing field. As a result he was always outward looking. His roles involved constant interface with politicians, business people, and the travelling public – all of which was to prove significant when he was in positions of authority at the top of the industry.

A formative period in Reid's career was a spell in Glasgow during the 1960s where he reported to the Divisional Manager James Urquhart. As Commercial Manager, Reid was frustrated by the overriding operational focus of the time. He had little respect for Urquart's commercial judgement and it was ironic that they would work closely together as Board members in the 1980s fighting for greater employee productivity; but 20 years earlier their relationship was far from harmonious. His daughter, Janet, recalls that when he was in Glasgow he developed a stress induced ulcer, went on a palliative milk based diet, and even talked about leaving BR due to his exasperation and unhappiness. However, his appetite for the railway was restored when he was appointed Planning Manager for Scotland, a post which he only occupied for a year but which transformed his prospects, enabling him to escape the clutches of Urquhart and giving him a much wider perspective of all aspects of the railway. Although for a while he worried about being sidelined in the role, it gave

---

[27] Politics, Philosophy & Economics

him 'a helicopter view' of the industry and when he left Scotland in 1968 it was to take up his first general management post as Divisional Manager Doncaster. In those days Divisional Manager was an essential stepping stone to a high flying career and he was a rising star.

In Janet's words "he wasn't really a deputy sort of person" and Doncaster offered him real power. He found it a very satisfying job but when he was promoted to Deputy General Manager of the Eastern Region in 1972 he again felt the frustration of not being in control. That would change two years later when he got his first big command as General Manager of the Southern Region, a job he enjoyed "because he was in charge". Within three years he was appointed to BR's most senior commercial post, British Railways Board Member for Marketing, a role for which he was ideally suited; and in 1980 he was selected as Chief Executive, seen as the man to get a grip on BR at a time of severe public sector spending restrictions.

During his progression to the top, Reid had filled every significant senior role in regional management. As a result he acquired an unrivalled knowledge and understanding of the territorially protective ethos of the Regions and a complete appreciation of how the power structures operated, not to mention the personalities and motivations of the senior managers running them. He was well versed in railway politics and had the scars to show for it. As Board Member for Marketing, he had been at the epicentre of the management matrix in which the General Managers of BR's five Regions exercised substantial influence, to the extent that if they chose, they could frustrate centrally driven initiatives. He was very open to any initiative that would assert a more commercially directive approach and, given his temperament, he would undoubtedly have resented these obstructions to his role. An example from that time relates to mould breaking work in BR HQ to determine the profitability of freight traffic flows, which fell within Reid's oversight. It showed that so called merry-go-round working of coal to power stations was hugely profitable based on methods developed jointly with the National Coal Board and the Central Electricity Generating Board. However, its massive profitability obscured the uneconomic activity of most other freight. Generally if the customer was involved in loading and unloading its own traffic it was profitable. Otherwise it was not. Within the all-powerful Regions there was no focus or impetus to correct these inefficiencies.

Although the Regions were responsible for running the trains, the overall economics of freight activity were not visible at that level – a consequence of 80% of freight traffic crossing regional boundaries. According to John Edmonds, who was to become a prime mover in organisational change in BR and Railtrack's first Chief Executive, but who was then a senior manager in BR Freight HQ, the Regions "derided" the methods being developed to specify costs which they claimed could not usefully be attributed to specific traffics. Downward pressures from the centre were frustrated by regional control. "The Regional General Managers were still Gods at this stage," John recalls. Increasingly these frustrations were aired with Bob Reid, already sceptical about the regional role and who by this time was in overall charge of BR's commercial activities. After moving to become Freight Manager on the London Midland Region in 1979, John recalls that in one such discussion with Reid he urged the Board member: "You know the Regions. You can sort it out."

Reid's advocacy and approach to implementing Sector Management in the early 1980s was shaped by such experiences of the priorities and accountabilities within BR, gained over many years and in many roles. From conversations I had with him at the time of Sectorisation, his stint in Scotland under Urquart unquestionably left its mark. Others have pointed to similar influences. Frank

Paterson, who worked closely with Reid as his deputy on the Southern Region, believed he had a "jaundiced view" of functional departments, borne partly from his time as Deputy General Manager of the Eastern Region where he felt that functional managers did not support him. He bore resentment from these episodes and he was not someone who easily forgot, or forgave.

He was notably disdainful of the engineering functions within the railway; not necessarily of engineers per se; but of their departments. "The more money you give them the more they want", was Janet's way of describing his views. "They were a bottomless pit" was another condemnation. When he reached the top he was merciless in their pursuit to drive change. A simple illustration is encapsulated by a situation I encountered when I first went to work as his Personal Assistant in November 1981, the very moment that the implementation of Sector Management was confirmed. Reid chaired what was known as the Railway Executive Group which comprised all the senior railway management including the Regional General Managers, Functional Directors and newly-appointed Sector Directors. One of my humble but fascinating duties was to act as the minutes secretary of the Group. Preparation for meetings included placing engraved tiles on the conference table to indicate where people should sit. Reid would be at the centre of one of the long sides of the oval table with his most trusted colleagues seated either side of him. Others in favour would sit at strategic points around the table, often at the far ends, from where they could make visible but welcome interventions. Some, in or out of favour, would sit on the same side as Reid but out of his sight lines, whilst the person who sat immediately opposite him was unquestionably in the firing line. This unfortunate individual was invariably an Engineering Director, specially selected for harassment on the grounds of his department's perceived profligacy and inefficiency.

I came to see over subsequent years that in many gatherings of senior managers he would deliberately pick an argument with someone "pour encourager les autres". A drink or two at the start of the evening always did something to get him warmed up. I was the victim of this approach myself a few years later when General Manager of the Eastern Region. Although he would land punches directly onto the immediate object of his assault (in this case me), his messages were really meant to be picked up by everyone else in the room. It was an effective method and one he used remorselessly in propagating his message of change.

At the time of Reid's appointment as Chief Executive, there were two dynamics driving work to understand the specifics of railway finances in greater detail. The first was the increasingly professional commercial approach, especially within freight, to identify costs and revenues. The second, which was more pressing, was Government's increasing frustration with BR's overall financial results. According to Reid himself this was partly motivated by Government's reluctance to provide taxpayer funding for commercial freight flows and for the InterCity passenger business[28]. Moreover, it was a time of severe financial stringency brought about by a global rise in oil prices in the late 1970s – a period which had seen the Callaghan Government's infamous application for an IMF loan. When the Thatcher Government was returned in 1979 her Chancellor of the Exchequer, Geoffrey Howe, introduced the concept of a 'cash limit' above which the BRB could not go to finance its activities. Restrictions on public finances had been a feature of the years before, but the focus became much sharper from the early days of the Conservative Government. This immediately brought a new imperative to BRB's priorities, although the Board did not react in the way that might have been expected.

---

[28]Taped interview with Gourvish in December 1987

A year earlier BR had appointed Ian Campbell, an engineer who had been chairman of BREL [29] and BR Research, as Chief Executive. He appears to have believed that the railways were being singled out for tough funding when the whole of the public sector was subject to the same regime. He persuaded the Board to seek a deputation to meet the Tory Minister of State, Norman Fowler, to call for a review of the Government's funding plans for the railway. In January 1980 BRB produced a Statement of its Policies and Potential for the next decade. One section read: "The heart of the problem is the need for more resources to undertake necessary investment. Our locomotives, rolling stock, signalling equipment, buildings and the permanent way itself will soon need to be renewed or replaced on a significantly larger scale than in the past. To undertake this would reflect our desire to provide Britain with a modern, clean and efficient railway and would positively support national policies for the conservation of energy and the environment." Making the case for additional funding, the statement acknowledged the need for BR to make better use of its resources but pointed out that efficiency alone would not be sufficient to free up the additional funds required. It concluded: "If BR is to take the path of progress we must also have a new financial regime. Under the prevailing system it has been impossible to undertake the long term investment programme which the railway requires. Financial ceilings, shortage of cash, the need to divert 'investment' money to meet shortfalls on current account have all militated against such a course."

Investment proposals were ambitious and included main line electrification schemes; Channel Tunnel operations; tilting Advanced Passenger Trains on lines from London to the North with HSTs cascaded to other routes; new lightweight trains on rural lines; new stock on electrified commuter routes; and dedicated services to airports, notably

---

[29] British Rail Engineering Limited

Gatwick and Stansted. The programme would be underpinned by the use of technology to reduce the unit cost of the infrastructure and by new working practices including single manning of trains "in appropriate circumstances". It would require timely approvals from Government including the "authority in agreed circumstances" to raise investment funds from the private capital market. BRB also sought "a form of contract for the Social Railway" providing "incentives, a clear sense of direction, and a workable financial framework".

None of these objectives were unreasonable but the approach was naïve and lacking political nous in the context of a Government whose Chancellor used his first budget to herald a programme of public spending retrenchment. In his budget speech on 12th June 1979, Geoffrey Howe had said: "There is a need to reduce the burden of financing the public sector, so as to leave room for commerce and industry to prosper." He went on to explain that he was compelled to take "painful action" to reduce public spending and borrowing in the immediate future, and that the Government intended "to continue on that path in the years ahead". The context could not have been clearer and over the next decade public spending as a proportion of GDP fell from 45% to 34%[30].

Initiated when Callaghan was Prime Minister and with the left of centre BR Chairman Peter Parker still believing he could take the unions with him, the Campbell thrust might have stood a chance. Post IMF intervention and in the light of Howe's budget, there was never any realistic possibility of Government endorsement. On the contrary, it would look to the railways to become much more cost efficient within their existing operations without the upfront investment that might enable this to occur over time. The need to improve the public finances was urgent and immediate; and capital spending was spending nonetheless.

---

[30] UKpublicspending.co.uk

So the pressures on BR to reduce the cost of its operations actually ramped up a gear. A target was set to reduce staff numbers by 35,000.

One outcome of the Board's misdirected approach was the replacement of Campbell, who had also been personally associated with the perceived 'failure' of the project to introduce the Advanced Passenger Train (APT). Peter Parker's then Personal Assistant and subsequent BRB Secretary, Peter Trewin, recalls that this was "used as the excuse" to remove him "but it was not the reason". Reid was Parker's choice to replace Campbell; a view shared in Whitehall by John Palmer, Head of the Department of Transport's Railways Directorate. The Department saw Reid as possessing "huge focus, determination and ruthlessness" and was "the man to take on the operators" who were believed to lie at the root of the railway's financial problems. He would indeed go on not only to take on the operators and engineers, but the unions too. According to Janet he saw himself as being "an old man in a hurry".

Sector Management was developed against this background, building on official encouragement for the extension of bottom line responsibility to management levels below HQ. There remain different views among managers of the time as to who was its principal architect, ranging from Geoff Myers – a close ally of Reid's who succeeded him as Board Member for Marketing – to a collective dawning during analytical exercises at HQ. Reid himself described the idea as having been "rolling around for years". However, what cannot be disputed is that he was the instrument for its implementation. Someone was needed to make it happen. "That was my contribution," he told Gourvish. He set about the task with vigour and determination, saying at one point: "I was determined for it not to get bogged down like Field", a failed attempt at re-organisation thwarted by the unions in the early 1970s.

Given the entrenched and equally determined opposition to Sectorisation he would encounter from the Regional General Managers, whose role would inevitably be diminished by its creation, these qualities were essential – as was some astute political manoeuvring.

A predecessor of mine as Reid's Personal Assistant recalls a meeting he held with the five Regional General Managers in the summer of 1980. It is instructive of the tensions and power play at the time. Reid had long viewed the railway's financial management systems as a barrier to efficient decision making and was determined to instil a bottom line market based approach to it within BR. Ostensibly the meeting was called to enlist the General Managers' support for introducing profit and loss accounting and to discuss how it could be achieved. However, it seems probable that Reid set it up as a way of flushing out the response he got. The overriding memory is of the very hostile body language of certain General Managers, which translated into a "let's see this daft proposal off" approach cataloguing the reasons it was not credible. Penetrating lines, cross border services, freight/passenger mix were all cited as making the proposition infeasible and expressed to Reid in terms of "well you should know that anyway". The meeting lasted no more than an hour. With hindsight it served to give him licence to say "they've had their chance so we're going to do it my way". Work on developing the structure and tools for Sectorisation accelerated and became the number one priority in Reid's in tray. His desk diary entries for the year 1981 reveal how the project gained momentum. "Dinner with the General Managers" gave way to "Sector Director Breakfasts", the latter invariably preceding the monthly Railway Executive Group.

Throughout 1981 Reid convened a plethora of development and progress meetings with the objective of implementing Sector Management in January 1982.

Participants generally included the head of the BR policy unit (Bill - now Lord - Bradshaw, a prominent Liberal Democrat), Professor John Heath (a leading business strategy academic from the London Business School), and usually Philip Sellers (Director of Finance). Sometimes specialists in particular fields would attend, especially when the financial systems that would be crucial to the creation of business Sectors were being developed. Ad hoc meetings, always referenced in the diary as "SM", involved many key players in the project and by July 1981 the enterprise had built up sufficient head of steam for Reid to convene a Sector Management Seminar for the entire railway leadership group at the Great Eastern Hotel at Liverpool Street. According to Reid this was the crucial meeting. Most senior people present accepted that "we should just get on with it", though in some quarters, support was "grudging".

The principles of Sector Management were articulated by Reid on many occasions but were best expressed in a memorandum prepared for a meeting to present the finalised plan to trade union leaders. Dated 6th October 1981, this explained the intention to "focus the management of the overall rail business into five business Sectors and the arrangements to bring this about". Freight, Parcels and InterCity passenger services were three commercial Sectors required by Government to cover their direct costs of operation and to make a sufficient contribution to indirect costs so as to meet Government's required rate of return on future investment. The other two Sectors, one comprising Provincial passenger services and the other those in London and the South East, were not seen as having the same financial objectives, but they were required "to provide services at levels and costs very broadly determined by Government". In other words, irrespective of whether or not there was a necessity to make a commercial return, each Sector would need to operate within clearly determined financial limits. Furthermore, systems would be introduced so that "the financial results of each Sector can be expressed on an income/expenditure basis avoiding as far as possible arbitrary allocation of cost". The memorandum pointed out that there was only "one point where total costs and revenues are [currently] brought together", namely at Reid's own desk which he saw as "highly unsatisfactory for [him] personally and for the effectiveness of decision making". It was necessary to change this "if we are to react effectively to Government support by Sector". Doing so would allow "a better form of management of the rail business".

The document went on to set out the inadequacies in the Regions' accounting systems explaining that they "were in no way an expression of net revenue in profit responsibility terms; rather they summarise the receipts and expenses" arising from activities in their localities. "Thus some Regions generate a lot of traffic and incur little in the way of expenses, whilst others that receive the traffic spend substantial sums of money in providing services for which they receive no revenue".

In the light of debates on the structure and accountability of the privatised railway that continue to rage to this day, Reid's explanation of the benefits of the financial framework that would accompany Sector Management is noteworthy. "The development of costing methods makes it possible to bring together nearly all the expenses and revenue of each business. It will be possible to draw up profit responsibility statements which will show the operating, engineering and administrative expenses associated with each in a way which will enable managers to propose effective action to pursue beneficial opportunities or remedy unsatisfactory trends." Put simply, it would enable them to run a business. The sophistication of these financial systems would ultimately enable precise bottom line accounting, not only at Sector level but at Subsector profit centre level too. The way Government chose to re-structure BR for privatisation a decade later effectively destroyed this. The industry has struggled to achieve a similar alignment of whole business costs ever since, despite frequently expressed aspirations to do so.

Although the new Sector organisations would assume the Regions' responsibility for budgeting, service planning and marketing, Reid stressed the importance of understanding that "the five Regional General Managers would retain their present responsibilities for managing the railway within their geographical areas". They would continue to provide regional inputs to planning and budgetary processes and have the "responsibility for ensuring that the agreed quality of service together with their revenue and expenditure targets are actually achieved". Implementation would be on 4th January 1982.

However, even as the trade unions were being informed of these imminent changes and as interviews took place to appoint Sector Directors, the General Managers were meeting to devise a proposal for an alternative Regional accounting structure for the freight business. It was a last minute bid to halt Reid's Sector Management plans. Ongoing and active tactical debate at the General Managers Informal (a regular private meeting) was led by Eastern Region General Manager Frank Paterson. Only eight days after Reid's meeting with the unions, a letter from Frank to other General Managers was circulated with a paper proposing ways to allow some means of "establishing bottom line responsibility on a Regional basis". Even at that late stage the General Managers thought it might still be possible to secure the support of the Freight Director, Henry Sanderson, to whom the letter, dated 23rd October, was copied. A post script suggested a chance that the Freight Director might be someone the General Managers could get on side. It read: "I gather John Edmonds had radically different views (i.e. from the Regions) and has undertaken to give Henry Sanderson a paper which proposes the development of Profit Centre Commodity Managers geographically located. This would appear to suggest a degree of reorganisation far greater than we had previously accepted as desirable."

Frank's paper followed hot on the heels of a memorandum from Ian Campbell, by now Board member for Engineering, which made a pitch for separating engineering activities from Reid's approach. Picking up the business bottom line mood music, Campbell's memorandum proposed an "asset management company" which, together with BREL, "would be responsible for the design, manufacture and maintenance of track, signalling, traction and rolling stock". He advocated this as preferable to "the introduction of Sector Management that produces a third [management] dimension which will confuse authorities and compound the difficulties" of administering the present organisation of centralised functions and the regional management of engineering activities. Under Campbell's proposal which presumed engineering 'companies' at HQ, Regional and local levels, "general management would have the task of running trains to Sector Management requirements, providing common services such as personnel and finance, and dealing geographically with such public affairs and commercial matters as are allocated to them".

It is difficult to avoid the conclusion that these were last ditch attempts to thwart the Sector proposition. At the same time they demonstrate with clarity the lack of single focus business accountability that existed on the railways at that time and illustrate why Bob Reid was right to do what he did. That the General Managers were continuing a rearguard action through private, off piste discussions at the same time as the Board had adopted the Chief Executive's policy and advised the unions of its implementation speaks volumes about the lack of accountability that existed. Even after the General Managers accepted that their counter proposals had failed, lobbying continued in an attempt to dampen down the application of Sector Management. In November 1981, only two months before Sector Directors took up the reins, Frank Paterson wrote directly to Peter Parker following an evening session held with the Chairman away from the office. Referring to "there being a lot of spirit left in your Barons in the Field" (an apt description of how the General Managers were seen at this time), Frank expressed his concern that Parker had unrealistic expectations of the benefits Sectors could deliver for BR's finances and meeting Government funding targets.

"The fact that you see this as being one of the key features during your next two years really bothers me," he wrote to Parker. "Up to now I had always felt that you saw the main reason for Sectorisation as meeting a political demand for more information about where the Government support money finished up. For the first time, it came through that you had a strong personal belief that Sectorisation would so sharpen up the minds of the managers who were given the bottom line responsibility that there would be a tangible measurable improvement in our overall performance." Outlining why he felt Parker was misguided, Frank continued: "I'm afraid I feel strongly that the concept is irrelevant to our real needs today. This attitude does not derive from a resistance to change; it stems from a widely held belief that we know what changes we have got to make; the difficulty is in implementing them. Sector Management, with the sharpest focus and the best will in the world, cannot, I believe, do very much to speed up the processes. Perhaps I have got it wrong but I believe that the right calibre of people motivated to achieve optimum results will be doing so today and will not be constrained by organisation structures. It follows, therefore, that if you are relying on people from within the organisation to achieve the conceptual benefits of Sectorisation you might be backing a loser."

Frank went on to explain that despite his opposition to Sector Management, he had accepted it as Board policy and that his concern now was "to do whatever I could to make the concept work". Finishing by asking that Parker should "tear up after reading" the letter, he stressed that he and his senior managers "really don't understand" the emphasis being given to Sector Management "when there are so many more vital issues to be faced and we have a shortage of good quality people to tackle them". Parker replied with a short note that was respectful, but made clear there would be no change of course. Dated 10th November 1981, it read: "I take your strong points: I truly do not expect too much, and I am extremely grateful to you for your experienced warning. One thing that I am sure about, and that is that you are not afraid of change, I have seen no signs of that. And your strength of mind and your constructiveness will continue to be the thing that matters. I have destroyed the letter but I will keep your advice very much in mind."

The last attempt to halt the Sector juggernaut had failed and a General Managers' meeting including dinner was arranged to confirm "the bad news". By this time the Steering Group, advised by Professor Heath, had decided on the future top management structure for the organisation that would apply throughout the remainder of Bob Reid's tenure as Chief Executive and subsequently Executive Chairman.

Despite the robust opposition to Sector Management from the Regions and engineering functions, even after the Board had formally announced its intention to proceed, it would be a mistake to regard their stance solely as a defence of existing power structures. This may have been true in some individual cases and power politics undoubtedly played a part but to portray it purely in that light would be to unfairly denigrate some significant and eminent personalities. Frank Paterson, the principal opponent of the policy, had a track record of substantial achievement and had worked closely with Reid in a number of roles, both commercial and operational. Although other General Managers shared similar views, Frank was the most articulate and formidable. In a recent conversation I had with him, he explained his belief to this day that Reid's reforms should have focused on creating methods for bottom line financial accountability within the existing Regional structure. He argued that this would have avoided the distraction of a major management restructure in a period when BR faced significant challenges. He had a reasonable point that the objectives the Conservative Government had set for BR, particularly a target of saving 35,000 posts, required all-out management concentration and focus. In opposing Sectorisation, his concern was that the teamwork required to achieve targets would be complicated and possibly compromised by creating a third senior tier of management on top of the Regions and Headquarters Functions.

In Frank's view effective teamwork was and remains the key to achieving objectives and securing maximum benefits in their delivery and most railway managers would agree with him. Frank believed that the same outcomes could have been achieved by "an organisation that had existed for 150 years": he favoured Regional structures as the means of delivery because "they worked". Frank acknowledged that the Sector organisations irrefutably delivered huge improvements in the years that followed, but pointed out: "We don't know whether the old regime would have done the same, better or worse." While I respect Frank's views, I disagree. My opinion is that in the BR of that time, a Regional approach to bottom line responsibility would not have worked, not least because huge volumes of freight traffic, and many passenger flows too, crossed Regions' boundaries.

My experiences as Parcels Sector Business Manager on the Southern Region in the period 1982/83 demonstrated clearly to me the benefits of taking decisions from a market based perspective. In this case I fought successfully to reverse Regional management's disastrous proposal to save costs by closing parcels offices at 3pm – just before the peak hours for dispatching them. It was only my newly created Sector role that could provide the evidence to show the proposal would not only have decimated the parcels business but lost money. I am not convinced that a Regional accounting system could have provided the same perspective given the volume of parcels traffic that crossed the Southern Region boundary. To me this episode was symptomatic of the benefits that Sector Management started delivering right from the start. When I became responsible for the Red Star national parcels business it became increasingly apparent that the Regions' myopic view of what by then was an international market was frustrating the business overall due to the narrow, territorial and cost focus of Regional managements. Nonetheless, given the subsequent debates about how privatisation could have been implemented, not least through 'regional companies' once advocated but dropped by John Major, Frank's thinking does not today seem quite so out of kilter with accepted wisdoms in the rail industry as perhaps it did when he was first making the case. The integration inherent in this form of organisation, though not market based, would have been a better model of privatisation than the fragmented structure that was chosen.

In terms of practical railway politics at the time all that matters is that the Regions' opposition came to nothing. Reid was determined to implement Sector Management. Although he may not have thought of it himself, its alignment with markets chimed precisely with his commercial perspective and he understood from the start that it was a mechanism that could transform the railway and its culture. So when the time came to introduce the new structure he did so with a ruthlessness that even 40 years on seems breathtaking. Using his powers of appointment, he removed people he saw as standing in his way and replaced them with others who would implement what he wanted. In a matter of months in 1982 the General Managers perceived as 'recalcitrant' were either retired or moved to positions where they couldn't pose a threat. They included Leslie Lloyd (Western), John Pallette (Southern), and Leslie Soane (Scotland). At the same time he appointed the new Sector Directors and gave them an equivalent status to that of the General Managers. Interestingly Frank Paterson was spared on the promise that he would retire within three years and Jim O'Brien (London Midland) would go on to sit on the BR Board. Reid's treatment of Frank reveals a side to him that not many were aware of, although as his Personal Assistant it was evident to me. Though professionally hard, he was fundamentally a kind and empathic man who valued those with whom he worked most closely. Frank was one of them and, despite the challenges he posed, he was not dealt with in the way of others because of the respect Reid had for him.

Reid's decisiveness in dealing with the General Managers was matched by his enthusiasm for promoting younger people who he saw as change agents for his new regime. The whole enterprise opened up pathways for a new cadre of younger managers as Sector Management developed across BR. The formerly pivotal role of Divisional Manager (geographically configured within each Region and accountable to the General Manager) was replaced by that of the Profit Centre Business Manager, accountable to the Sector Directors, the selection of whom was critical to the early success of the new system. It was carried out with the assistance of Board Member for Personnel Cliff Rose, but apart from Peter Parker, Reid said "no one else knew what I was doing"[31].

---

[31] Interview with Gourvish

The most adventurous appointment was Cyril Bleasdale who moved from MD of Freightliner to head the InterCity Sector. Cyril had a buccaneering commercial approach which Reid had noted when chairing Freightliner Board meetings. He was a person who amused Reid and the two men shared reservations about many aspects of BR. Cyril was hypercritical of much that he saw around him – overstaffing, bureaucracy and resistance to change among unions and management alike. Reid said of him: "He is a very lively guy. I knew he would be loyal. He has always been an innovator." Cyril's background was very different to his Chief Executive's, and of most who reached senior positions in BR. He left school at 15 and, with two years National Service behind him, became a station master at the age of 21. He set about resuming his education, taking Chartered Institute of Transport exams as well as A Levels, and was accepted on the traffic apprentice management training scheme. Bobby, later Sir Robert, Lawrence, the London Divisional Manager at Euston, took Cyril under his wing and was a significant influence on his varied career on the London Midland Region. It included spells as Senior Freight Salesman for the West Midlands and as Depot Manager at Camden Freight Depot. A stint promoting British Transport Advertising in Scotland followed.

With several senior managers having noticed Cyril's energy, enthusiasm and adaptability, he was sent on the senior management course at Woking Transport College. This was usually a stepping stone to higher things and on completion he was posted back to the London Midland Region where Lawrence appointed him Motor Industry Business Manager, another commercial post. Promotion to Regional Freight Manager followed and by this time he was clearly on the escalator to higher general management, initially as Divisional Manager Doncaster where, still in his 30s, he succeeded Bob Reid. David Bowick, BR's Chief Executive at that time, was a frequent visitor to the

Scunthorpe iron and steel complex in the Division where Cyril seems to have continued to make his mark because in 1975 he was appointed Managing Director of Freightliner. The business was losing £2m but when he left in 1982 it was making the same in profit. A controlling stake in the company was meanwhile transferred back to BR from the National Freight Corporation. This proved significant because Peter Parker began to take a direct interest in how Freightliner operated as a commercial business at the very time the debates were taking place on creating similar structures within the BR mainstream. He told Cyril that he wanted to "spend time with you on a one to one basis", and at one meeting asked: "How can we establish something similar on BR?" and "can you write me a confidential paper?", which Cyril did with the support of Rob Mason, one of a group of young, bright, commercially minded people on his team, which also included Richard George and Richard Brown. All of them would go on to pursue notable careers in the future railway. Parker must have been impressed by Cyril's contributions during this planning phase. He promised that if Sector Management was implemented "I want you to be one of the first appointments", which Cyril assumed would probably be freight. In late 1981 he was called in to see Parker and Reid, and to his amazement was offered the InterCity role. Expressing surprise and saying that he didn't know anything much about the passenger business, Reid retorted: "Then it's about time you learned."

The appointment to head what was known at the time as the Provincial Services Sector[32] was John Welsby, a civil servant who had worked on secondment at BR's strategy unit since 1979. Reid liked and saw eye to eye with Welsby on most issues, as he did with several DoT civil servants of the era, notably Peter Baldwin, Peter Lazarus, and John Palmer. He had a natural regard for Welsby's intellect and

---

[32] It was later renamed Regional Railways

appreciated the role he could play in carving out a sector which, as the recipient of a large subsidy at a time of cutbacks, would receive considerable attention from Government.

David Kirby's appointment was a different matter. On the face of it his background in BR's Sealink Shipping Division was ideal because it was viewed as operating in a competitive market and as more switched on to meeting customer service needs than the railways. He was appointed as both Sector Director for London & South East and General Manager (Southern) where he was supported strongly by Gordon Pettit. Kirby's urbane persona hid a lazy intelligence but some of his colleagues harboured doubts about his contribution to Sealink. Following his subsequent elevation to BRB Chief Executive when Reid succeeded Parker in 1983, the new Chairman developed a low opinion of him. After a particular incident during an industrial dispute when Kirby told Reid he was returning home to Cornwall at the insistence of his wife, Reid came to the conclusion that "he was hopeless". Kirby was said to have been in tears, torn between domestic demands and those of the job. Other contemporaries held similar views of his ineffectiveness, which they characterised as indecision.

The Freight and Parcels Sectors retained their chiefs. Henry Sanderson and Mike Connolly had both been managing their businesses successfully, overseeing changes to improve accountability to their customers. Nonetheless Reid expressed regret that he had not injected new blood into freight leadership from the start. "It was a mistake," he said in an interview, but one that he moved to correct when other younger managers were added to the mix as Sector Management developed. Following a significant early career in freight, Brian Burdsall replaced Connolly as Parcels Director when still in his 30s. Chris Green was encouraged to transform the Scottish Region (quickly rebranded ScotRail) at a similar age and John Edmonds was appointed to head the Provincial Services Sector when Welsby was transferred to report on the restructuring of BREL[33].

I place myself in the category of new appointments designed to promote younger managers and fresh commercial thinking. Following my spell as Southern Region Parcels Manager, I was appointed Business Manager (Red Star) in 1984 taking bottom line responsibility for the parcels business nationally. Much to my initial surprise in view of the historically hierarchical, and somewhat command and control culture that I had previously experienced in line management, I was given substantial space and freedom to pursue product development, sales and customer service strategies without interference. As a result, at Red Star my team was able to introduce numerous innovations, some of which were not only firsts for the railway but for UK industry[34]. Virtually all these initiatives involved increasing the cost base on the basis that the return in revenues would be substantially greater. In less than four years, Red Star's profitability quadrupled. This was exactly what Sector Management was designed to promote. On a cost obsessed railway, with overhead reductions targeted through a regional structure, it would not have been possible. Similar successes were being delivered across the railway. Five years after Sectorisation began, Reid highlighted that BR had reduced PSO funding from Government by 25%. "Devotion to the bottom line provides the impetus for change," he said.

Despite my record in the Parcels Sector, I was a very unconventional and surprise choice for my next appointment, as General Manager of the Eastern Region in November 1987. I was barely 40, the youngest person ever

---

[33] At the time British Rail Engineering Limited was seen as a problem child; monopolistic and expensive; and had been the subject of a review by the Monopolies and Mergers Commission.

[34] See also Chapter 2

to become a General Manager, and had spent practically my entire career in commercial roles. I had never occupied a mainstream operational post and by this time in the evolution of railway organisation, the Regions were fulfilling the production delivery role that Bob Reid's memorandum to the trade unions had promised. I had virtually no hands-on experience of production management, little professional contact with engineers and no in-depth appreciation of their activities. I was, of course, fortunate to have worked directly for Bob Reid and that obviously helped, but what mattered more was that the success of Red Star and the manner in which it was achieved demonstrated an ability to promote and manage change. It was Reid's way of making a statement, one that was symbolic of the ascendancy of the commercial over the operational railway, on a Region moreover that had a reputation for being amongst the most traditional. My appointment, just like those of John Edmonds as Director Provincial Services and Chris Green as Director London and South East had been, was designed to send signals about the direction of travel and the need to move with pace.

Change was happening everywhere. In Chris Green's case, Reid had supported him in Scotland where as General Manager he was allowed to meet the competitive threat posed by bus deregulation with vigour. In Chris's words he was encouraged (as I had been at Red Star) to "get on with it". The same applied when he moved to the London and South East Sector. Reid told him "to do a ScotRail" and transform it into something "modern". Even though Chris may admit to high spending in rebranding the Sector as Network South East and the accompanying initiatives, he believes Reid allowed him to "get away with it". John Edmonds was used as a similar force for change, though in a very different, almost opposite way to Chris. After Provincial, his next job was to carve out from the Eastern

Region, a low-overhead, market-focused Anglia Region. He had a remit to "shake a few trees". Creating Anglia was aimed at streamlining Regions whilst aligning them better with Sectors. He thought the eventual abolition of the Regions could be seen as implicit but that it was never explicit in his remit.

From its introduction in 1982 to the end of Bob Reid's tenure in 1990, Sector Management evolved significantly, notably through the creation of route and market based Subsectors as profit centres within their parent Sectors – for example East Coast in the InterCity Sector and Regional Railways North East in the Provincial Sector. Despite this, it was not until the end of the decade that the Regions themselves came under serious threat. When they were eventually subsumed within the Sectors in 1991/92, it was really a result of a merger of commercial and production activities that by then had already become increasingly aligned, rather than one taking over the other.

The intervening period was at times stressful for those who had to manage within what came to be known as BR's matrix organisation, a balance of power between the Sectors and the Regions. The initiation of Sector Management did indeed lead, as Frank Paterson and other General Managers had feared, to a period of tension between existing and emerging forces. Reid characterised this as "constructive tension", although to many working at the interfaces in this developing matrix organisation, the tension was often personal as much as it was organisational. Frank describes the early period as "an unhappy time" and felt Bob Reid's treatment of some individuals was unacceptable. My own experience from 1987 when I was appointed Eastern Region General Manager, the same role Frank had occupied, was also personally stressful. This was mainly because by this time the relationships between Sectors and the production functions run by the Regions had in some cases become quite confrontational. What Bob Reid saw as constructive tension occasionally manifested as unpleasant and acrimonious. Subsector managers, accountable to Sector Directors at the centre, found themselves in a difficult place, rubbing shoulders day by day with regional managers who they had formerly seen as colleagues, but with whom they were often at odds as a result of policies determined from above. This was especially true when it came to setting budgets. Formerly the responsibility of the Regions, this essential function passed to the Sectors, resulting in often quite young and junior members of the Subsectors challenging budgets proposed by senior, long serving functional managers, notably civil and signalling engineers with substantial safety responsibilities. As General Manager I became a mediator of disputes.

Gradually the dynamic changed with an acceptance that the Sectors had primacy and that the Regions' production functions were their suppliers. Once I had got my feet under the table and began to understand the dynamics and capabilities of the production functions for which I was responsible, I realised two important things. The first was that the managers in them were overwhelmingly capable and adaptable. Civil engineers were a prime example of a cadre of management which was capable of harnessing its skills to the needs of the businesses without any risk to safety or performance. I struck up a particularly good relationship with Bryan Davies, a colossus amongst civil engineers, subsequently making him my Deputy General Manager, and was able to work through him to bring about fundamental changes across all the production activities.

The second key enabler of change was that as relationships matured, the Subsector managers gained greater knowledge and awareness of how the production functions could serve the needs of their businesses, and also of the safety and risk management dynamics of the operational railway. I facilitated the development of these relationships by implementing changes to the way functions were structured. Operations and engineering were created as mirror images of the Subsectors to which they became suppliers. Eastern was also the first Region to establish a significant part of the engineering organisation as a 'profit centre' trading with other departments including Sectors. This worked so well that similar initiatives were developed in other parts of the Regional organisation. Pretty soon we had developed internal customer facing production organisations at local Area level that, for the first time, were aligned not just geographically but commercially. For example, the Area Manager, Kings Cross was aligned with the commuting business of the Great Northern Division in Network South East as well as with InterCity East Coast. The former Doncaster Area Manager's organisation was split two ways, into InterCity and Yorkshire Freight. Further north Leeds and Sheffield became Areas that were aligned principally with Regional Railways passenger services. The Newcastle and Middlesbrough Areas became passenger and freight respectively, following on from the North East Coal organisation already established at Sunderland. Elsewhere Immingham became a freight only Area with local passenger operations transferring to the control of a South TransPennine passenger Area, headquartered at Sheffield.

The civil engineering organisations were restructured in a similar way with an InterCity South and North configuration covering only the East Coast and Leeds main lines. A freight equivalent was based at Doncaster and a Regional passenger organisation at Leeds. Signalling and Telecommunications were similarly divided, and a new Doncaster-based Electrification Engineer was established following the electrification of the line to Leeds and Scotland. In this way, a completely new commercial-facing production organisation was established with its component parts aligned with passenger and freight businesses in all five Sectors.

Even with the passage of time it is difficult to exaggerate how radical these developments were in the context of their day or their importance in commercialising the railway. They meant that commercial managers gained an appreciation first hand of the practical and safety aspects of railways while the operators and engineers, through their new found understanding of market and customer requirements, were able to contribute ideas and solutions that enhanced the overall result. Neither were these the only changes made. Following a model established in the new Anglia Region, the infrastructure departments were brought together under the leadership of Bryan Davies so that best practice, better co-ordination, better project planning and improved productivity could be driven faster, heralding future more radical changes that would take place in the early 1990s.

The changes made on the Eastern Region created much closer interfaces, similar to those that existed between Network South East and the Southern Region where there was a geographic and market proximity between the two. Gordon Pettit's experience as Deputy and then General Manager of the Southern Region was that this worked well within Network South East where he was included in Chris Green's team. This may have had something to do with the fact that Gordon's own background was a mix of operations and commercial responsibilities. Elsewhere Gordon observed that the relationships between Regions and Sectors "depended on the people". On the other hand, Chris Green, who after Network South East went on to head up InterCity, felt that it only worked "because we chose to make it work".

Towards the end of Sir Robert Reid's tenure as Chairman there were plenty of pressures on him to merge the production and Sector activities as integrated businesses at the Subsector level. I became a strong advocate of this. I had seen the effectiveness of aligned working relationships on the Eastern Region, and from my experience at Red Star

I understood that a key dynamic in our achievements was the shared identity everyone working for the business felt. I thought that having infrastructure and operations directors sitting round the same table as the finance, personnel and marketing directors, would have a double edged benefit. The production directors could contribute to the development of business strategy whilst the commercial side of a business would equally come to have a greater appreciation of the parameters of what was safe and operationally feasible. With a Managing Director leading the business and holding the ring between the various directors, the creation of these entities represented a final incremental step in creating genuine businesses.

Not that Bob Reid necessarily saw the benefits in the same way. On his frequent tours of Regions and businesses he would explore the issues time and time again, apparently agonising whether this would be a step too far. It was strange to see someone who had made such bold and controversial decisions in 1981 balk at the prospect of making what to many of us in 1990 seemed a logical next step to take. He had certainly been pleased with the constructive tension that had existed previously between the businesses and the production functions. Is it possible that he still preferred this as a galvanising dynamic in the railway? Or was he perhaps concerned, as some in the industry were, that the safety of the railway might be compromised if the production functions were fully incorporated into business-led Sectors? Was his thinking influenced by the aftermath of the tragic Clapham rail crash, which had brought about a massive re-appraisal of safety management in the industry, or with his term drawing to a close, was he simply prepared to leave the decision to his successor?

Two months before he retired in March 1990, Reid was invited to make a valedictory address to the Chartered Institute of Transport. Looking back over his career, he said that before Sectorisation in 1982 BR had been "organised as a bureaucracy; that it had been engineering based, union dominated and production led". The customer took a back seat to the "more important engineering and operating expediency led priorities" which only served to "produce demands for ever larger subsidy". Following his decade at the very top of the industry, he considered the period one of such transformation that it had left BR in an unprecedented position of strength. Casting an eye to the future he said: "I would be foolish to predict what the competitive environment for the railway will be in the year 2000. However, it will be very different to 1990 and not what we now may expect."

Never were truer words spoken. In fact the story of change over that period proved to be more far-reaching, more extraordinary and occurred far quicker than Reid could have envisaged. Shortly after his retirement, BR would embark on its Organising for Quality (OfQ) programme which would fully integrate railway management. Yet little more than a year after it was completed in 1992, the same managers that had implemented OfQ would be tasked with taking it apart in preparation for a privatisation that would destroy the very structures and relationships they had themselves created.

Moving BR from vertical integration to fragmentation would occupy the next five years.

CHAPTER FIVE

To Vertical Integration and Back

Sir Robert Reid's successor as British Rail Chairman had enjoyed a career that was almost a mirror image of that of the great railwayman but in another industry. He also shared the same name! Like his predecessor, Bob Reid II (as I shall refer to the new Chairman) had worked almost exclusively for a single organisation, but in his case it was in the private sector oil industry, the last 35 years at Shell, where he was Chief Executive from 1985 to 1990. He had many good attributes for the BR job. His career had revolved around the management of safety-critical, heavy infrastructure and capital intensive projects, which helped him gain a good understanding of the railway from the start. Personally he was open, honest and straightforward – all good qualities in managing a large people orientated-business. He brought a freshness and ebullience to the upper echelons of BR, demonstrating an immediate empathy with managers in the field and for all types of railwaymen and women, often turning up unannounced at work locations to share thoughts and conversations at odd times of the day and night. Unlike other railway industry leaders brought in from outside the industry following privatisation, he did not come merely with the self-confidence of someone who had been successful in his own previous sphere; neither did he present himself as someone who knew all the answers. He displayed no arrogance and was someone who listened. He showed respect to industry professionals and they in turn respected him.

In the post Clapham period and with BR moving in an increasingly business focused direction Reid II was the ideal successor to his namesake. He picked up the baton of organisational change and it didn't take him long to acknowledge the sense of moving to the integrated Sector based structures, described at the end of Chapter 4, and favoured by many in BR. Coming from the heavy, yet highly commercial, structure of the global oil industry, he needed little persuading of the merits of creating equivalent structures in the railway. These were the norms in the industry he knew.

At this point in my narrative I pause briefly to reflect on how far management thinking and attitudes had changed in a very short space of time. In Chapter 2, I described how two or three years earlier I had been remitted by BR's Chief Executive, David Kirby, to review the interaction of production interfaces with the Sectors and to make recommendations for their improvement. It was a mark of the lack of clear thinking and reticence among some in the top echelons of BR at the time that, faced with my proposals, Kirby protested almost with incredulity that they heralded the demise of the Regions. His initial 'shock-horror' reaction to bury my recommendation of redefining the production functions as suppliers to the businesses demonstrated the nervousness and indecision that existed. On the one hand there was a recognition that something had to change; that parallel Region and Sector power structures could not continue to exist as equivalent; yet moves towards the primacy of Sectors were still seen to be fraught with risk. It wasn't until John Edmonds was elevated from the Anglia Region to the BR Board in 1989 and given the task of determining future organisation nationally that more radical changes began to gain ground, culminating in the creation of vertically integrated businesses as profit centres during Reid II's Chairmanship.

John masterminded this next stage in BR's development, known as Organising for Quality, supported by project lead Richard Goldson. Richard recalls that it was introduced on the simple business principle that vertically integrated railway companies would operate more efficiently than those in which the production and commercial functions existed in separate organisations, regardless of the extent of the alignment that had taken place in the preceding years. Encouragement came from the Department of Transport which accepted the business principles on which it was based. Upfront costs were seen as an investment worth making in a system that it was believed would deliver a more efficient railway, evidenced subsequently by the profits made at both InterCity and Network South East in their final years of existence.

In preparing to launch OfQ, the first task was to brief the Regional General Managers and the functional Heads of Engineering in HQ whose roles and departments would be merged into the Sectors. This time the mood was very different to the resistance that had accompanied Sectorisation a decade earlier. Nevertheless John Edmonds was nervous of the reaction of Signalling and Telecommunications Director Ken Burrage whose department had been through a significant re-evaluation of safety process following the Clapham crash two years earlier. According to Richard Goldson they had clashed over the management of safety standards during John's creation of the new Anglia Region, but Burrage nevertheless co-operated on the detailed, critical work needed to transfer safety roles and responsibilities to the Subsectors under OfQ. In fact a key aspect of the preparation included the creation of a bespoke safety validation process which mapped in detail how safety critical tasks would migrate from Regional posts and departments to equivalent new ones in the Sectors and Subsectors. This would subsequently prove significant because the same process would be used again when privatisation came along.

The whole enterprise was managed through a network of project managers reporting jointly to Richard Goldson and to senior management in the functions and Regions. His team included a young and then junior manager, Andrew Haines, who was to rise to the very top of the industry as Chief Executive of Network Rail, a post he would take up in 2018. Some of the principles for structural reform Andrew started to introduce when he took up this new role clearly reflect this earlier experience. Richard describes Andrew as "very bright, capable, energetic, hard working, ambitious, good with people", and a man "who knew the railway in every dimension"; something that in my opinion distinguishes him from all his predecessors at the top of Network Rail.

Implementing OfQ in the Eastern Region was straightforward due to the changes I had already made to align production activities with the Subsectors' markets and geography. The process was completed in April 1991. It meant the Region was replaced by five vertically integrated passenger Subsectors, only one of which (Regional Railways North East) fell pretty much entirely within its boundaries. Three InterCity businesses were created (East Coast, Cross Country, and Midland Mainline), each of which had straddled more than one Region, whilst in the Network South East Sector Great Northern routes were merged with West Anglia routes from the Anglia Region. Because Regional boundaries no longer existed there was further reduction in interfaces and simplification of structures that went beyond merging of production functions into the Subsectors. For example, InterCity East Coast broke a long held taboo in that it included staff and physical infrastructure in Scotland as well as England. I became the first Managing Director of this newly integrated business, reporting to the InterCity Managing Director, John Prideaux. In the process I had made myself redundant as General Manager.

In BR's other Regions support in creating the new structure came from Southern's General Manager Gordon

Pettit and in Scotland from John Ellis. In the Anglia Region, where David Burton was now General Manager, the groundwork for the change had already been laid by John Edmonds two years previously. It was only in the geographically large and complex London Midland and Western Regions that more time was needed to fully implement the OfQ changes, but here too it was completed in short order.

The single biggest task in establishing the new integrated organisations was, in Richard Goldson's words, "to create the belief in middle management that it was going to happen". This was an important factor in my experience too. On the Eastern Region the engineers who had initially felt threatened by Sectorisation came to see being part of the new integrated businesses as "a route back" to the mainstream from which some of them had felt isolated, especially when Sectors came to control budgets and were perceived to threaten their professional judgement. Others, cynical in the light of earlier failed attempts at re-structuring, such as the Field Re-organisation, soon started to march to the beat of the drum when it became clear beyond doubt that the whole Board and the Regional General Managers were four square behind the changes; in stark contrast to the skirmishing they had witnessed when the Sector organisations had been created in 1982. Full integration across the railway took place in 1992, a time when further senior management changes were made to underpin its implementation. These saw Chris Green move from Network South East to take over at InterCity while I was appointed to head up NSE. John Prideaux took up the lead role in developing the Channel Tunnel Rail Link, a project close to the heart of Bob Reid II. This also saw John Armitt brought in from Laing as lead engineer and Chief Executive of Union Railways, the entity established for the purpose of constructing the new high speed railway. He would later become Chief Executive of Railtrack when the company was in administration and then the first Chief Executive of Network Rail.

It is worth reflecting on the change that had occurred within BR over the previous decade in which it had moved from geographically based on five Regions to being founded on the business Sectors. A common misconception today is that as a nationalised industry BR was by definition vertically integrated simply because all its assets were owned by a single party. I hope that the description of the railway in the previous chapters makes clear that, although the railway's assets and personnel were all part and parcel of British Rail, the ways in which they were organised and managed, were by no means clearly focused and integrated. Key related and interdependent tasks and functions were often under different managements with separate accountability structures. Prior to 1982 the term silo management could almost have been coined with the railways in mind.

Sectorisation re-orientated the railways so that the focus was principally on markets and not geography, even if these coincided in many cases. Despite having its origins in the Government's desire to separate the commercial from the subsidised railway, it was a more logical way of marshalling resources to meet the needs of passengers and freight customers. Even those Sectors that continued to be loss making benefited from the single minded concentration of effort that was the consequence of aligning all related activities in a single organisation. With everyone and every department pointing in the same direction it was easier to motivate people to find solutions to problems and to create accountability mechanisms that enabled managers to do their jobs better.

Sectors were defined by their market profile and characteristics more than by anything else. There were obvious differences between the rolling stock and timetable specifications of long distance InterCity routes compared with those that applied to commuters or in rural situations. Focusing attention on each one individually led to solutions tailored to the needs of passengers in those markets. The type of rolling stock provided followed naturally from this. Furthermore, the way track and signalling systems were configured to accommodate the trains and the way timetables developed to meet specific needs were far, far more likely to provide the best outcomes if the key managers responsible for delivering them were seated round the same table, accountable not just to a single Chief Executive but to one another in a tightly managed, well-motivated team. The same would be true today if this form of organisation were readopted. When maintenance engineers understand the commercial imperatives of the business they are more likely to come up with innovative solutions that enable them to apply their technical and professional expertise to meeting customer needs. If they are embedded within the business alongside the marketing and finance directors, they are even more likely to do so. Furthermore the safety and operational standards which are so crucial to railway performance and for which production managers are responsible (often in law) would also become embedded in the thinking of those managers who are not directly accountable for them.

So in the decade from 1982 BR moved progressively from a start point where nationally created Sectors worked initially alongside geographically based Regions in a state of tension to the position that by 1992 it had created unified structures. During the early to mid 1980s the Sectors took on an increasingly market focused dimension with the creation of profit centres (or Subsectors) based on discreet markets (many of these incidentally also defined by fairly narrow geographical limits) such that by the end of the decade it became a logical next step to align the regional engineering and operations functions with them. Then in 1991 they were amalgamated into unified, multi-functional businesses, each with its own accountable management team. Genuine vertical integration had arrived and was accompanied by the melding of formerly BRB engineering and functional headquarters staffs into the businesses as well. It would not be wildly imaginative to envisage a similar development occurring today involving Network Rail and the train operating companies.

In the case of BR, Sectors delivered amongst the most significant and innovative changes in modern railway history, some of which I was involved in during my period in the Eastern Region. They included the on-time and on-budget electrification of the East Coast Main Line from London all the way through to Edinburgh and on to Glasgow accompanied by the introduction of associated Class 225 traction and rolling stock; substantial increases in the frequency of interurban services across the Pennines using new rolling stock to generate increased revenues whilst reducing costs; and devolution of all aspects of running the Great Northern commuter services to a unified management at Kings Cross so that it recorded the highest standards of punctuality and performance in London and the South East.

When the new fully integrated businesses were created it presented the opportunity for even greater change.

I was appointed Managing Director Network South East in January 1992. NSE was the largest of the three vertically integrated passenger Sectors established by OfQ and had the biggest bottom line responsibility on the railways. Although the Managing Director job title sounded similar to the Sector Director title that preceded it, it was in fact a different role. Previously NSE had existed as a marketing, planning, business development and budgeting department, specifying service requirements to the Regions which delivered them. Under OfQ, NSE had total responsibility for all operations and engineering including safety. In the case of major infrastructure investments, the Sectors' role had previously been one of project sponsorship rather than delivery. Now they were responsible for project implementation as well. I was not the only new Sector MD who had previously held major production and safety responsibilities. In fact it was notable that all three integrated passenger businesses were headed up by former Regional General Managers. I led a team of 15 Divisional directors, nine of whom were individually responsible for running the profit centres. The others were functional heads responsible for the major activities of fleet engineering, operations, marketing, finance, personnel and infrastructure. On this occasion my experience as a Regional General Manager put me at an advantage. I was used to managing large teams of people with ego but I had also acquired my own views about the principles on which the railway should be run. By then I was not only thoroughly in favour of integrated railways, I was also an advocate of devolved organisations supported by effective accountability systems.

I decided to make my views known at an early stage and worried about how this would go down with the functional directors in NSE HQ, some of whom would be almost bound to regard devolution as a loss of power. Management jobs were rewarded on the basis of size and some people saw the prospect of devolution as diminishing their status. I didn't see it that way at all. My view was that by changing the nature of the 'headquarters' role to strategy, standard setting and monitoring, I was not diminishing 'control' but improving 'accountability'. Devolution by these means actually improved control. The Divisions would be strengthened to fulfil more of the integrated railway delivery role than ever before whilst HQ departments would either become focused on strategy and standards or be re-established as 'profit centre suppliers' providing services to the Divisions which would become their customers. Instead of calling the shots, many HQ departments would need to develop a customer facing approach. They would succeed solely on the work they received from their customers.

There was a big human consequence of these changes. When I went to NSE in 1992 the organisation employed around 35,000 people and as many as 5,000 were classified as HQ. I considered this to be ridiculous and by the time of privatisation had reduced the number to less than 50 by following the principles of devolution and commercialising activities. Of the rest about half migrated either to the Divisions or to the new 'profit centre suppliers' whilst the remainder left the industry, facilitated by generous redundancy terms. The new arrangements not only saved millions of pounds but also improved the capability of the Divisions to run a more efficient railway. One outcome was that they got a firm grip on the punctuality of the NSE railway such that it improved for 24 consecutive months to reach its highest recorded levels in 1994/95. Every Division bar one improved and at the same time the focus on quality management techniques and devolution resulted in huge financial benefits that moved NSE into profit. Operating under a network wide strategy and a well-resourced change management programme, my role became a relatively straightforward task of monitoring performance through a series of monthly review meetings that ensured accountability. These allowed for flexibility in discussing issues of local importance but otherwise operated to a standard format reviewing in turn safety, operations and finance, a process supported by the use of key performance indicators including customer polling, the first time this had been adopted anywhere on the railways as a means of driving improvement. The review systems laid down at this time have been in large measure followed by franchise owning groups ever since and subsequently by Transport Focus, the public body charged with monitoring passenger satisfaction with railways. When in recent years Network Rail proclaimed the benefits of devolution to its Routes I often thought that it should adopt a similar approach to the one implemented in NSE in 1993/94 and it seems that Andrew Haines has started to do so.

In Chapter 2 I described the period of vertical integration within NSE, some of its achievements and the challenges that had to be met. Overall I would describe this as a considerable success. Given the focus that continues to be given to what could be done to create more effective management structures, a brief description of what these looked like in a NSE Division is a worthwhile diversion at this point in my narrative.

Each Division was a profit centre headed by a Managing Director. They varied in size and scope according to operating circumstances but some were substantial, the largest being South Western, South Central, South Eastern, and Great Eastern. I no longer have to hand the exact numbers of personnel but they would have been in the order of three to five thousand for each Division. People were employed in infrastructure and train maintenance, station and train operations, as well as in non-operational functions including health & safety, finance, marketing, human resources, and projects. Each function was headed by an experienced manager, (professionally qualified in the case of the engineers). The largest and some smaller Divisions were pretty much self-contained operationally. Others shared tracks with larger profit centres, mainly in the InterCity Sector. Thames and Chiltern shared tracks with InterCity Great Western; the North Division, with InterCity West Coast; Thameslink with both InterCity Midland Main Line and South Central; and West Anglia/Great Northern with InterCity East Coast. Some of these NSE Divisions were not large enough to support their own teams of specialist engineers so it worked instead through customer/supplier relationships with the equivalent teams in the larger Division. These relationships were underpinned by contracts providing clear lines of accountability for delivery, including of safety. To get best value from the relationship, each of the smaller Divisions had specialist, professionally qualified Engineering Directors to ensure that their own requirements were properly met. It worked very well.

A quarter of a century later it still seems an irony that as OfQ got underway and began to make a positive early impact, the Government chose to privatise the railways in a form that would destroy these integrated profit centres. It was a further irony that the OfQ reforms and the preceding Sectorisation would actually assist a privatisation that the Conservatives had shied away from committing to until the dying days of Margaret Thatcher's time as Prime Minister.

During the Thatcher Government's huge privatisation programme of the 1980s the focus had been on the sale of industries that, despite being public utilities, were in essence profitable. The view was that disposal would not only be beneficial to the Treasury, but that profits would enable investment in infrastructure. When BR was considered, subsidiaries[35] such as hotels and shipping that were essentially standalone commercially viable businesses were disposed of. This made sense because within BR these assets made claims on investment funds that might otherwise have been available to the mainstream railways and the British Railways Board was not opposed to their sale.

The railway itself did not escape scrutiny. However, various Treasury-led exercises undertaken to consider privatisation options highlighted that there were significant differences between BR and other utilities slated for sale. Assessments recognised issues specific to rail, notably the impracticality of promoting effective competition, difficulties in breaking up the network, the perceived power

---

[35] In the 1980s several BR businesses were sold. In addition to hotels (1982-4) and Shipping (1984), these included Hovercraft (1981), British Transport Advertising, Doncaster Wagon Works (both 1987), British Rail Engineering, and the catering division Travellers Fare (both 1988).

of the trade unions; and the difficulty of selling, then supporting, a loss making industry dependent on Government funding. The Department of Transport adopted a posture of identifying options to the Treasury and listing the pros and cons which, according to John Palmer, DoT Deputy Secretary at the time, showed the cons were sufficient to discourage any serious attempt at drawing up privatisation proposals. There were also strong political reservations even amongst most senior Tory ministers of the day. Apart from the ongoing need for public subsidy, the railway had a proven track record of producing political controversy at the slightest whiff of a threat to services. Thatcher's natural leaning was to regard it as a high risk political venture which led to clashes with her Chancellor Nigel Lawson. Though she came round at the very end of her tenure, subsequent events have proved her initial nervousness about the political fall-out was right.

As BR Chairman, Sir Robert Reid did little to discourage these doubts and his relationship with Secretaries of State for Transport, notably Nicholas Ridley who was in post from 1983-86, helped to stave off any serious talk of privatisation at that time. The two men were similar in character and got on well. They shared a passion for fishing and even went on holiday together. Reid undoubtedly discussed mainstream railway privatisation with Ridley. Although not necessarily anti-privatisation himself, ownership was not Reid's prime concern: meeting market needs was. "Would there be customer benefits?" would be his starting point. "How could Government financial targets best be met?" would have been another huge consideration. He saw no contradiction between a commercially-led and publicly-owned railway and as a 'railway integrationist', opposed to the fragmentation of the industry that most privatisation models would have entailed, he would not have seen the benefits. It seems highly probable that Ridley was influenced by Reid in advising Thatcher against railway privatisation. Although generally a free market economic liberal, Ridley was a man of independent spirit and on railway privatisation he was a noted sceptic.

It was in the late 1980s towards the end of Reid's tenure that the political mood on rail privatisation began to change. The first public statement announcing potential privatisation options came towards the end of 1988 from Paul Channon who had been appointed Transport Secretary the previous year. Scenarios ranged from privatising BR as a single entity; as integrated Regional or Sector businesses; or under a track authority model. The latter option would create a standalone body to manage the railway infrastructure with train operating companies responsible separately for running services. The models put forward reflected options aired in the preceding 18 months in a series of policy papers from right-wing think tanks such as the Adam Smith Institute and the Centre for Policy Studies. These precipitated a series of reviews to examine the options, but the difficulties were again highlighted, and political opinion remained divided. It was only in the last Conservative Party conference before Thatcher was ousted in November 1990 that her then Transport Secretary Cecil Parkinson announced that the question was not whether to privatise but how and when. In her first, and last, clear public statement in support, Thatcher confirmed in her speech that a new wave of infrastructure privatisation would include the railways. "We've trebled the number of shareholders in Britain and privatised 20 major industries. That's good, but not enough. We want more shareholders and more workers to own shares. So we'll privatise the major ports; then tackle British Rail with more to come," she said to applause from the delegates.

Although these conference speeches gave no indication of urgency, work had already been stepped up, initially under a cross-departmental group including John Redwood, Minister of State at the DTI, Francis Maude, Secretary to the Treasury, and Transport Minster Roger Freeman. There the free market held sway. Jim Coates, a senior civil servant at the Department of Transport at this time, recalls a meeting where he advised that BR was working well under its Sector structure; that this had proved successful; and breaking it up would lose the advantages gained. The response left little room for debate. He sums up Ministers' attitude as: "Competition must prevail and if it doesn't work it doesn't matter. The market will have decided." It was this free market ideology that ultimately determined how BR would be privatised under the new Prime Minister John Major. In retrospect Major is viewed as a centrist and his interventions in the Brexit debate certainly cast him on the moderate side of the Conservative Party but he would not have won the vote to succeed Thatcher without being seen to pursue the more economically liberal policies of his predecessor who endorsed his campaign. He wasted little time in confirming his commitment to rail privatisation after he became Prime Minister, even if his speeches gave no detail on the form it could take.

Behind the scenes though, Government departments involved became engaged in an increasingly fraught attempt to formalise a policy for the 1992 General Election. Debates over the various options were swaying towards the Treasury's preference for a highly liberalised structure based on creating a separate infrastructure authority and promoting the maximum possible competition. Vertically integrated Sector or Regional organisations (said to have been Major's initial preference) were seen as limiting competition and presenting practical difficulties in a privatised environment given the number of cross-boundary routes. The dynamic was given added impetus by the European Commission's Directive in 1991 promoting the separation of track and train. As with many such Directives, the British Government chose to apply it to its ultimate limits by creating Railtrack not only as an organisation to control the infrastructure but to do so, moreover, as a FTSE 100 company. Elsewhere in the EU the separation was usually one of accounting methodologies rather than physical management separation. The Directive was useful cover for the free market zealots and sealed the fate of anything resembling an integrated railway.

Another factor influencing Government thinking was concern over how to engage private sector interest in owning and operating the railway. That meant reducing risk. The major capital value in the railway was in its infrastructure but that was where the greatest potential for risk lay. There was a feeling that some of the more obvious potential bidders for rail franchises, particularly bus companies, would be put off by any requirement to take on infrastructure risks. It contributed to a privatisation model of 'thin' train operating franchises, with limited asset ownership and responsibility, gaining ground. However, with splits in Government and the civil service repeatedly delaying a White Paper, it was not until the Conservatives' 1992 manifesto that separate management of infrastructure and train operation was announced formally as the basis of policy. It stated a central belief that "competition and private ownership are the most powerful engines of economic efficiency, innovation and choice". This would involve restructuring the railway. "One part of BR will continue to be responsible for all track and infrastructure". On the train operating side, the Government would "sell certain rail services [such as freight], and franchise others". Franchise areas would be decided following "technical discussions with BR".

When the Conservatives were re-elected in April 1992, the new Transport Secretary John MacGregor was given just six weeks to finalise the White Paper, published in July 1992. Railtrack was mentioned for the first time as the name for the new infrastructure manager with services including maintenance to be contracted to the private sector. At this stage though, there was no commitment to sell the infrastructure. Objectives for franchising rail services included letting contracts to operate InterCity services by line of route to maintain a basis for a future outright sale. Regional and NSE services would be franchised by geographical area. Although billed as a consultation, in reality the decision on separating track and train had been made.

Meanwhile the British Railways Board's relationship with the Government had degenerated into an unpleasant stand-off in which the Board and its new Chairman exerted little influence and held few cards. The same straightforward and forthright approach to business which made Bob Reid II an effective leader of BR's structural reforms and major projects was probably less well suited to the political manoeuvrings of the time. As an experienced executive with a lengthy career in another substantial industry where integrated organisation mattered to safe, efficient decision making, he was wedded to the OfQ changes he had been bedding in. His view, and that of the Board, was that privatisation should be based on integrated structures. It found him in desperate opposition to the emerging direction of the Government's privatisation policy. Twenty-five years on, few now would be likely to question the fundamental wisdom of his position.

Initially Reid II had enjoyed a comfortable relationship with the Secretary of State. He had been Cecil Parkinson's appointment and there was some personal connection. Parkinson had attended the same school as Reid's wife. It was not to last. When Parkinson resigned in protest at Thatcher's forced departure as Prime Minister, Reid's relationship with the new Transport Secretary, Malcolm Rifkind, was very different and at times antagonistic. The pair had clashed over the routing of the Channel Tunnel Rail Link, a project which was very close to Reid's heart. On occasion Reid was publicly critical of Rifkind's announcements on the emerging privatisation agenda.

One issue that contributed to the tension was the Board's reluctance to provide the co-operation Rifkind asked for in promoting competition from private sector passenger trains in line with the Government's approach to implementing the EU Directive. A number of businesses expressed interest, notably Richard Branson's Virgin Company which sought to hire three BR train sets on the East Coast Main Line to compete with BR's InterCity service. Brian Burdsell, then Managing Director of InterCity East Coast, recalled that the Board rejected it because revenue abstraction would have wiped out InterCity's profit. In the event the only initiative that went ahead was for Stagecoach to buy space on, and sell tickets for, two branded carriages attached to an Anglo-Scottish train. The experiment failed after six months. The Board's approach probably did little to assist more moderate voices within Government promoting a more incremental, less radical form of privatisation.

In a bid for compromise between its advocacy of an integrated railway and emerging Government proposals, Peter Trewin, the BRB's Secretary at the time, recalls that the Board offered a new option. BR would remain in overarching control of the infrastructure and strategic planning, effectively as the industry's directing mind, while franchising train operating businesses to the private sector and contracting out engineering works. The response from Government was that the proposal was too close to a BR monopoly. Ministers also considered that it would not address their dissatisfaction with previous utility privatisations which in hindsight they believed had failed to inject sufficient competition to the market. Nonetheless, Trewin says Reid II continued to believe he could "turn things around" including through covert lobbying. His pursuit of a change in policy included a meeting with John Peyton, a Conservative peer and former Transport Secretary in Ted Heath's Government, who remained a prominent member in party committees and was an opponent of the

Government's proposals. Despite agreeing with him in principle, the Chairman's approach and criticisms were seen by a number of his colleagues on the Board as unrealistic, out of line and contributing to an "irrepairable" relationship with Government. It led them to reflect that he had seriously misjudged the politics and that he had acted initially as if "he expected Government to accept whatever advice the Board gave". By the time of the 1992 election he was a marginal figure in the policy-making process.

Some believe Reid II's illustrious predecessor might have been able to temper Government policy, but in my view that is doubtful. A measure of the political paranoia during this period is that when John Welsby was appointed BR Chief Executive in January 1990 he was required to sign a loyalty oath, despite his background as a civil servant and strong public service ethos. Although his favoured model would have been a vertically integrated structure based on BR's existing Sector framework, Welsby nonetheless supported privatisation and committed to carrying out Government's instructions regardless of his personal beliefs. It was also apparent in his last days as Chairman that Sir Robert Reid did not enjoy the same influential relationship with Parkinson during his brief tenure as Secretary of State, as he had with Ridley or even Paul Channon, whom he found supportive in the dark days following the Clapham disaster[36]. He saw Parkinson as a brick wall. He noted that Parkinson's eyes would glaze over when he explained situations to him and seems to have doubted he had sufficient grasp of or energy for the situation.

For me, the overwhelming recollection from that period is the extent to which professional advice was either disregarded or not even sought. The form of privatisation chosen was not only contrary to the advice of the BR Board,

---

[36]

but the views of most railway managers and almost every organisation with an interest from passenger representatives to the Commons Transport Committee. Contrary views to the hard line right wing ministers, Treasury officials, think tanks and political activists promoting separation of track and train were often distrusted, sidelined or even gagged. The antipathy to the consultative and legislative process sometimes bordered on contempt. There were minimal soundings taken among the executive managers who would be running the privatised railway and the few there were clearly demonstrated that ministers appeared, wrongly, to believe that they were inherently opposed to privatisation and would try to hinder the process. The only time the senior Divisional Directors below Board level were actively asked their views was at a meeting shortly after the 1992 General Election which Transport Secretary John MacGregor agreed to attend with his Minister Roger Freeman. The universal advice was that the railway should remain vertically integrated. Not one senior manager present believed separation of infrastructure from track was likely to prove an efficient way of running a cost effective and reliable service, and I never heard anyone involved in running the passenger railway argue in favour of it. It was also pointed out that BR had been through a major restructuring in the previous two years of OfQ reforms and should not be pulled apart and reorganised again. However, it was abundantly clear from MacGregor's body language and comments on the side that he was going through the motions in attending. The overwhelming impression was that he had anticipated a pre-determined plan to close ranks against the Government's chosen option, and perhaps privatisation itself, as if the Board had briefed its managers to do so. That was emphatically not the case.

A significant number of BR's profit centre directors supported privatisation in principle, if not the form. At InterCity several Board directors had come in from the private sector specifically because they saw the opportunities privatisation could present. Many existing mid-career managers were also excited by the prospects, not because they believed in the structure being proposed, but because it would offer the chance to make a fortune. Others had a more practical view. Adrian Shooter, then Managing Director of Chiltern, was one who favoured privatisation because, in his opinion, Government involvement impeded railway management, regardless of the party in power. As he put it: "The Treasury suppressed good ideas." He saw it as "an institutional problem". Adrian had been influenced by a visit to Japan in 1986 where he examined privatisation there, and also by a period at Red Star from 1987 where he had seen what "massive engagement with the private sector" could achieve. In Japan, he had been impressed by the organisation of geographically discrete, vertically integrated companies, not to mention the 100 or so smaller private companies that displayed substantial commercial innovation, which the six regional businesses there subsequently emulated. He provided advice to the Conservative Party in its period in opposition during the Blair Government, influencing among others Chris Grayling, then Shadow Transport Secretary, to the benefits of a policy of vertical integration. There is more than a hint in the setting up the most recent review of railway structures[37] that Grayling, in charge of the transport brief as I write, entertains a return to his earlier thinking. In any event it is clear that he will need an alternative policy to pitch against the Labour Party's endorsement of public ownership models at the next General Election.

The few railway managers who supported the Government's position in 1992 were in the freight business. Some had become frustrated by BR decision making processes which they believed prioritised passenger services over freight. One was Mike Jones, who had co-authored the

---

[37] The Williams Review

Adam Smith Institute's *The Right Lines* paper in 1987 advocating privatisation of the infrastructure and train operations as separate entities. In Mike's case, though, the prime motivation as a committed "privatiser" and long standing Conservative activist was political. For many years he was National Vice Chairman of the Young Conservatives and mixed with Party chiefs including Thatcher and her successor John Major at Tory gatherings. The latter's constituency was Huntingdon where Mike lived. His experience in promoting privatisation reflected the Government mood music.

Mike first tried to persuade Thatcher of the benefits of privatisation before her 1979 election victory. When she became Prime Minister he had a conversation with the Secretary of State for Transport, David Howell, to present his views but claims to have been ridiculed, prompting a complaint to the party hierarchy. Yet by the late 1980s it was Thatcher herself raising the issue with him. On one occasion she asked him "why aren't we doing something with rail?" Mike recalls that his response was to explain his view that: "The railway is not a sunset industry but it would be if it remained nationalised." That is not to say Mike was at the heart of decision making, but to illustrate the opportunities he had to air views to figures at the top of Government and to command attention, not only because they were already being advocated by free market thinkers in the Conservative Party, but because as a railwayman his ideas carried weight.

My own attempts to engage with Government advisors confirmed the impression that politics rather than effective railway operation was the primary consideration in policy making. One of the 'bright young things' at the No.10 policy unit was, at my instigation, offered a secondment to NSE to inform his views. I had hoped that he would come to see the benefits of integration and the practical constraints there were on competition. However, his all too brief exposure to reality on the Great Eastern did nothing to calm his ardour for the free market. Informal meetings with consultants advising the process also confirmed that minds were set. I had several 'working breakfasts' with Christopher Foster, a former senior civil servant and secondee from Coopers Lybrand as John MacGregor's personal advisor. Others met him too but it was clear he was less interested in reporting back on the merits of different options than keeping his finger on the pulse of the mood within BR. This was important at a time when Management Buy Outs were seen as a 'life saver', backstop position for rail franchising, in the event of limited private sector interest; as they had been in bus and coach privatisation.

Neither was there evidence of Ministers considering international experience. Even though Britain was a forerunner of rail privatisation in Europe, there were other parts of the world where relevant models were being developed. A particular oversight appeared to be a lack of knowledge or interest in a vertically integrated franchising structure introduced in Argentina which had been designed as a means of modernising a railway with high investment requirements. I visited Buenos Aires and produced a report on the potential benefits of the Argentinean approach. Although Public Transport Minister Roger Freeman agreed to meet me to discuss my findings, it came far too late to influence opinion. The die was cast.

Others were unsuccessful in influencing policy too. After publication of the 1992 White Paper, the Commons Transport Select Committee, headed by the Conservative railway enthusiast and privatisation sceptic, Robert Adley, started to gather evidence and marshal views. Along with Chris Green, my predecessor at NSE but by now my equivalent running InterCity, I was called to give evidence. This appeared to cause ructions amongst the powers that be in the civil service. They were obviously concerned that a combination of Adley's committee and the practical views of senior railwaymen might prove something of an unstable cocktail. I was presented with a legal document to sign which might best be described as a 'gagging order'. I declined because it could restrict my ability to offer my professional opinion. Both Chris and I answered the questions put to us honestly and straightforwardly. It was fairly obvious from the line of questioning that Adley had already made up his own mind and when it was published, the committee's report was highly critical of Government policy. It too was ignored.

The level of opposition meant the Railways Bill only scraped through Parliament by the skin of its teeth. From its publication in January 1993 to the time it was enacted on 4th November 1993, there were no fewer than 1,435 amendments with numerous compromises required to ensure it passed into law. They included one proposed by Lord Peyton to allow BR to bid for franchises. In the event BR did not do so. It is not clear whether this was a BR decision or if Roger Salmon, Director of the new Office of Passenger Rail Franchising (OPRAF), prevented them from doing so. Either way there would have been political pressure for BR not to do so. The previously announced intention to keep Railtrack in the public sector for at least the lifetime of the Parliament was also reneged on in order to maximise the amount of money gained from privatisation. John MacGregor quickly broke that promise when his advisers told him the Government would be able to raise hundreds of millions through Stock Exchange floatation. This occurred in 1995. I attended its launch celebrations, held fittingly in the Dinasoaur Hall of the Natural History Museum. Within five years Railtrack would be a defunct relic too.

In many ways, the primary political aims of the 1993 Act – private ownership of the railways and promotion of competition – were almost a sideshow in terms of the impact on railway management. The Act led to the recently integrated OfQ structures being dismantled and went further by fragmenting BR into over 100 parts for sale. Not only did it split infrastructure and train operation into separate companies but it also created a myriad of new companies to supply them. It precipitated the most intensive period of restructuring in the railway's history. This began following the publication of the privatisation White Paper in July 1992 and gathered pace in earnest after the Railways Act was passed in November 1993. It was completed less than six months later when BR started operating the 'shadow' companies that would form the structure of the privatised railway.

The shape of the passenger franchises to be privatised was one of the first things to be established, a process that was aided when one of my director colleagues at NSE, Chris Stokes, was appointed Deputy Director at OPRAF. This was a good appointment since Chris had an unequalled understanding of the railway, not least from an economic point of view. Another good appointment to OPRAF was that of Nick Newton. Although by some accounts civil servants were not keen at first on encouraging bus companies to bid for franchises, Nick's arrival did give this idea significant impetus. On the recommendation of London Transport Chairman Sir Wilfrid Newton, Nick came hot foot from his role in tendering bus contracts to the private sector and immediately started a dialogue on rail franchising. Several aspects of the policy made franchising attractive to bus companies. These included examining the potential to create relatively small franchises, not only to reduce risks and increase competition, but to provide a discrete operating environment of a kind with which bus companies were familiar. A rational franchise map was achieved, though not without a degree of pain.

The process led to some bizarre theories being tested. At one meeting with Treasury officials on franchising in what is now the South Western Railway, I was asked to advise, with no notice, on a proposal they were considering to create up to eight different train operating companies. The experience reinforced how little the fundamental principles of railway operation were being considered as an essential pre-requisite to successful privatisation and told me everything I needed to know about the dogma driving the politics. Whilst there was an obvious case for separating the Isle of Wight railway and a possible case to be evaluated for the DMU[38] operations between Waterloo and Exeter, the more radical options were plainly impractical. The operational and commercial implications of so many companies running into Waterloo were made evident to the Treasury and the plan was dropped.

In the end the shape of the British franchise map was based almost exclusively around the markets and geographies of the Subsector business units BR had created, with some relatively minor exceptions, largely designed to increase the number of franchises available to the market. In NSE the suburban Thames and Chiltern services, which had been managed as a single unit, were set up as discrete businesses. This was a good move as it created operating units focused more sharply on markets. In addition, Island line was separated from South Western. In the Regional Railways Sector similar thinking applied with the Cardiff Valley Lines separated from Wales and West. In the InterCity Sector, Gatwick Express was formally separated from Anglia, which was itself reorganised to include local feeder services separated from the Regional Railways Central Division. I thought this too was a good idea as the local services in and around Norwich provided essential connections into the main line service connecting this part of Norfolk and East Suffolk with London.

Despite general dismay at the form of privatisation delineated by the 1993 Railways Act, it was a mark of the public service ethos prevalent within BR that it quickly

---

[38] Diesel multiple unit

established an effective structure for managing Government's preferred outcomes. Ironically, the project management techniques used to implement OfQ were adopted again to dismantle the very integrated organisations they had been designed to create; only this time, instead of establishing project teams within the Regions, they were established within the new business units. In some cases the personnel were the same.

The first step was to disaggregate all of BR's businesses and migrate the various parts, personnel and assets, to the nascent organisations that would underpin the privatised railway. In London and the South East, this meant building on the devolution measures previously taken under OfQ and reducing the HQ organisation to the bare bones (about 25 people). At the same time NSE's Divisions were split between train operating unit activities (commercial, train operations and maintenance), and the infrastructure (track, signalling and electrification systems) which was in turn split between the owner (Railtrack in waiting) and new companies known then as IMUs (infrastructure maintenance units), which were to be sold outright. Other activities (specialist maintenance, design and architecture, for example) were separated off and made ready for outright sale. Roughly speaking each of NSE's nine Divisions was split at least three ways to create around 30 new entities.

Rolling stock assets were re-assigned to three newly created rolling stock leasing companies (ROSCOs) in waiting. The sale of at least two of these (Porterbrook and Angel) would deliver fortunes to the people appointed by BR to run them when they were subsequently sold on. Although some of those who picked up windfalls manoeuvred into position to do so others benefited simply by being in the right place at the right time. The creation of the myriad of companies occasioned by the industry's fragmentation meant that BR was struggling to find sufficient qualified people to populate them. The technical and safety aspects of ROSCOs required the appointment of a chartered engineer to the Board of each of them. In one case there was nobody obviously available and at the meeting at which it was being discussed it was pointed out that one person present had an appropriate qualification and was appointed there and then. Within a very short space of time he picked up several million pounds when the company was sold. Similar good fortune was visited upon others.

The period from when the White Paper was published in 1992 until the last franchise was let and the last business sold, was the most intensive period of restructuring activity in the railways' history. BR's last business (BR International[39]) was sold seven minutes before the purdah deadline date[40] for the 1997 General Election which was announced on 18th March. The last franchise to be let, ScotRail, started operating the following month, almost five years to the day that the Tories had been re-elected and one month before they were ousted. The defeat was universally expected by this time and for many months if not years it had been obvious that Labour would win the 1997 election. Less than three weeks before the official announcement of the election the Party had won the Conservative held seat of Wirral South with a swing of 17.2%. In fact the Tories had lost every seat they had defended in every by-election since the 1992 General Election, a trend which ultimately deprived them of their slender Parliamentary majority, itself a factor in how the railway privatisation was progressed[41]. The impending political tsunami was almost certainly a

---

[39] BR International sold and marketed BR fares and services from offices abroad, including New York

[40] The date in advance of a General Election after which normal Government transactional business ceases.

[41] One of the seats it lost was Christchurch, one of its safest, following Robert Adley's death.

factor in the hastening pace of franchising that occurred in the period from mid-1996 to March 1997.

By now Bob Reid II had served his five year term as Chairman and had been succeeded by John Welsby, who also retained the role of Chief Executive, in 1995. John was a very substantial and significant figure but one who was unfairly judged by those who did not know him well. Some believed him to be seriously at odds with the Government and an obstacle to its aims. In my experience this was untrue. As a former senior civil servant himself he knew well the roles of giving advice and of accepting instructions. Whilst it was true that he would have favoured a form of industry structure based on BR's vertically integrated companies, he was nonetheless a believer in privatisation. He was also a very great public servant and it is without question true that the success of the whole complex BR privatisation process between 1993 and 1997 was an achievement that could be laid at his door. He was the man with the intellect to understand what needed to be done. I like to think that I was one of those able to get things done.

After the passage of the Railways Act in November 1993, franchise preparation took place within new South & East and North & West organisations, headed by myself and Paul King respectively. I had an excellent team to work with in creating the new train companies and preparing them for sale. Euan Cameron was my right hand man, ably assisted by Peter Wilkinson who would subsequently join me in various ventures in the private sector[42] and who in 2012 was himself to take on the role of Franchising Director following yet another industry crisis. David Burton, someone whom I had known since our first induction course as management trainees in 1968, worked closely with me making sure that safety and operations (and a lot more) were not overlooked in the rush to privatise. Together with

---

[42] Peter Wilkinson was Managing Director of Consulting company First Class Partnerships of which I was Chairman

Ian Cross (Group Finance Director) we created a cadre of Non- Executive Directors for all the new companies, each of which I chaired as part of the accountability tree that passed from the train operating companies through me to the BRB Chairman. In the North & West group a similar functional team was created which included Richard Goldson as Euan Cameron's opposite number.

Developing the structure and organising the management teams was the easy part of creating the shadow franchises that would operate until privatisation. Assets needed to be allocated and contracts drawn up between the first organisations planned for privatisation and their 'suppliers', businesses that would be sold later[43]. At the same time, BR teams were overseeing preparation of the new railway structure needed to form relationships with various bodies to progress vitally important aspects of the planning with numerous new bodies like Railtrack and the ROSCOs, that would become part of the privatisation architecture This was a more complex task.

Creating the franchising documentation with OPRAF involved producing financial data and describing the risks and opportunities for all franchises. Due diligence meetings involved 20-25 people going through the tender documents line by line to make sure there were no inaccuracies bidders could use to challenge contract awards. All needed to be in place so the first franchises could be let in late 1995 with all 25 operating by March 1997. It created some tension between the teams responsible for oversight of the shadow franchises and OPRAF which was under pressure to get things moving to hit the deadlines required by a Government that was becoming nervous of its political prospects and of its ability to attract interest in bidding for franchise contracts.

My own working relationships began to re-focus as new elements in the structure were created. I forged an

---

[43] A special Sales Unit was established for this purpose

especially good relationship with Nick Newton (a few years later a Chief Executive of the Strategic Rail Authority) whose initial role was to mobilise the new franchises at OPRAF. His boss, Roger Salmon and mine (John Welsby) simply did not gel. John appeared to have little time for Roger who irritated him with his high intellect and seemingly low railway knowledge. At times the atmosphere was frigid but the better working relationships at my level enabled progress to be made. Franchising steering groups which we all attended were aimed at reconciling issues but I often felt that my role was to help keep warring factions apart. Nick and I worked well and together with Patricia Hudson, a private sector adviser from Samuel Montague, and Euan Cameron, a programme for the creation of franchises based on NSE was steadily constructed.

The shadow franchises or train operating units (as they were designated), came into being on April 1st 1994 alongside the new Railtrack and infrastructure maintenance organisations, all of which remained for the time being in BR ownership although the future Chairman and Chief Executive of Railtrack were also nominated. Although I am an admirer, it probably didn't help the cause of recruitment to Railtrack that the Chief Executive was John Edmonds whom many, perhaps most, railway engineers of my acquaintance eyed with suspicion as someone perceived to be hostile to their role. Neither did the haughty and seemingly arrogant Chairman, Bob Horton, inspire many to want to join him. Fears appeared justified when Railtrack was developed as a lean and mean organisation contracting out most of its basic functions. Quite quickly Railtrack by both accident and design lost all but a handful of its most capable engineers. This would prove to be a mistake.

John Edmonds, with whom I got on well and whom I respected for the excellent work he had done in earlier Sector roles, asked me on many occasions to join Railtrack but I had little time for its developing ethos or for some of the people on its Board who I considered to be motivated mainly by prejudice against railwaymen and women and arrogance born of their own (in their view superior) private sector experience. It was probably inevitable that the vast majority of the railway's best senior managers gave the new company a wide berth. Looking back this could have been one of Railtrack's major problems. It did not employ enough people who understood railway markets and business economics. In failing to enlist the support of enough good engineers the company lost much of that capability as well. This lack of sufficient talent may have been a crucial factor in the company's catastrophic failure in the year 2000.

The vertically integrated organisation I had gone to lead at Network South East having been split up, I was left with 13 train operating units, each of which I chaired until they were franchised. Gatwick Express and Anglia InterCity were added to my nine Network South East Divisions which were further separated into 11. Generally the network shapes of these units were sensible although it was unfortunate to lose a Network South East brand that had strong public recognition. This made it more difficult to market railways in the London and South East area. When Transport for London was created three years later it inherited a fragmented network that made its job positioning integrated public transport more difficult. NSE might have been a better franchising authority.

In the meantime the caravan moved on and the next task was for OPRAF to sell the franchises.

CHAPTER SIX

Letting the first franchises

For many managers across BR, the period following the creation of shadow businesses in 1994 until franchising and sale were completed in 1997, was one of multiple responsibilities but huge excitement too. At the same time as running the railway, they needed to understand how to work within the new matrix of organisations and contractual structures being prepared for privatisation. On the side they were building management buyout teams to prepare bids for the franchises, ROSCOs and IMUs, attracting expertise from within and outside the industry to their teams and negotiating finance with backers. Management teams installed fax machines in their homes for document sharing at a time before mobile devices and email were common, and prepared at weekends for bid team meetings after work during the week. They received active encouragement in their ambitions from a Government that remained nervous about the prospect of attracting sufficient bidders and saw management buy outs (MBOs) as a 'backstop'. Another reason to encourage management to compete for franchises was that their bids would provide rational benchmarks against which submissions from parties outside the industry could be measured.

In addition to developing their own MBO ventures, Train Operating Unit (TOU) management teams were required to assist the franchising process, providing information to OPRAF for bid data rooms and leading presentations to the private sector companies they were competing against. Measures had to be in place to prevent conflict of interest and guarantee equal access to information. MBO teams were often cautious in their approach to demonstrating impartiality, in some instances reading presentations word for word to different bidders to ensure they could not be accused of providing partial information. John Welsby set the tone clearly for how TOU management should prioritise their time, telling all Managing Directors that BR would support their MBO by funding the necessary financial and legal advice while emphasising that the "core job" was to run the railway. The MBO must be considered an out of hours, "marginal activity". Dick Fearn, whom I had appointed to lead the South Eastern TOU recalls John saying: "I'm running the shop until the shop closes and I require you to do it properly." He added: "Remember this. I will be keeping a loose hand around your throat." John delivered this message in his own inimitable style to all prospective franchise bidders from the BR fraternity.

These multiple activities were reflected in my role as Managing Director (South & East) too. Part of my job was to manage personal aspirations. I had to keep an ear to the ground to prevent 'bid fever' adversely impacting day-to-day management relationships and judgement. In a few cases the cracks began to show. Usually it was possible to manage these situations through reminding people of their responsibilities but in a small number of cases I needed to move managers to different roles. One was Jim Collins, Managing Director of the Thameslink TOU. I held Jim in high regard as a strategist and, like me, he had been a Personal Assistant to the great Bob Reid during the 1980s. However, he was pushing for the early franchising of his TOU at a time when I thought decisions on future investment in the planned Thameslink 2000 scheme were needed first. Jim was appointed to the vital task of setting up the railway's first National Telephone Enquiry Service. He did a great job and did not appear show too much resentment at my decision, at least not to me.

An altogether more difficult situation developed at West Anglia Great Northern (WAGN) where the Managing Director, Ken Bird, and his Commercial Director, a recent entrant to the industry, created an MBO team from which key members of the TOU's management were excluded. The first I knew of this was when I got a phone call from Julian Drury, one of the excluded managers, asking for a private interview. He told me that management was effectively divided into "us and them", which if true would not have been conducive to smooth operation of the business on a day to day basis. I confronted Ken, who confirmed what I had been told. I transferred him to head up LTS, a railway he had managed previously. The switch was possible due to headline grabbing events at LTS, which I will turn to shortly, but the timing meant he would not have the potential opportunity to profit from an MBO. The Commercial Director's year-long contract which was about to expire was not renewed and subsequently I successfully defended a charge of unfair dismissal made against me. My deputy, David Burton, was transferred to WAGN where he took a more inclusive approach to leading the MBO team. Ironically, Julian Drury and Ken Bird would later become colleagues in the same private sector owning group when franchising was completed and Julian would follow Ken as a Managing Director of the LTS franchise when it was owned by National Express.

Reporting lines put in place in preparation for privatisation also created tensions in running the operational railway. In some cases managers who had been among BR's 'biggest beasts' found themselves subordinated. The most notable instance was in Paul King's North & West group where Chris Green had been appointed Managing Director of ScotRail. In this capacity he was accountable to a Board headed by Paul. Previously they had equal status when Chris was Managing Director of InterCity and Paul MD of Regional Railways; and of course Chris was a substantial railwayman of huge reputation. Richard Goldson recalls that Paul, who came from a commercial background outside the rail industry, was wary of this creating a potentially combustible situation from the start, confiding to him: "I don't know how I'm going to manage Chris Green." In fact he treated all TOC Managing Directors the same. After the first Board meeting Chris, who had been given a fairly hard time, approached Richard asking: "Is this how it is going to be?" Unable to tolerate the new regime, Chris left the railway and joined English Heritage as its Chief Executive in 1995. After little more than a year he would return as a consultant and later to one of the most demanding roles in the franchised sector when he was appointed by Richard Branson to lead the Virgin Trains portfolio.

All the while Government was making substantial efforts to court interest in the rail privatisation, marketing the various opportunities internationally and nationally to airlines, shipping firms and utility companies as well as to listed bus groups, whilst also providing them with substantial access to ministers. Although a large number of organisations attended briefings and expressed interest, it is fair to say that initially it was far from clear whether it would translate into bids. Mike Jones, who had used his Conservative Party connections to make the case for privatisation, recalls John Major berating him at a time when attracting bidders looked problematic, complaining: "You bloody told me this would work." Mike replied: "Relax John, it will." Ultimately, in terms of attracting sufficient interest from the private sector at least, Mike was right.

The history of the involvement of bus companies in rail privatisation and their motivation is of particular significance because it turned out to be fundamental to successful completion of the first round of franchising. The deregulation of bus and coach operations in the 1980s and the privatisations of National Bus Company subsidiaries,

PTE companies, and municipally owned operations were followed in the early 1990s by consolidation as the initial owners looked to cash in by selling on. As a result a number of stock market listed bus operators were already on the scene and viewed rail privatisation as a natural opportunity for business growth. The players most active from the start were Stagecoach, National Express and FirstGroup. Others were more reticent. Go-Ahead secured two franchises after entering relatively late, but Cowie (rebranded Arriva in 1997)[44] failed to win any after entering later still towards the end of 1996. Ultimately, bus companies would win or have a stake in 18 of the 25 franchises let.

Among the bus industry players that participated in rail franchising, the role of Prism is of particular interest. Initiated by the same dynamic unleashed by bus privatisation, the founders raised their own funds to bid for contracts and when successful quickly floated the business on the Alternative Investment Market (AIM). The 'AIM route' was quite different to the larger listed bus groups and was only replicated by one other bidder, GB Railways, in the first phase of franchising.

Prism's roots can be traced back to Stuart Linn's interest in examining the potential to form an integrated transport business on the Isle of Wight by adding the Island Line to his Southern Vectis bus company. From this beginning an informal group of bus entrepreneurs met to discuss the prospects for rail franchising. It was at these meetings that Bob Howells and Godfrey Burley, who owned businesses at opposite ends of the country, came to know each other. Both already knew Giles Fearnley from their time at the National Bus Company, where Giles and Bob had made an unsuccessful MBO bid in West Yorkshire. All three

---

[44] The Cowie Group, which had its roots in car dealerships, became the largest bus operator in London during the privatisation of London Buses in 1994. Its acquisition of British Bus in 1996 made it the second largest bus company nationwide.

subsequently went on to acquire bus companies following privatisation. In forming Prism, they were joined by Len Wright, a coach operator who had made a profitable niche in the market for ferrying rock stars and their roadies to and from gigs. Ken Irvine, co-author with Mike Jones of *The Right Lines*, had also attended the same informal meetings and Giles, Godfrey, Len and Bob drafted him in as an employee in an advisory role. They met weekly to understand the nuances of privatisation and initially set their sights low in terms of bidding prospects, targeting the LTS franchise as a relatively simple operation that was easy to understand. "It didn't frighten as a prospect over a 15-year term," Giles said, and the group's observation of fraudulent travel gave them cause for optimism that revenues could be boosted.

Ministers, DoT officials and OPRAF all courted the Prism team, encouraging them at every stage. Building relationships was assisted by the fact that they knew OPRAF's Nick Newton well from his role at London Transport managing bus franchising. Giles recalls: "We were called in every month in 1994/95 to see [Transport Secretary] John MacGregor and [his Minister] Steven Norris" who were keen to learn of Prism's preferences which, in addition to LTS, were Midland Mainline and WAGN. They were assured that Prism was "always mentioned at Cabinet", where Scottish Secretary Malcolm Forsyth was a particular advocate of the company's involvement. The impression Giles and his team received was that "we were made to feel important and to expect to be successful at some stage". Ultimately Prism competed for 18 franchises, was shortlisted for 12, and won four – a decent hit rate. Only National Express won more.

Prism was one of a limited number of companies to feature prominently in the bidding for the first tranche of franchises – LTS and South West Trains from my South & East area of responsibility together with the Great Western

InterCity business. All three were due for award in December 1995 with the first services in the private sector scheduled for 4th February 1996.

Despite expressions of interest from nearly 40 organisations - the result of a softening up process that had begun after the publication of the Government's White Paper on rail privatisation in July 1992[45] - there was at this stage considerable nervousness in the private sector about entering a new and untested market where the potential risks (operational, contractual and political) were initially perceived to be high. There was a general reticence and caution over bidding for franchises, illustrated by the fact that shortlists for all three of the initial competitions featured both Stagecoach and the BR management team. Typically Stagecoach Chief Executive Brian Souter had been among the first to see the possibilities that entering early offered in terms of making highly profitable, low cost bids before more red-blooded competition emerged later. The only businesses outside the UK bus/rail fraternity on any of the shortlists were Bermuda-based shipping company Sea Containers, which pulled out due to misgivings over the structure of the contracts on offer, and CGEA, the transport division of French utility group Compagnie Generale des Eaux. The bidding contingent was made up by GB Railways founded by Canadians, lawyer Max Steinkopf and transport consultant Michael Schabas, with Jeremy Long from the motorway services sector and Jim Morgan, a senior railway civil engineer. Schabas and Steinkopf had both played a significant role in a number of UK projects including the Jubilee Line Extension and Channel Tunnel Rail Link. Chris Stokes, who was Deputy Franchising Director, recalls that OPRAF "would have preferred wider interest" but

---

[45] "New Opportunities for the Railways" was published on 14th July 1992, only two months after the Conservative election victory. Expressions of Interest were sought but initially only received from MBOs, bus companies, Virgin, and Sea Containers.

believed that the intervention of Labour's Shadow Transport Secretary, Claire Short, was off putting to some potential bidders, because she had threatened renationalisation if the Party returned to power. A further limiting factor was the pre-qualification process put in place in order to "rule out the Boy Scouts".

All three initial competitions featured considerable controversy, some of which amounted to high drama. The first franchise, awarded on 19th December 1995, was South West Trains (SWT), which Stagecoach won with a bid that shaded Peter Field's MBO team by a fraction. Its plan for the franchise offered almost nothing in terms of service development or investment and had little risk attached; and it was on the right side of impending growth trends in London and the South East which began to re-emerge very quickly from a low point following London's financial recession of the early 1990s. The cost cutting theme of the bid also bore some resemblances to Stagecoach's template for assessing opportunities during bus privatisation which was summarised for me by one competitor as: "What is the redundancy cost for the entire workforce?" and "What routes are self-sufficient?" The same approach of seeking to maximise cost efficiencies in the rail industry led to some initial early miscalculations, most notoriously around the SWT's failure to retain sufficient train crew a year after it started operating the franchise. This error, and the embarrassing headlines that followed, would almost certainly not have occurred under Peter Field's leadership.

While the SWT franchise competition appeared to have been relatively orderly from a public perspective, there was a moment when Stagecoach threatened to withdraw claiming that the MBO bid was unfairly advantaged by its inside knowledge of the likely financial impact of a bespoke performance regime[46] negotiated with Railtrack. In the face

---

[46] The contractual mechanism for determining payments between the parties for delays and cancellations

of what would have been the unwelcome withdrawal of a genuinely strong private sector bidder, OPRAF decided instead to apply the generic performance regime. Whether or not this action influenced the competition outcome I cannot say, though it may have been one factor. A more likely consideration was that at the same time both the LTS and Great Western franchises were set to go to companies led by BR managers. Awarding all of the first three franchises to rail industry managers would surely not have been the result favoured by politicians when they were trying to encourage wider private sector interest in the process. The outcome of the SWT competition left the incumbent managing director Peter Field high and dry. Despite his significant contribution to the industry, Stagecoach dispensed with his services. Although he was to move on into senior posts at Transport for London, it was ironic that someone who was clearly capable and had ambition to lead a private sector railway was denied the chance. His departure from mainstream railway leadership was a blow to the industry, one of the first casualties of highly competent managers whose faces for various reasons didn't appear to fit.

In the case of LTS, the drama was greater and very public. The day after Stagecoach won SWT, OPRAF awarded the LTS contract to the MBO team which pushed Prism into second place. The decision would only stand for a matter of weeks before being withdrawn the day before the MBO team was due to start running the business as a privatised company. Strangely enough, in this unfolding of events there was a connection with SWT, where I had attended my final Board meeting as its Chairman on 1st February 1996. Had I not received the information I did then, the end result of the LTS saga might have been even more embarrassing to the Government than the rapid unravelling of OPRAF's decision that followed.

Leaving SWT's Friars Bridge Court offices for the last time I had just shaken hands with everyone to wish them 'bon voyage' when Peter Field came after me and asked what I thought about a season ticket audit at Upminster – one of two stations LTS shared with London Underground. I looked blank. He told me that an audit by the Association of Train Operating Companies had revealed that season tickets intended for sale at Upminster had in fact been issued in bulk at Fenchurch Street station. The consequence was that the industry's ticketing and revenue management system would allocate a much higher proportion of the revenue for those transactions to LTS at the expense of London Underground. As I travelled back to my office at Euston House the enormity of this sunk in. Whether or not any of those involved realised it, what appeared to have happened was potential fraud. The value of these sales is brought to account as time passes rather than when tickets are issued because a season ticket is essentially a purchase of future travel. As LTS was about to pass into the ownership of its managers and staff, this transaction, if deliberately engineered, would be to their personal benefit as shareholders in the company and therefore a self-interested action. I ordered a further audit that evening by the British Railway Board's Chief Internal Auditor. His report was available to me the following morning on Friday 2nd February, two days before LTS was due to pass into the ownership of the MBO team. The potential consequences could not have been more serious and proved to be so because the audit confirmed the irregularities.

After I had notified Denis Tunnicliffe, Managing Director of London Underground, I called the Commercial Director of LTS, Colin Andrews to my office and confronted him. He confirmed the practices identified and that he had ordered them, but denied that the motivation was personal gain. Nonetheless, it was clear to me that the intention to improve LTS's revenue line, in effect, amounted to the same thing. On the basis of this admission I removed him from his post, which resulted in the bizarre situation that he remained a director and major shareholder of the company that was about to acquire the business from which he had just been dismissed. I followed up by interviewing the Managing Director, Chris Kinchen-Smith, and his Finance Director. While I was completely satisfied that neither had been aware of the practice previously, I concluded that they had essentially both been negligent in their own duties. It was agreed that I would accept their resignations from LTS but that they would be redeployed to support the general privatisation process that was by now in full swing across the railway.

Events moved quickly. On the same day I briefed OPRAF, landing Franchising Director Roger Salmon with a call he would have preferred not to take. Could he allow the transfer of ownership to the MBO in such circumstances? To me it was obvious that he couldn't but the political stakes were high. The phone lines were hot between OPRAF, me and the Secretary of State, George Young, whose initial reaction was to, more or less, accuse me of trying to sabotage the Government's privatisation policy. Fortunately cool counsel and common sense prevailed. Although the incident did generate unwanted headlines, had the Government permitted this deal, the fall out would certainly have been far worse for the politicians when the knowledge of what had happened became public. Labour MP Brian Wilson exemplified this in a Parliamentary debate prompted by the debacle when he described Enterprise Rail (the MBO team's bidding company) as "a railway for spivs handed over to them by the Government of sleaze. One more fraud investigation and we may even rename it Sleazerail". [47]

The next day Rail Regulator John Swift convened an improvised inquiry into what I had found and announced

---

[47] Hansard 7th February 1996

that he would be holding an official one, the first such to be invoked since the Railways Act had been passed. OPRAF and the Secretary of State were given the cause they needed to announce a pause in the LTS franchising process but sadly the whole episode took a very much nastier turn than anyone could have anticipated. The police got involved and made dawn raids on the homes of the former key company directors taking away many files and papers in black bin bags. This was very unfortunate and I felt for the people concerned, not least the wives and children who would have been around at the time of the raids. Thankfully nothing more was found and no charges were brought.

Subsequently the franchise was re-tendered to the other shortlisted bidders and Prism won by a whisker from Stagecoach. Giles Fearnley attributed the winning margin to Prism's assessment of fraudulent travel as making the difference. The factors underpinning the bid were new trains to replace two thirds of the ageing fleet, ticket gates to pick up 'lost' fares, and "renegotiated drivers' contracts based on annual hours, which optimised costs and allowed drivers more time off". Giles remembers ASLEF General Secretary Lou Adams as pragmatic and the union as supportive.

A key issue that MBO teams and new companies such as Prism faced when bidding for franchises was satisfying OPRAF's requirements to show they could finance a multi-million pound performance bond should they be successful. Its purpose was to provide a guarantee that the cost of any early contract termination would be borne by the company rather than the Government. Prism's plan for financing the £8m bond OPRAF required for the LTS franchise was devised by Philip Moody, a partner at its accountancy advisor Solomon Hare. An initial private shares placement to institutional investors raised the bulk of the funding and was followed by flotation on the Alternative Investment Market on 29th May 1996; days after the franchise began operating. As Prism won further franchises over the following six months, the rapidly rising share price provided the means to finance performance bonds at these businesses as well. Two rights issues netted £24m, which was remarkable given the lack of an established trading record. The balance of the bond funding for the largest franchise, WAGN, was provided by a £7m bank loan. The strategy worked because despite their personal holdings being diluted through the issue of new shares, Prism's founders and two bus industry associates, Peter Shipp and Stuart Wilde, still owned 30% of the business and with the share price nearly six times higher than at flotation, their combined stake was worth over £40m.

Like LTS, the competition for Great Western also involved a U-turn on OPRAF's original selection to run the franchise, although in this case it occurred before the contract was awarded. Initially OPRAF had nominated Resurgence Trains as the preferred bidder – a bid vehicle formed by Mike Jones and John Ansdell, formerly a director of a "failed" double glazing company[48]. Resurgence's bid was being bankrolled by the Union Bank of Switzerland and supported by Touche Ross (Deloittes) and venture capitalists Philips and Drew. Time ran out on the bid because of last minute nerves from the Gnomes of Zurich which meant Resurgence missed the deadline to demonstrate it had financial backing in place. Interestingly, UBS failed to guarantee the bid because it had committed to support the successful Stagecoach bid for SWT at the same time. The perception of the combined risk was too great for the UBS credit committee to accept. As a consequence the Great Western franchise passed to the second placed bidder, which meant the MBO bid, led by Managing Director Brian Scott and devised by Richard George, emerged as the winner. The management team was backed by FirstGroup,

---

[48] "Failed" was how it was reported in the media at the time, in part I thought, to convey an aspect of sleaze surrounding the process

which held a 24.5% stake in their Great Western Holdings Company, as did venture capitalist 3i. Intermediate Capital Group and The Royal Bank of Scotland provided funding while KPMG's accountancy support was led by Dean Finch. He would make the most of his early exposure to rail privatisation, subsequently moving on to head Great Western before becoming a Board member at FirstGroup. Later, as National Express Group Chief Executive, he would withdraw NEG from UK rail franchising altogether in 2017, musing that high financial risks and low returns on capital were such that he wouldn't be prepared to invest his personal money in the sector.

The Great Western contract itself was an unusual arrangement. It can best be described as offering little in terms of service development under a preliminary seven-year franchise award but with scope for a replacement 10-year deal if a full investment and improvement programme could be agreed with OPRAF within two years of the start date. This was exactly what happened with the contract being amended to deliver a quality and growth-led strategy including commitments to faster journey times, increased train frequencies and new trains.

A notable feature of the winning bids for all three of the initial franchises was the lack of any stressful commitment to reduce subsidy, reflecting the early wariness of companies over bidding for contracts and prevailing economic conditions as the UK emerged from recession. OPRAF was wary too. Chris Stokes told me that the early franchises did very well mainly because "nobody expected revenue to take off" in the way that it did, notably in London and the South East and on long distance InterCity services. Bids were principally based on "cost reductions" and although these generally did not occur, they were more than compensated for by revenue growth. The law of unintended consequences seems to have applied.

Stagecoach's winning bid was based almost entirely on cost savings which appeared to reflect its experience from bus privatisation. It meant they barely needed to develop the market at all. An assessment I carried out suggested that, after potential cost savings, the SWT bid could be delivered with revenue growth of just 1-2% in total over the entire seven year franchise period to meet financial targets. The Great Western and LTS bids were scarcely more stretching. Even when Great Western's initial seven year award was renegotiated into a 10-year contract, I considered that it still only needed revenue growth averaging 2% annually to hit targets, despite its franchise plan being billed as a vision for "emptying the M4". Neither was the requirement for growth of 13% over 15 years on LTS ambitious given the investment in new trains and the new revenues these would generate. In the event, the benefits of getting in early would see LTS together with the large SWT and Great Western franchises do extremely well. As the economy picked up and the companies sought to develop the market over and above the limited initiatives in their bids, SWT and Great Western would become cash cows for their owners generating profits as high as £40m per year.

To help secure a smooth transfer to private sector ownership, BR had prepared a number of systems which came in to play between franchise award and contract start. One that provided interesting insights on how companies would manage their new businesses was the arrangement for the successful bidders to nominate two people to attend TOU Board meetings in the transition period before they began running the service. This worked well as a means of ensuring that decisions taken under BR ownership with substantial implications could not be implemented without a new franchise winner's approval. As Chairman of each TOU in the South & East area, I retained the ultimate legal responsibility to override their wishes if I thought safety might be impacted, but this situation never arose. It was also evident in the case of the early awards that directors appointed to the TOU Boards by the franchise winners were respectful and this also proved to be the case in subsequent transition phases when further contracts were awarded. I do not recall a single instance when there was a significant difference of view on the matters under consideration.

Nonetheless, it was apparent that the world of railways was very new to them and there did not always appear to be a ready understanding of what was being taking on. At one level this was hardly surprising but as franchising progressed, it did bring home to me that the tight timescale, coupled with the multiple bidding approaches adopted by the limited number of companies in the field, meant that new entrants were often flying by the seat of their pants. It was unsurprising that they would be acting initially on the basis of their own business experiences (driving down costs in the bus industry for example), and then applying them to rail. I think there was also a perception that as a state run industry BR was, like the utilities the Conservatives had privatised previously, overstaffed and full of opportunities to reduce costs. In fact this was not generally the case. While there were some, BR had already started pursuing several, such as restructuring driver terms and conditions. Being an industry that recorded substantial deficits, the continuous downward pressure on subsidies from successive Governments had rendered BR the most cost effective railway in Europe.

The lessons learned from the work undertaken by BR and OPRAF in preparing the early franchises created the confidence to proceed at pace with others, especially in the South & East where the many similarities between them made it simpler than we had envisaged to complete the process. The second batch of franchises, awarded in March and April 1996, benefited from our early experience and, from an evolution of the private sector's approach driven by an increasingly competitive bidding environment. As the trend towards fiercer competition gathered pace and bidder confidence grew over the coming months, it would result in a number of contracts being let on highly improbable financial terms.

The four franchises awarded in the second batch were interesting in different ways, featuring greater ambition in service delivery plans; the first awards to companies outside the bus and rail fraternity; and the first to overseas companies. They also illustrated the difficulties MBOs faced in bidding against private sector rivals with deeper pockets and often a different view of the market.

The recognition that more ambition would be needed to secure contracts was apparent in bidders' approach to the next franchise off the block, East Coast, which I had run five years earlier as an integrated business. Although patronage had been affected by the recession and remained weak, the route had recently received a massive BR (therefore taxpayer) funded investment[49]. As a result it was highly likely that it would soon be on a path to substantial revenue growth. The MBO team led by Brian Burdsall, with CGEA holding a 25% stake as a partner, was well aware of the opportunity, and also had the benefit of being supported by accountancy firm Grant Thornton which had worked on the winning Great Western bid and whose advice influenced the MBO team's bid strategy. This involved basing its bid pro rata on the £320m subsidy OPRAF had agreed for Great Western but with a reduction applied in recognition of the stronger competition for contracts that was emerging. Even so the MBO team was hamstrung by the banks backing its bid and to some extent by its own caution. Brian's team had wanted to go further in offering OPRAF a reduced subsidy but the banks took a

---

[49] The electrification of the route from London to Edinburgh & Glasgow including a fleet of new trains.

conservative view, concerned that revenue was flat lining at the time. They were also wary of EasyJet's recent launch of competing air services to and from Scotland. These factors meant the management bid would be based on cost control rather than growth.

The successful bidder was Sea Containers, which took a more bullish view of revenue and, according to Brian, adopted the MBO's cost plans as well once they took control. Brian was asked to remain for six months to support the franchise's Chief Executive Christopher Garnett who had led the Sea Containers bid. In fact the entire BR management team was retained demonstrating a respect for the value of high calibre railway experience which was not shown by all new franchise owners. In the event, Brian himself did only one month as MD to Garnett's CEO, being retained on an 'as and when basis' to support various initiatives. Leadership passed to Sea Containers and with it a new and successful philosophy based on cultivating customer service, consistent with the values deployed in its operation of the high quality Orient Express.

Sea Containers' initial preference was to re-name the service Great Northern and it attempted to acquire the brand from BR. I was called by John Welsby who told me the company's founder, James Sherwood, had been in touch about the possibility, and asked for my views. I was against the move, pointing out that the branding was already part of the West Anglia Great Northern TOU's identity and had significant passenger recognition on the route south of Peterborough. To accept Sherwood's request would involve substantial rebranding at a high cost for the commuter services at the southern end of the East Coast Main Line, not to mention the need to re-name WAGN. Instead, Sea Containers christened the operation Great North Eastern Railways (GNER) and rapidly built it into a well-regarded brand, one that is still remembered fondly by passengers.

The strategy was underpinned by £17m of investment to refurbish rolling stock and upgrade station facilities.

Meanwhile, bidding had opened for Gatwick Express where the management team created following its separation from InterCity Anglia was a strong one. Led by Rob Mason, former Marketing Director of InterCity, the company had developed a very effective operational and commercial approach under BR. However, the MBO team's record and experience did not bring the success that might have been expected, losing out to National Express Group whose bid also saw off Virgin's first appearance on a franchise shortlist. NEG offered little encouragement for the management to stay; rather the opposite and the entire team of top directors departed. A clash of cultures, possibly of personalities, appears to have been partly to blame but the main reason was management's dismay at the keenness of the winning bid which they thought was unattainable. They felt National Express had trumped their MBO bid, which they considered superior, by throwing money at OPRAF. Neil Atkins, the team's Commercial Director, says the management expected to win. "We were a good team, a view I think that was generally shared by our peers and we knew both our business and our market (Gatwick Airport) extremely well," he recalls. "We were also able to choose from a quality list of bidding partners, eventually opting for British Airways who were dominating Gatwick Airport back then. Because we had a partner like BA and were also receiving great support from BAA, who were then running Gatwick Airport, we felt our bid was invincible and spent months refining every small detail. Colleagues at OPRAF who were running the franchising process also appeared supportive of our MBO. Although they could show no bias we could sense they appreciated our thoroughness and professionalism. When the result was announced our bid had been blown out of the water by National Express who bettered it by an unbelievable 25%. When NEG shared their numbers with us, without disrespect they looked as if they had been configured on the back of a fag packet."

Neil also points out that "we were then living in a world where every time a listed company won a rail franchise it put a pound on the share price and that's what really mattered to them at that time". In addition, OPRAF and the Treasury were very happy to accept keen bids on a "succeed or fail" basis. Neil's view of the Gatwick Express situation was shared widely in the rail industry. My own assessment at the time was that National Express's bid was undoubtedly racy requiring 3% real terms annual revenue growth to be maintained for 15 years (although this would look positively conservative compared to certain bids later in the franchising process). Yet it is also fair to say that National Express's bid had some interesting plans to generate new business through fleet replacement, filling gaps in the timetable to provide a 15-minute service from 5am to midnight and experimenting with overnight trains. In the event NEG did achieve its profit targets at Gatwick Express for several years until thrown of course by the 9/11 2001 terrorist attacks in New York which had a devastating impact on air travel.

Shortly afterwards, National Express also won the Midland Mainline franchise against another strong MBO team led by Richard Brown. This successful bid had some genuinely innovative aspects, again involving new rolling stock but also a new timetable offering stopping patterns to deliver a very significant expansion in services and reduced journey times. It was a well thought through plan with a balance between potential cost reductions, service expansion and marketing initiatives that meant NEG had a good chance of meeting the payments offered to OPRAF assuming the expansion plans went well. In this instance, Richard Brown was retained to lead the business and he would later be appointed to NEG's Board.

CGEA's entry into the market was a different matter. It had gained experience as a partner to the MBO bids for both SWT and East Coast and enjoyed early success when chosen for the South Central franchise which it would operate through its Connex subsidiary. However, CGEA had very little rail experience and exaggerated that which it did have. I was struck by its press statement at the time of the South Central award portraying itself as an international transport company with significant experience of running trains in France. In fact its only experience appeared to be operating a small regional line near Rennes.

In seeing off its rivals for South Central – National Express Group and a management bid partnered by Stagecoach – CGEA appeared to me to benefit from special factors. NEG, for example, was bidding for Gatwick Express at the same time and won it shortly before South Central was awarded. Gatwick Express and South Central provided competing services between London and the airport, and the franchising rules in place back then would not have allowed the same company to run both. There was also a view that competition issues could work against the MBO/Stagecoach bid because of the award to Stagecoach of the adjacent SWT franchise. However, that theory proved to be unwarranted when CGEA took South Central's other neighbouring franchise, South Eastern, four months later. It did so against competition from GB Railways, Stagecoach and an MBO team which experienced irritation in its relationship with its partner, FirstGroup. The initial agreement was that the management would hold a 51% stake in the joint venture bid, but the bus conglomerate insisted on an equal share before putting pen to paper. The outcome left the French company with two of the largest and most important railways in the country accounting for 13% of passenger journeys. For CGEA, the prospects must have looked so good in those early, heady days after breaking into a market which it had targeted heavily from the start. However, it would fail to complete its contract term on either franchise, exiting the UK industry amid passenger dissatisfaction and a reputation for mismanagement. This is covered in detail in Chapter Seven.

The link between Connex in London and CGEA Paris was the urbane and outwardly assured Antoine Hurel, who led the successful bids. Despite a display of cultured professionalism from Hurel and his team, it was evident to me during TOU Board meetings in the period before Connex took over that the company was complacent and lacked knowledge about the challenges it would face. Chris Green, who advised CGEA's bid team and whose presence as a Non-Executive Director on the Connex Board gave some gravitas to the organisation, formed a similar impression. He was horrified by its approach and felt CGEA "hadn't a clue about what it had bought". He recalled that during bid discussions someone had asked: "East Croydon, where is that?" showing a startling lack of awareness of one of the key areas on the South Central network. It was clear that everything was "run from Paris and they thought they were buying a utility company" where financial return would come from cost efficiency. Not that Connex's revenue assumptions were modest because the bids themselves were comfortably the most aggressive to win any franchise at that point. Both followed a similar pattern of huge subsidy reduction commitments in the first three years, which indicated considerable optimism in the potential for cost savings but risked heavy early losses. The task of growing revenue was much tougher than it appeared because commuting accounted for a high proportion of revenue and the impact of fares regulation meant there was a risk that unrealistic growth would be needed on off-peak services across the life of the contracts to meet financial forecasts. In Chris Green's opinion "they lost interest when they couldn't make la monnaie". This was to prove pivotal in subsequent events.

The technical requirements were at least as challenging as the commercial task. Given that these were two of the most heavily trafficked railways in Western Europe, operating and engineering competence would be the key criteria for running them successfully, coupled with a strong project management capability to deliver the investment in new trains that was the central feature of the South Eastern contract. At over 400 carriages, it was comfortably the largest fleet replacement programme in any franchise let. As Managing Director of Network South East I had overseen previous projects on the South Eastern routes including introduction of new Networker rolling stock on the inner suburban Kent Link lines [50]; associated infrastructure enhancements; and new maintenance regimes on the Dover Main Lines to complement the imminent introduction of Eurostar services[51]. My experience was that their successful delivery was assisted significantly by the integrated management approach BR had developed under the OfQ reforms. I saw the changes to the industry structure brought about by the privatisation framework as importing risk to the pressing needs of the railway operation in the South of England, especially on South Eastern at that time.

While there was an inherent performance risk in the separation of track and train, before Connex took over steps has been taken to mitigate it. The new Railtrack Director for the route was the former NSE Divisional Director, Geoff Harrison-Mee, who had a complete understanding of the

---

[50] Heavily used commuter services operating throughout the South East London metropolitan area via various routes to such destinations as Hayes, Dartford and Sevenoaks.
[51] Then operated between London Waterloo and the Channel Tunnel

complexities and interactions of track, train and passengers in the region. I had also made sure that his replacement in charge of the South Eastern TOU prior to franchising was the competent and personable Dick Fearn whom I promoted from Thames and Chiltern because of his involvement in total route modernisation there. It was exactly the experience required at South Eastern and initially Connex seemed to think so too offering Dick a 30% salary increase to stay. Sadly, his services were dispensed with after a year just when his skills were needed most in the run up to and during the introduction of new rolling stock. He would go on to demonstrate his abilities as a well-regarded Zone Director at Railtrack and later as head of Irish Railways. Meanwhile at South Central, Connex also lost management continuity when the Managing Director of the TOU, Graham Eccles, joined Stagecoach after forging a strong working and personal relationship with Brian Souter during the unsuccessful MBO/Stagecoach bid for the franchise. Graham, a highly competent railway operator, moved to Stagecoach's Perth HQ where he became the group's Rail Director. He was replaced at South Central by Geoff Harrison-Mee.

The scale of the rolling stock challenge Connex would face was exacerbated by Government decisions. When I appointed Dick to head South Eastern, I had been confident that he was the right person to oversee the next phase of modernisation scheduled to be the replacement of the Kent Coast 'garden shed on wheels'[52] trains that were over 30 years old. It would have been entirely logical and sensible for BR to commission a further build of Networkers, suitably modified for longer distance running, to replace the

---

[52] Longer distance services operating to coastal destinations such as Margate, Ramsgate, Dover, Folkestone, and Hastings, serving intermediate places like Chatham, Canterbury, Tonbridge, and Tunbridge Wells. The soubriquet accorded to the rolling stock was coined by my Fleet Director, Cliff Perry at NSE

existing trains. So in advance of privatisation I made a submission to the British Railways Board to this effect. Frustratingly it was rejected on instruction from the Government which, I was led to believe, wished to demonstrate that rolling stock investment would be achieved effectively through its franchising programme.

There were several undesirable and avoidable consequences from this decision. The first was that a very large and complex rolling stock replacement programme would not only be delayed but overseen by an untested new owner. The second was that the York Carriage Works, where the trains would have been built, closed down because of a lack of orders. At the time it claimed to be the most modern train assembly production line in Europe. The situation was made more painful for me personally because my house in York overlooked the factory, which more or less declined into disuse over the next two or three years. More serious for the local economy was the loss of an important manufacturer and many hundreds of jobs. York's rail sector has never recovered from this loss; neither have the relatively highly skilled jobs been replaced by similar employment in other sectors. Like much of the rest of the UK, the manufacturing sector has declined to be replaced by lower paid, often insecure jobs in the hospitality sectors. To this day I remain angry about what was an avoidable catastrophe for my home city.

In the next batch of franchises, Chiltern Railways was the first award with the MBO team led by Adrian Shooter winning out against CGEA and Stagecoach. Its bid company was named M40 Trains in reference to ambitions to develop the service to win passengers from the motorway. Uniquely, the management team's partners included a construction company, John Laing plc which held a 26% shareholding, while venture capitalist 3i owned a 23% stake. Laing's involvement arose from a desire to gain a broad perspective of the industry as part of its plan to build a rail infrastructure business via privatisation of the IMUs. It gave M40 Trains in-house skills that no other winning franchise bidder possessed. A second more significant factor in the way the business would develop was that even though the initial contract awarded was a short seven-year franchise, the bid had been submitted on the basis of a 15-year business plan designed to exploit a growth market. It was only after bids were submitted that OPRAF ruled a short term franchise would be let, leading Adrian to assume, wrongly as it turned out, that his team would be unsuccessful. In fact their proposals were exactly what was required – a vision based squarely on growth to build on recent investment in the line.

While on the face of it the bid contained a tough subsidy reduction profile, Chiltern was coming off a major total route modernisation in the early 1990s with new signalling from a single control centre at Marylebone and new trains based at a spanking new maintenance depot in Aylesbury. Patronage was growing at a rate well above anywhere else on the railway and served an area of rapidly expanding population. Although a small franchise, there was plenty more to go at, not least because in the run up to privatisation, when I was still Chairman of the TOU, Chiltern secured a track access agreement with Railtrack (also in shadow mode) that enabled it to increase its train frequency to Birmingham. It enabled the company to provide competition to West Coast services on a potentially high earning parallel route at a time when major planned infrastructure upgrades would cause significant disruption on the West Coast Main Line. Although these would eventually open Chiltern up to more severe competition, the company was able to secure a valuable market niche in the early phase of its franchise which it would sustain and build on. It was a far cry from the late 1970s when a commuter protest had famously saved the Chiltern route from partial closure with its Marylebone terminus sold-off and trains diverted into Paddington.

M40's strategy recognised the opportunities available with plans designed to keep pace with high demand and drive further growth through service quality and capacity enhancements. Uniquely at that time, these included infrastructure investments specified and overseen by a franchise owner, notably redoubling an 18-mile section of track, while an initial order for new trains would allow more services on the London-Birmingham route, and faster journeys. Other infrastructure projects provided for a vast increase in car parking at stations in areas of substantial population expansion. They would act as magnets in attracting car users, often from a wide geography. Additionally the franchise funded and built a major new facility in Warwick Parkway station, virtually adjacent to the M40. This was so successful that additional car parks were constructed there in subsequent years.

A few years later I joined the Board of the Holding Company and recall a discussion about Warwick Parkway in which we were informed that Railtrack, by then in its supposedly FTSE 100 entrepreneurial mode, had declined to build and own the station on the grounds that "it wasn't in that sort of business". Consequently the station was built by Laing Rail and as far as I am aware, remains in its or its successor's ownership to this day. Even if the company were to lose the franchise it would continue to reap the rewards derived from owning the station. Laing went on to deliver further projects for Chiltern including a new Wembley depot, while the original 15-year plan formed the basis for progressive development of the route when M40 Trains retained the franchise.

There are two lessons to be drawn from this. The first, which has been demonstrated time and time over as the years rolled by, is that Railtrack, and latterly Network Rail as infrastructure owner, placed itself so far from the market needs of the passenger railway that it was pretty much disconnected. The second lesson is that a train company that understands its markets, has a long term perspective on them, and which also understands the nature of railway operations and infrastructure, can profit from an approach that integrates all aspects of railway activities on its routes. Adrian Shooter and his team understood this and the phenomenal growth of Chiltern Railways on the back of these early and subsequent infrastructure enhancements demonstrates clearly the advantages of taking an integrated approach to running a railway; one which can facilitate investment that delivers benefits downstream. The success of Chiltern illustrates what could have happened across the railway as a whole if franchising structures, based on BR's former profit centres, and incorporating a long term vision, had formed the basis of the original privatisation model.

Adrian's leadership is very much associated with Chiltern's achievements but when he was appointed Managing Director he was not the clear choice. The vacancy arose when Thames Trains and Chiltern, which had been managed as a single unit within Network South East, were separated as part of the preparation for privatisation. The unit's Managing Director at that time was Roger MacDonald, a former Great Western Commercial Director, whom I had appointed after promoting Dick Fearn to lead South Eastern. Roger was subsequently chosen to head the Thames TOU and a selection process began for an MD to lead Chiltern.

The British Railways Board had decided that applications would be invited only from the most senior managers and a shortlist of potential candidates was drawn up. Adrian, who had succeeded me as MD of the Red Star Parcels business when I was promoted to General Manager of BR's Eastern Region in 1987, applied but some BRB members had doubts over his suitability as a TOU MD. This was due to a series of lurid and embarrassing national newspaper stories in the late 1980s alleging loose management of certain Red Star supply contracts, which had also been subject of a Police investigation. Although no charges were brought, Adrian, as head of the parcels business, became the unfortunate fall guy for the reputational damage perceived by the Board. A professional engineer, he was moved from the parcels portfolio to advise the Board Member for Engineering on locking mechanisms to prevent passengers falling from trains with 'slam doors'. There had been unwanted press headlines about this too, and in this case Adrian successfully completed the important assignment at about the time Chiltern was set up as a standalone entity.

Following a tussle amongst Board members about whether he should be considered, my opinion was sought. My view was that his exclusion would be unwarranted. To my mind there had never been any suggestion that Adrian had been personally implicated in the contracts that were being scrutinised. Even if some members had reservations, "everyone" as I put it when asked, "deserves a second chance". Given the stunning development of the Chiltern franchise, driven by Adrian's vision, expertise and determination, I like to think my support for him was vindicated.

M40 Trains also attempted to take the neighbouring Thames franchise, but there the existing management was successful. Unusually, though, in this case Roger MacDonald's MBO team was a minority shareholder in the bid company, Victory Holdings. Its partner, Go-Ahead, held a 65% stake, and victory secured the bus group's entry into rail after it had opted not to participate in earlier tenders[53]. The winning bid again highlighted an advantage the

---

[53] Evidence of City pressure on bus companies to engage in rail privatisation

management had in understanding the opportunities for growth provided by total route modernisation. In Thames's case, those benefits had not been fully realised at the time of franchising, partly because the upgrades were completed later than on Chiltern and partly because Thames had been affected by industrial disputes and safety incidents. The bid lacked the innovation displayed by M40 at Chiltern; neither were there similar opportunities for service development, although it did include plans to increase core London-Oxford services and to generate faster journey times. So while the subsidy reduction Victory Holdings offered looked demanding, particularly in view of competition on the route from Great Western, it was bid by people who knew the franchise's commercial potential.

The Thames team contained a good mix of experienced and upcoming managers which, by accident rather than design, included the excellent David Franks. In the run up to privatisation a mistake had been made in selecting an Operations Director from outside the industry who proved unsuited to the role. Although a solid enough manager, his lack of knowledge at a time of fast moving change was a disadvantage and a parting of the ways became inevitable. Fortuitously, I was able to appoint David to fill the vacancy. As operations director at LTS he had been an innocent victim of the ticket scandal which had seen the original award of the franchise to the management team overturned. His move to Thames gave him another opportunity to participate in an MBO, although it did not confer the riches on him that winning LTS almost certainly would have. After Go-Ahead bought out the Thames management in 1998, David went on to forge a successful career at National Express where he played a leading role in restoring the industry's confidence after the Hatfield crash. Later, he would succeed Dick Fearn as Chief Executive of Irish Railways before trying his luck in Australia as head of Keolis Downer.

At the same time as Thames, OPRAF announced the award of the Cardiff Railways and Wales and West franchises. Similarly to Thames and Chiltern, the Welsh TOUs were separated from each other in the run up to privatisation to increase bidding opportunities and competition. In the event, both franchises went to the same company, Prism, an experience replicated days later when Stagecoach won the tiny Island Line franchise that had been part of SWT. When it came to the Welsh franchises, there was limited interest from the larger players and in the case of Wales and West there was none from management. Its MD John Mummery, whom Paul King had recently appointed to replace Theo Steele, had no appetite for an MBO so Prism's competition came from Great Western franchise winner GWH and from MTL, formerly the bus division of the Merseyside Passenger Transport Executive which had become an employee-owned private company during bus privatisation. Both already operated either within or adjacent to the franchise area. For Cardiff, the bidders joining Prism on the shortlist were Stagecoach, an MBO team led by Managing Director John Buxton, and consultancy Halcrow which had acquired BR's Transmark transport consulting arm in 1993 – the first railway business to be privatised.

The contracts had not been among Prism's priority targets either and this was reflected by an apparent lack of sophistication in its bids which placed significant reliance on reducing fraudulent travel and restructuring driver terms and conditions. As described earlier these were themes Prism had developed as cornerstones of its bids for London and South East franchises and were much more applicable to that market. The plan for the Welsh franchises was also dependent on opportunities to save costs by integrating aspects of the businesses and extending the reach of Wales and West's Alphaline services to destinations on the Cardiff network as part of an expansion strategy for interurban routes. There were some unusual and interesting incremental aspects to the bids as well which looked beyond regular railway operation, such as brokering regional integrated transport tickets, park & ride sites and a commitment to evaluate a Cardiff light rail proposal. However, the commercial potential of the initiatives bore little relation to the subsidy reduction Prism had signed up to. At Cardiff, the bid was particularly ill-judged. To make the sums add up I calculated at the time that the company would need to all but double revenue over the seven year contract while halving costs, and this on a railway where patronage had fallen around 30% since 1989. The Wales and West prospects were scarcely any better requiring revenue growth double the recent trend on top of deep early cost savings at a business with fairly limited growth potential due to the mix of services. "They were stupid bids," Giles Fearnley acknowledged in retrospect.

Two months later in December 1996, Prism gained a further contract, the WAGN commuter franchise providing services into London from Hertfordshire and Cambridgeshire. It was one of three East of England franchises let within days of each other, with GB Railways making its entry by winning the Anglia InterCity contract and FirstGroup capturing the Great Eastern commuter business focused on Essex and East London. All three provided significant opportunities to compete with other operators' services. As such, they would be a potential test bed for one of the benefits privatisation was intended to deliver through innovation and service development stimulated by on-track competition. In WAGN's case, Prism's plan seized the opportunity to develop its tiny share of the London-Peterborough market dominated by Sea Containers' GNER business. The bid included using new Networker trains, which I had secured on lease in the period before privatisation, to increase frequency on the route and, along with keen price reductions, win passengers from faster GNER services. The company was able to maximise competition, and increase services on other routes as well, through a new maintenance arrangement with the unions at Hornsey depot which significantly increased the availability of trains for off-peak services. After building its market share to a respectable level on the London-Peterborough route, WAGN would also attempt to extend competition to GNER further north by applying for open access rights to Doncaster, a ploy that failed following a regulatory inquiry[54].

At Anglia and Great Eastern, the winning bids included plans to step up competition from high revenue earning stations on the Great Eastern Main Line. FirstGroup introduced additional peak Great Eastern services to London from Ipswich, a core Anglia stop, while the Anglia plan included increasing competition to Great Eastern from Colchester, as well as an option to do so from Chelmsford by taking up unused access rights. Arguments would rage then and in later years about the added value of such competition. When the initial Anglia and Great Eastern franchises expired they would be amalgamated, in part to eliminate the inter-company rivalry. I felt this was a mistake that removed the benefits for passengers of keen competition and was later shown evidence to that effect.

At Anglia, GB Railways' proposals for competing services formed part of one of the more imaginative franchise bids, with a core commitment to double frequency on the London-Norwich route to half hourly throughout the day with an order for new Class 170 trains. My feeling at the time was that this represented a massive step forward for a region that was buoyant economically yet geographically isolated. The way the franchise was let, combining the InterCity service with local branch lines, also encouraged bidders to consider development of the BR service pattern.

---

[54] Instead additional services were allocated to GNER and Open Access operator, Hull Trains.

GB Railways' plan included extending services beyond Ipswich and Norwich to provide (and in several cases restore) direct trains from destinations off the main line that had been poorly served. It did so by procuring a new diesel fleet to supplement the existing electric trains, creating flexibility to improve local and regional connections as well as significantly upgrading the passenger offer in a part of the country that was used to picking up hand-me-down trains from the more favoured InterCity routes. Like Prism, GB Railways floated immediately after winning its first contract and also like Prism its share price more than doubled on the first day of trading.

As the Anglia franchise progressed, GB Railways developed other proposals for innovative new routes from the Great Eastern Main Line. The company would also branch out into new spheres, backing my Hull Trains open access venture, starting a rail freight business from scratch[55] and exploring opportunities overseas. It bought a stake in Australia's interstate train operations and an Estonian rail company. It was the most truly entrepreneurial business in the privatised UK rail sector.

The eastern franchises had strong existing management teams which the new owners retained. At WAGN, David Burton had led the MBO bid (partnered by FirstGroup) despite having no personal aspirations that privatisation could meet. However, he was not in any way ill-disposed towards the franchise's new owners with whom he worked effectively and happily until taking an early retirement. As one of BR's most experienced managers, he not only knew the job backwards, but as a previous General Manager of the Anglia Region, knew the patch well, not least the workforce with whom he engaged particularly effectively.

At Great Eastern, I considered Bob Breakwell to be the most effective Managing Director in my South and East area. He had a solid track record of delivery from his

---

[55] GB Railfreight

previous command at WAGN and when Ian Dobbs left Great Eastern to head up transport operations in Melbourne, I appointed Bob to the Liverpool Street job. Although he could always be relied upon to deliver change, Bob was someone whose immediate reaction to the prospect could seem negative; and he was apparently opposed to privatisation, in particular to the abandonment of vertical integration, a point on which the two of us most certainly agreed. Yet despite reservations Bob had a tremendous commitment to his railway and to his team. Although he probably felt something like a fish out of water, he too led a MBO bid (partnered by CGEA), strengthening his team by bringing in a Commercial Director from the private sector. After some initial reservations, FirstGroup, the victors, came to value Bob's skills and retained him even after his retirement as part of the company's bidding machine.

At Anglia, the management team, led by Andy Cooper, was capable but relatively inexperienced. Andy was always open to new ideas, but only lasted two years with GB Railways, becoming a management consultant. He worked for a while through my consulting business First Class Partnerships in shaping franchise bids for Arriva where he eventually settled as Managing Director of Cross Country. Other members of the team who would go on to higher commands included Andy's successor, Tim Clarke, and John Smith who founded GB Railways' freight business.

Two further franchises let before the end of 1996 featured winning bids that were startling in their own ways. If Prism's Welsh bids had stretched the boundaries of credibility, MTL's for Merseyrail took the process into the realms of fantasy as it saw off competition from Stagecoach and Go-Ahead. Uniquely, the franchise was let with the regional Passenger Transport Authority, Merseytravel, retaining revenue risk across the franchise area, making the competition for the contract very much one of cost reduction. MTL's winning bid proposed to deliver that in spades. The problem was that in committing to reduce subsidy from £80.7m to £60.8m over seven years, the company was effectively proposing to eliminate 70% of costs within its control. The scale of the challenge can best be illustrated by the fact that the cost reduction required was equivalent to all the company's staff costs. In fact the contract provided relatively little scope for staff savings given the type of rolling stock on the network and the PTA's requirement for all stations to be manned first train to last. Potentially, a solution could have existed through making the case for a metro-style overhaul of the system including new trains suitable for driver only operation and features such as automatic ticket issuing and collection; or even automated operation of the train service. Such a transformation could have given Merseyside a world class rapid transit system and involved exactly the sort of innovation that privatisation was, in theory, intended to unleash. However, there was little indication of any such intention in MTL's announcements, and given Merseyside's industrial relations history it would have been fraught with difficulty. Over 20 years on, the PTA's efforts to introduce something similar are being dogged by union opposition.

After winning the franchise, MTL retained a young but fairly strong management team, led by Richard Parkyn; one that could have held its own in a larger company. Richard had attempted an MBO in which he was supported by Roger Cobbe, but his team did not make the shortlist. Sadly he died young and was succeeded by Roger who would later become Arriva's Bid Director.

Virgin's widely anticipated entry into the rail sector came with the CrossCountry franchise. By its very nature, the business interfaced with numerous other TOUs, none more so than InterCity West Coast – Virgin founder Richard Branson's primary target. Both businesses shared points of common reference on the West Coast Main Line with significant passenger interchange at stations including

Birmingham, Manchester, Liverpool and Glasgow. At the same time, rolling stock procured by both franchises for long overdue service upgrades would need to be mutually compatible to capitalise on Railtrack's plans to modernise the WCML. So while the businesses had very different market characteristics and there was clear justification for free standing and separate franchises, there was also a case at that time for a degree of common management of the operating environment.

That was certainly how Virgin viewed the situation. Its bid for CrossCountry provided for new 125mph rolling stock with tilting capability to maximise speed and dovetail with its strategy for the West Coast franchise, where there were suggestions that Virgin's path to the contract was being facilitated. Brian Burdsell, who had joined Railtrack as its Passenger Business Director after leaving GNER, was convinced Virgin was being "primed" to win West Coast. When I interviewed him, some months before his death from cancer in 2017, he reflected on his time at the infrastructure company where he was responsible for negotiating contracts with train operators. Brian recalled that Virgin had much greater access to Railtrack than the other bidders which included Sea Containers, National Express, Stagecoach and a management team led by Ivor Warburton.

For CrossCountry itself, Virgin's plan committed to a complete overhaul of the service including refurbishment of the existing loco-hauled stock and HSTs followed by fleet replacement and a total timetable revision in 2002 with shorter trains running more frequently. The subsidy reduction promised was ambitious, seeking to turn the £127m received in the final year of BR operation into a £10m premium payment to Government 15 years later. To achieve it, revenue would need to nearly double in real terms; this against a background of static revenue in the four years before privatisation at a business where the nature of the routes had made providing reliable services elusive; and there was significant competition from other operators. It was a level of commercial risk and backing for a genuine transformation programme that I felt few companies would have been willing or able to take on. It was more than enough to see off rival shortlisted bidders Prism and Mike Jones's Resurgence team. Mike remembers seeing the writing on the wall at an early stage.

The remaining seven franchises were let in a rush in February 1997, leaving sufficient time for all services to start operating in the private sector before the Conservatives were ousted from office in May that year. In each case, the award was complicated by difficulties that were inherent or emerged during the franchising process. They included the InterCity West Coast business where the route had been starved of much-needed investment over the previous decade due to Government funding constraints. Originally OPRAF had earmarked West Coast for inclusion in the first batch of franchise awards. However, it was delayed until the end due to bidders' uncertainty over how to respond to a new £1.5bn West Coast infrastructure modernisation programme developed by Railtrack and which the company had opted to fund itself in line with Government requirements for the works to be financed by the private sector.

Railtrack's plan was underpinned by a Core Investment Programme based on the replacement of conventional signalling with moving block cab signalling technology – a concept identified by the company's consultants to reduce costs so that it would be attractive for the private sector to finance the modernisation works. Despite the fact that moving block signalling was not in place on any main line railway in the world, Railtrack's Board endorsed the approach, with Engineering Director Brian Mellitt, who had been involved in work to begin installing the technology on London Underground's Jubilee Line, a particular advocate. Brian Burdsall recalled that he was shown a copy of a

Railtrack Board minute by Company Secretary Simon Osborne in which Mellitt committed to the Board that cab signalling would be completed in short order. This assumption and the absence of any credible strategy to deliver it, would play a significant part in Railtrack's downfall and the unravelling of operators' plans.

When the franchise was eventually awarded, Virgin's winning bid was, at last, one the Government could claim to be mould breaking as a statement of intent. Devised by Jim Steer, it catapulted the West Coast modernisation plan to another level as part of a strategy to double patronage through additional infrastructure upgrades and replacement of the existing fleet with new Pendolino tilting trains. As well as taking up an option to increase line speed on the West Coast from 110mph to an initial 125mph by 2002, it included an agreement with Railtrack for a further £600m of infrastructure upgrades to allow for an extra four services per hour and 140mph operation by 2005. The additional works were to be funded by Railtrack with Virgin paying higher access charges and the remainder coming from a revenue sharing agreement with payments dependent on passenger numbers. In many respects it was a litmus test of the potential for privatisation to transform Britain's railways.

The extent of the transformation could be gauged in Virgin's expectations of the franchise's financial performance. From receiving £77m subsidy in the first year, Virgin planned to return £1.2bn to Government over the last 10 years after route upgrades had been completed. Although there had been general astonishment at the payments promised, closer examination suggested that Virgin had carried out a considered assessment of the service's prospects. While not without significant risk, the revenue increase needed to meet the payments was consistent with West Coast's performance relative to other InterCity routes following previous investment programmes.

Initially, Virgin appointed CrossCountry TOU managing director Chris Tibbits to lead both of its franchises. I had worked closely with him at Network South East during the period when devolution to profit centres was my top priority and he had led a very effective change management team. He was selected in preference to West Coast managing director Ivor Warburton, a privatisation skeptic, who took up a business development role. When Ivor left the company on Chris Green's return, Chris Tibbits was retained as Operations Director.

The most problematic franchise to be let in my South & East Area was Thameslink [56] where arrangements were complicated by discussions surrounding the plans for what was then known as 'Thameslink 2000' – the infrastructure and rolling stock scheme intended to provide a high frequency service from Great Northern and Thameslink stations north of the Thames to multiple destinations south of London via London Bridge. Delays occurred in shaping the franchise early on because of the difficulty of specifying the network over which the franchise would operate. Decisions were yet to be made about how the immediate franchise proposition would fit into the wider Thameslink 2000 framework and until these were resolved I was of the opinion that it should be one of the last to be let. I was conscious that the management team at Thameslink was very keen to go earlier and felt that this was obscuring the bigger picture about a strategically very important project for London and the South East. Revenue flows would be critical to return on capital and until train service patterns over the extensive north-south geography had been determined, the financial projections for the Thameslink

---

[56] Thameslink operated services on a North to South axis from Bedford via St. Pancras/ Kings Cross to Brighton and some south west London suburbs including Sutton and Wimbledon

2000 project could not be properly assessed. So it was that Thameslink came to be the last franchise let in the South & East.

Although not a natural privatiser myself I did care a great deal about Thameslink 2000 and could see the potential for the private sector to fund the central core infrastructure on the back of the revenue generated by the new services. Rather naively as it turned out, I presumed a Conservative Government that was unwilling to commit public money might be attracted to the idea of a privately funded project based on the integration of track and train. I couldn't have been more mistaken, as Stephen Norris, the Minister of Transport for London, made clear to me following a presentation I made to him at a breakfast meeting hosted by BR's Chairman at which the Lord Mayor of London and other City notables were also present. It rapidly became apparent that the Government's principal interest was in disposal of the franchises as quickly as possible, and certainly by the time of the General Election in 1997. Yet when the Government reversed its initial decision to retain Railtrack in public hands, the floatation prospectus was considered to be enhanced by a strategy that rested in part on its future growth prospects, which included delivering Thameslink 2000.

With major construction works expected to begin during the seven-year franchise term, it was a difficult contract to bid for with relatively little scope for early service enhancements. The shortlist contained a capable cast of companies including Virgin, GB Railways and an MBO team partnered by Cowie. The constraints were reflected in the winning bid which came from Govia, a partnership between majority shareholder Go-Ahead and a new entrant, French urban transport group Via-GTI. It included few plans to develop the business beyond a commitment to provide additional early morning and off-peak services on the core Brighton-Bedford route, and these appeared to be largely motivated by a desire to compete for passengers at Gatwick Airport. While a lack of ambition in the bid was understandable, it was clear that the franchise plan would be inadequate to cater for any continuance in an extraordinary level of recent growth on the service, which BR managers were unable to fully account for. This would be especially true if Thameslink works were delayed; a distinct possibility given the need to obtain legal powers for construction.

The most interesting aspect of Govia's franchise plan was actually an assumption that operations could function with only one depot, so the one at Brighton could be closed. As Govia had dismissed the Thameslink TOU management team led by Cliff Perry, it was left to Euan Cameron as his successor to demonstrate that the idea was unworkable.

Ultimately, work on the Thameslink programme would not start for another decade and it would take another 10 years to come to fruition. When it did, in May 2018, its implementation proved to be an unmitigated disaster. It was so badly co-ordinated between the infrastructure provider (Network Rail, back in the public sector), the train company (GTR) and the Government (DfT) that large numbers of services were being cancelled from its inception such that an emergency timetable had to be introduced more or less straight away. Not for the first time since the Railways Act 1993 did I find myself reflecting on how much more effective the project delivery might have been had it been masterminded by a company in full control of all the parts.

Sitting to the west of Thameslink, the franchise covering the former North Division of Network South East was awarded at the same time, completing the process within my area of responsibility. Rebranded for privatisation as North London Railways, it was a rather unbalanced amalgam of the high performing suburban lines out of Euston towards Watford, Milton Keynes and Northampton together with the down at heel orbital routes in North and West London packaged together as a job lot. It was not one of the more enticing propositions, particularly as revenue on the orbital section had been falling for several years. The BR management team was solid enough though insufficiently streetwise to mount a convincing MBO attempt.

Against this background the winning bid from National Express rested on a plan to compete against Virgin and Chiltern in the London-West Midlands market. Services were to be extended beyond Northampton to Birmingham with increased frequencies in the peaks as well. A new marketing team was introduced to promote a new Silverlink brand. Perhaps unsurprisingly the bid neglected the low revenue, run down London orbital routes – a situation that would continue until their transfer to Transport for London[57]. Although the subsidy reduction contracted with OPRAF was not especially large compared to other franchises, I felt that it could prove one of the tougher challenges. Experience had shown that turning round commercial performance on routes that had reached their nadir was usually a slow and difficult process without investment in new trains.

By this stage the franchises left to be awarded from Paul King's North & West group were the four major regional businesses – Central Trains, Regional Railways North East, Regional Railways North West and ScotRail. They presented significant obstacles. Before any could be let, it was necessary for OPRAF to gain the agreement of the metropolitan Passenger Transport Authorities which were controlled by Labour-run councils and fundamentally hostile to what the Conservative Government was seeking to achieve through its privatisation process. ScotRail had been included for franchising as early as the second batch nearly a year beforehand but was suspended. Previous legislation that remained in force alongside the Railways Act effectively gave the PTAs a veto and a period of horse

---

[57] Branded London Overground, it was transferred to TfL in 2007

trading opened up between ScotRail and the Government. The situation was replicated in dealings with PTAs in regional cities in the North of England and the Midlands.

Towards the end of 1996 the deadlock had reached a point where there was a significant risk that the regional franchises would not be let before the May 1997 election, which the Conservatives looked certain to lose by some distance to Labour (and did). With West Coast looking problematical at the same time, John Welsby called me to his office and explained it was likely that BR would need to establish a management organisation to continue operating a number of the remaining TOUs in the public sector after the election. He wanted me to head it if it was needed. Ultimately, the election acted as the catalyst for the Government to make concessions over service specification and funding that were acceptable to the PTAs. At the same time the Leader of the Labour Party, Tony Blair appears to have persuaded the local political leaderships to accept the privatisation as a reality.

The lateness of the hour of this political acceptance had unfortunate consequences. One was that the regional franchises with limited scope for financial improvement were let at a time that competition for contracts was at its fiercest. It was questionable whether the swingeing subsidy reductions that the winning bidders signed up to would prove feasible and with relatively low revenue, large cost reduction would be essential to deliver them. However, the scope for savings was restricted compared to other franchises due to the tightly specified service levels, and in some cases staffing levels, determined by the PTAs. In addition, restructuring opportunities that did exist were potentially problematic due to a history of difficult industrial relations, particularly at ScotRail and in northern England. The fact that, with the exception of Manchester and West Yorkshire, the PTAs had opted to retain revenue risk also meant there was some pressure on bidders to push the boat out when assessing the prospects for growth outside the metropolitan areas in order to submit the most competitive subsidy reduction to OPRAF.

At Regional Railways North West[58], the winning bidder was Great Western Holdings, which saw off Stagecoach and Prism to win its second franchise. Peter Strachan was installed to replace the TOU's Managing Director Bob Goundry to lead a growth and quality vision at a rebranded North Western Trains business. Commitments included new trains, innovative new routes and additional interurban services. Whilst laudably ambitious and potentially a real boost to the quality of the region's transport, it was clear to managers on the TOU team that there was a high risk of the programme costs exceeding new revenue gained. One service extension had been assessed by BR as a loss-maker and at £12m the funding NWT had committed for station improvements, on which it would not be possible to make a return, was several times greater than might have been expected. Most significantly, considerable revenue had been predicated on innovative new budget ticket routes from Manchester Airport, Rochdale, Bolton, Blackpool and North Wales to London. It was a bet on a limited market in north Manchester due to the protection Virgin received from competition on the West Coast Main Line under the privatisation architecture and, after a short period, the flagship Manchester Airport-Euston service was withdrawn in 1999 and plans for other services cancelled. Meanwhile performance on the core network was underwhelming and it quickly became apparent that efficiencies could not make anywhere near the necessary contribution to the £66m subsidy reduction promised to OPRAF over the course of the seven-year contract.

---

[58] Basically the network centred on Manchester, Cheshire, Lancashire, and Cumbria

On the other side of the Pennines, I was very familiar with Regional Railways North East[59] from my time as General Manager of the Eastern Region and, at an earlier stage in my career, had worked in close liaison with both the West and South Yorkshire PTEs. I had a high regard both for the PTEs' promotion of their networks and for the Regional Railways strategy of developing services between the major Northern cities. This was a substantial business and whoever secured the franchise would quickly become the focus of political and media attention much of which, if the operation did not establish itself as competent and efficient from the start, would inevitably become the subject of criticism. Unfortunately this occurred much earlier than might have been imagined.

The Regional Railways North East TOU Managing Director was Bob Urie, who moved into the role after Aiden Nelson was appointed BR Head of Safety. Bob opted not to participate in the MBO bid which was led instead by the Production Director Mike Hodson and partnered by Govia. They filed a strong bid but were pushed out by MTL which branded its new business Northern Spirit. The franchise plan set out some worthwhile initiatives, particularly for expanding the interurban TransPennine services. By May 2000, it committed to increase frequency on the core Leeds-Manchester route from three trains per hour to four and introduce a new Premier Class on board. There was also a commitment to assess the potential for additional interurban services. Nonetheless, it appeared probable from the start that heroic growth on the TransPennine routes would be necessary before then if the franchise was to remain in a viable financial position. There was general incredulity when MTL's proposals were compared with the second-placed MBO/Govia bid. Despite needing £50m more subsidy overall, it required lower payments than MTL in the

---

[59] The network including Northumberland, Tyne & Wear, Durham, Yorkshire, and Humberside

first two years. Its plan for a more gradual and less ambitious subsidy reduction throughout the course of the franchise seemed a fairer reflection of the potential to grow revenue and reduce costs.

The two remaining regional franchises, Central Trains[60] and ScotRail were won by National Express, taking its total to five. At Central the TOU Managing Director was Mark Causebrook whose MBO team submitted a joint bid with FirstGroup. Mark's career included extensive experience of working with Passenger Transport Executives and local politicians throughout the North of England and the Midlands and he continued to lead the business under NEG. At ScotRail, the last franchise to be awarded, the TOU's Managing Director was John Ellis, a former General Manager of the Scottish Region who had returned to replace Chris Green when Chris left for English Heritage in 1995. Although he knew the turf well, John had no interest in participating in an MBO and it was Finance Director Alex Lynch who led an attempt to win the franchise. Alex would stay on in the same role under Alastair MacPherson, previously Managing Director of National Express's Scottish Citylink coaching business. The rival shortlisted bidders for the contracts were a now established cast of Prism, CGEA, Stagecoach, Govia and the MBO teams.

While the committed subsidy reductions on both franchises undoubtedly represented a major challenge, to an extent National Express's task was less tough than at the other Regional Railways franchises in that the NWT bid was patently undeliverable and there was no cliff edge subsidy fall as at Northern Spirit.

As for its own prospects, Central Trains had potential advantages in that cost savings were likely to be available as part of a group of three Midlands businesses under National

---

[60] The rail network centred on Birmingham, Leicester, Derby and Nottingham, including Lincolnshire to the East; Shropshire, Staffordshire, and Mid Wales to the west.

Express ownership. NEG had also developed some strong marketing initiatives at its Midland Mainline franchise which could be exploited jointly. In addition, Central had some high value interurban routes to exploit across its sprawling geography. Stretching between the Welsh and East Anglian coasts, under BR it had been known as "Barmouth to Yarmouth". Meeting the subsidy reduction targets appeared to depend on high quality marketing to a significant degree, especially given the strong competition to Central's interurban routes from car and coach travel. I regarded the franchise as an interesting test of the private sector's ability to attract passengers from other modes through commercial initiatives without the obvious benefits of operating a premium InterCity rail route.

The ScotRail bid appeared altogether more challenging given the history of union militancy whilst commitments to enhance the level of services in the Strathclyde area would be likely to increase costs. The PTA had also devised a particularly tight specification for Strathclyde services constraining the company further. It seemed to me that delivering the required subsidy reductions would hinge on ScotRail's ability to grow the market very significantly on its main interurban routes connecting Scotland's seven cities, capitalising on an order for new Turbostar trains.

So with ScotRail now in the private sector it came to pass that the whole passenger railway was privatised; pretty much on the basis of franchises that resembled the operating units established by BR, but stripped of their prime infrastructure assets and the engineering expertise associated with them. In this way risk to the private sector would be minimised whilst risk to the Government would be lessened by reducing the term of a franchise to around seven years unless the operator had arranged investment (effectively in new rolling stock), in which case a longer term was justified. Sadly a consequence of the same approach, compounded by the way Railtrack chose to organise its maintenance activities at arm's length, was to substantially diminish the connection of the engineers with the operation and the market. This disconnection was in turn to import greater risks to the railway as a whole. These came in the form of poor operating performance, greater cost to the taxpayer, and in the short term, safety risk.

Despite these serious defects, such considerations were not uppermost in the minds of the architects of the privatisation and in their own terms it got them out of the starting blocks. Their policy had worked well in attracting more bidders for the initial tranche of franchises than might otherwise have been the case, so much so that the Government's parallel approach of encouraging British Rail managers to bid for their own businesses (which I saw at the time as an insurance policy) did not in the end need to be relied upon to the extent that it might have been had private sector bidders been put off by the perceived risks. MBOs were ultimately successful in the case of Great Western, North Western Trains, Chiltern Railways and Thames Trains, and for each one their bid was in conjunction with a major bus group, or in the case of Chiltern a construction company.

Of the 25 original franchises, the major bus groups won or had a share in 12 with a further four being acquired by Prism, founded by bus industry entrepreneurs, and MTL winning two. Connex Rail acquired two, whilst Richard Branson's Virgin Trains also picked up two. Sea Containers, GB Railways and M40 Trains won one each. Despite this, the only companies with an obvious experience in high end transport operations and marketing where customer service delivery was fundamental to success were Virgin (in airlines) and Sea Containers (in passenger ferries and hotels). Most of the rest were in it for the opportunity the Government had created to move from bus to rail and, as it turned out, were fundamental to the success of the first round of franchising. FirstGroup, Stagecoach, National Express and Go Ahead between them acquired, or had a stake in, half the franchises let.

Talking to senior bus industry figures about their venture into rail, what comes across strongly is the personal links and relationships between the 'busmen'. The similarities with the rail fraternity are almost exact. An industry that had been nationalised and within which careers developed and people networked naturally created lifelong friendships which in the commercial world eased the process of making alliances, consolidation and deals. Movers and shakers in bus privatisation transferred effortlessly to rail. Heavy hitters in bus like Brian Souter and Moir Lockhead became heavy hitters in rail. They were joined at the top of the industry by entrepreneurs like Giles Fearnley, while leading bus managers such as Phil White (National Express), Ian Buchan (FirstGroup) and Keith Ludeman (Go-Ahead) seized chances to take already successful careers in new directions and to greater heights. In Keith's case, experience in the rail industry would act as a significant step on his path to Go-Ahead Chief Executive. Ian would later become a Non-Executive Director at Network Rail, as would Keith. Many made, or added to, their fortunes along the way but above all they made the most of the opportunities that successive privatisations opened up for them. As Giles Fearnley was the first to admit; if rail had preceded bus, the boot would have been on the other foot.

It would be fair to point out that the sequencing of events and the perceptions bus and rail people had of each other did affect certain working relationships as people from different industries and cultures were thrown together. At National Express, the relationship between Brian Burdsall, a well-respected and empathic manager in British Rail, and the straight talking, don't take prisoners style of busman Ray O'Toole was only ever going to end up in a bad place. At Virgin, Ivor Warburton's spell on the management team was never likely to work out, even in the short term. Whilst some rail managers resented, or even disparaged, the success of their bus opposite numbers, there were almost certainly some bus people who suddenly found themselves at the top of the rail industry and felt threatened by new colleagues with greater experience. In the main these situations worked out to the disadvantage of the rail managers simply because they were not in a position to call the shots.

In certain cases, tensions emerged between businesses controlled by people from different industries, driven by early nerves surrounding privatisation as well as the way people from different backgrounds perceived each other. On some occasions it seemed irrational. After Prism started winning franchises, John Prideaux, who became Chairman of Angel Trains during the privatisation of the ROSCOs, led a delegation of his senior managers to Prism's Ludgate Hill office, specifically, Giles Fearnley claims, to announce that "we will never do business with bus people who don't know what they are doing". The meeting had been requested by Angel and lasted no more than five minutes.

This type of situation was by no means universal though and in other instances productive relationships were struck up from the start. Brian Souter found he had an immediate rapport with Graham Eccles at Stagecoach, recognising his abilities from the beginning. Great Eastern's Bob Breakwell survived the scepticism of Moir Lockhead at FirstGroup as a result of the intervention of the perceptive and more appreciative Ian Buchan. The intelligent and strategic Richard Brown undoubtedly made his mark early on at National Express leading the private sector's largest trains division and sitting on the company's main Board as its Commercial Director. However, it would end with NEG claiming that Richard wasn't sufficiently interested in its wider business outside the rail industry. Before long, Richard would resume his career as Chief Executive of

Eurostar and become a recognised 'eminence grise' in the rail firmament, not least when things started to go badly wrong at the Department for Transport after the West Coast Main Line farrago led to the suspension of rail franchising in 2012, a topic I return to in Chapter 9.

The stage was set and the success or otherwise of the industry would, from this point on, be seen through different eyes. The railway was now privatised. How would it work out?

CHAPTER SEVEN

Franchises get off the ground – some fly, some crash, one burns

In 1998, after a year's study of the successful bids, I published a detailed assessment of the first round of passenger franchising in the UK[61]. A year on from the last franchises being let, and following the election of a Labour Government that would be in power for another 12 years, I wrote that privatisation was a done deal and that the future ownership of the new train operating companies (TOCs) in the private sector did not seem to be in doubt. Although the regulatory and planning frameworks in which they operated could well be changed, I wrote that the essential contribution of TOCs would be as private sector companies providing public transport but in a highly regulated, structural environment that ran counter to most private sector norms. Twenty years later these words remain pretty much as valid as they were then, although the renationalisation of the railways remains a possibility should a Labour Government of a more radical hue than the previous one be returned at a General Election.

My 1998 review of all 25 TOCs examined the financial commitments made to Government in the context of the principal market and operational issues each company faced, focusing particular attention on the implications for revenue growth and cost reduction that the successful bids implied. I was able to do this not only on the basis of information publicly available at the time but on account of my own knowledge and understanding of each of those

---

[61] "Britain's Privatised Passenger Railways 1998 – a practical assessment", a First Class Insight Report

businesses, several of which I had recently chaired, and others of which I had had earlier management experience.

Noting that the pace of franchising had accelerated in the run up to the May General Election which saw John Major's Government defeated I observed that the franchising process had resulted in the creation of eight TOC owning groups. If their franchise commitments were successfully delivered they would have the effect of reducing the railway's annual subsidy from the Treasury by around £1.2bn by the end of the seventh year of franchising (2003/4), and by £1.6bn by the end of the year 2011/12. I estimated that total operating costs could, through a combination of initiatives, be reduced by about 14%, with around half coming from reduced track access charges and the indexing of train leasing charges, essentially 'gifts' from the Government in setting things up. By comparison BR had been reducing its operating costs by around 3% per annum for several years, so from this perspective the goal the franchises had to achieve was not out of line. However, such was the nature of the competition for contracts as franchising progressed that only a small number of the new train operating companies had any prospect of meeting targets to reduce subsidy without a substantial increase in revenues. For the industry as a whole I estimated that this would have to be of the order of 24% in real terms over seven years assuming the potential cost reductions were delivered. The effect by 2012 would need to be an increase in rail passenger journeys to levels last seen in 1958.

The overall position hid challenging objectives for certain TOCs. Some were positively heroic. My report forecast that Cardiff Valleys, newly created as a small, discrete company for franchising, would require revenue growth of 93% in seven years to achieve the committed subsidy reduction. In the same 'regional sector', Wales & West required 65% growth and North Western Trains 58%, both of which suggested the winning bids had taken a somewhat other-worldly view of the market. Real terms targets of nearly 40% at Central Trains, ScotRail and Regional Railways North East were modest only by comparison, given the contractual and commercial conditions on regional franchises.

By contrast some of the long distance franchises, where substantial investment had recently been made by BR or was promised as part of the franchise contract, had relatively soft revenue targets to meet. On the East Coast, where the benefits of route modernisation still had a long way to go before being fully realised, GNER (Sea Containers) needed to increase revenue by a modest 14% in seven years. Great Western required an even more modest 5% (and only 23% by 2006 following the introduction of new rolling stock) while Midland Mainline's equivalent challenge was 10% and 18%. Only Anglia Railways (59%) and Virgin's CrossCountry and West Coast franchises, both of which needed, in broad terms, to double revenue by 2012, had a substantially greater task. However, in Virgin's case, this was conditional upon the delivery of substantially improved traction and rolling stock as well as enhanced infrastructure promised by Railtrack.

Within the London and South East area, my report showed that revenue growth requirements for the first seven years of franchising were relatively modest for some: 22% for Connex South Central and South Eastern, 23% for Great Eastern, and a meagre 1% for South West Trains. Another batch was tougher. Silverlink required 38% growth, Thameslink 39%, Thames Trains 51%, West Anglia/ Great Northern 52%, and Chiltern Railways 56%. Moreover, a general challenge for all London commuter franchises was that peak fare rises were to be regulated below inflation as an inbuilt political sweetener provided by the Government, so pricing had limited potential to contribute towards these real terms growth targets. Achieving them would rest on both a large increase in peak hour travel (which did come about with a major revival in central London employment following the drop of 25% that had occurred in the aftermath of the 1992/93 financial crash), and the stimulation of off peak revenue, which would require substantial marketing effort in order to be realised.

The effects of fares regulation meant the need to grow off-peak revenue was disproportionately higher for some London and South East TOCs than others. Silverlink's growth target appeared improbable at the time it was let given the dependence of much of its business on flat rate travelcard fares in the Greater London area and its uninspiring performance in the latter days of BR. By contrast Thames and Chiltern, with apparently tougher targets on paper, would be less affected by the fares regime as they had a lesser dependence on commuting revenue and high potential for growth given recent route modernisation work.

Summing up the overall position, I wrote: "The implicit revenue required to meet [all] the bids will, if achieved, help drive the railways into becoming the most successful since just after the Second World War in terms of the numbers of journeys made. However, the revenue growth that the franchises need to meet their bids after anticipated cost savings will not occur naturally."

Looking back it is instructive to analyse what actually happened. In the first seven years of franchising passenger journeys increased by 26.3%, more or less in line with the progression implied by the first franchise bids. Most of this growth occurred before the Hatfield crash in October 2000. In the four years following the start of the first franchises in February 1996, the National Audit Office reported that passenger numbers had increased 24%[62]. After stalling for nearly two years post Hatfield, the growth trend resumed at such pace that by 2012 patronage had risen over 80% since privatisation. The 1958 industry figure of 1.09bn passenger

---

[62] Action to improve passenger rail services (2000)

journeys was actually surpassed in 2006/7, five years earlier than implied by my 1998 analysis. In 2012 itself, 1.46bn journeys were made, 40% higher than my earlier assessment.

Whilst there is some 'inflation' in the patronage figures since 1995 which include travel on different trains used in completing each journey, on the face of it, it seems safe to conclude that the structure of franchising was able to deliver, or at least contribute substantially to, the fastest and most sustained growth in the use of the rail network in modern times. The structure of franchising was one which, whether deliberately conceived or not, invited companies to chase marginal revenue because it would almost always exceed marginal cost. With a largely fixed cost base and in particular a leasing structure for rolling stock set against a timetable specification determined to a large extent by the Government, hefty charges were incurred irrespective of the utilisation of the assets. This encouraged the productive use of assets and led to a 'bums on seats' approach in which frequencies were improved; and in most franchises there was scope to stimulate demand. In a small number it also prompted investment in new trains beyond the commitments made in the franchise agreement.

How much of the growth was due to franchising itself, or indeed privatisation, is a matter that has occupied considerable debate. Looking back on the early days, there were undoubtedly other factors at play. The most significant of course was that franchising coincided with the recovery of the London economy which was on the road to becoming the power house for the UK's economic growth during the Blair-Brown years. The growth trend actually began picking up in the months before the first franchises were awarded and in some respects the growth achieved can be seen as a continuum. At the same time, the peace process was gaining momentum in Northern Ireland and in 1997 the IRA called off its mainland bombing campaigns in the run up to the

Good Friday Agreement. As one who had seen the impacts these atrocities had on propensity to travel by train when Managing Director of Network South East, I have no doubt that it was a significant but overlooked reason for the rail boom of the late 1990s, particularly for off-peak travel on London TOCs and journeys to the capital on long distance services. The rise of immigrant (often EU) worker populations who were less likely to own cars was another factor which contributed to early high growth on the London commuter franchises. During the late 1990s, immigration became the principal driver of population growth in the UK, and was particularly centred on London.

It would also be reasonable to point out that BR could have adopted similar marketing and asset sweating strategies to the TOCS, but equally reasonable to say that it might well have gone on to do so following the creation of the business-led, integrated profit centres that were overtaken by privatisation. We will never know what might have happened but if I had to speculate I would say that BR would have made similar moves, not least in response to the changing social and economic times. However, the fact of franchising meant that these issues were being looked at through new eyes and the competition for best value bids delivered the certainty of the more efficient use of expensive assets as new owners sought to keep up with or beat subsidy reduction targets. It is reasonable to conclude that franchising played its part in the rise in passenger numbers.

The overall growth requirements covered a variety of individual company outcomes. A key weakness in the privatisation process, and one graphically illustrated by my 1998 report, was that the Government's main objective in franchising was to get the process completed as quickly as possible. There was no strategy or objective for what the railway or even individual franchises should deliver. Inexperienced bidders were left to their own devices, designing bid plans in a policy vacuum. The effect was magnified by the rapidly changing sentiment among bidders as privatisation progressed and bids became more risky. Analysing the contract awards, it sometimes seemed that there was no rhyme or reason to many of the bids accepted. It made little sense that many long distance franchises, the ones with greatest commercial potential, had significantly lesser requirements to grow revenue than regional franchises – the group with least potential. Similarly, within the London and South East area, the revenue requirements covered a surprisingly wide range. While by no means identical, in many respects these commuter operators served broadly similar markets. The result was that some franchises such as SWT, where OPRAF accepted a very soft bid, and Thameslink, where patronage had been flying before privatisation, made what can only be described as supra-normal profits. Others such as Anglia struggled to break even. In some cases, franchises were in deep trouble from the start. A number are worth revisiting.

Even the most casual reader of my 1998 report would have thought it obvious that certain franchises were doomed. According to another report [63], published retrospectively in 2006 by the University of Leeds, it was soon "clear that those franchisees that relied on growth in revenue to meet their financial targets were achieving profits" while "those where fare box revenue was small relative to costs, and therefore cost reduction was the key to success, were in difficulties". That involved every regional franchise and would precipitate MTL's desperate departure from the transport industry in 2000. Prism would also leave in the same year after striking a deal with the Strategic Rail Authority (OPRAF's successor body) that removed

---

[63] Nash, C.A. and Smith, A.S.J (2006) Passenger Rail Franchising - British Experience. In: ECMT Workshop on Competitive Tendering for Passenger Rail Services, 12 January 2006, Paris.

substantial liabilities at its Welsh regional franchises, allowing its founders to realise maximum value from their rail portfolio when selling the business.

In the case of Great Western Holdings, the MBO-led company that had won the long distance Great Western contract and later North Western Trains, sale came earlier and, from the perspective of the owners, at exactly the right time. In March 1998, FirstGroup, a 24.5% shareholder in GWH, bought out its partners for £105m. The prime attraction was the Great Western franchise which had been let on very favourable terms early in the privatisation process and which FirstGroup pointed out was on course to make a profit of at least £25m that year. What it didn't mention was the issues that were about to unfold at North Western Trains and which it did not appear to fully appreciate at the time of the GWH purchase. Covering inter-urban services in the North West, metropolitan services in Greater Manchester and a scattering of rural operations, the NWT contract required a 35% reduction in annual subsidy from £191.9m to £125.5m, with the greatest falls coming towards the start of the seven-year franchise. In assessing NWT's daunting task, I estimated at the time that cost savings of £39m may be feasible, although complex to achieve. Even if fully delivered, a 54% increase in inherited revenue would still be needed on top. In terms of both cost reduction and revenue growth, this was phenomenally ambitious, especially given that the Greater Manchester PTE in particular had a major influence on service levels leaving the company with much less scope to impact costs and revenues. The contract looked highly problematic, and so it proved.

Initially NWT, like other franchises, addressed the need to cut costs with a redundancies programme which took out nearly a tenth of the company's staff. While a loss of £800,000 in 1997/98, the franchise's first full year of trading, could have been explained away by one-off expenses associated with the redundancies, it would rapidly become clear that actions to reduce the wage bill were doing little to counter the underlying financial challenges. A year later and following the sale to FirstGroup, losses exploded to close to £10m as subsidy fell by £13m. The more obvious options to cut costs had been taken, further large falls in subsidy were due and revenue growth was well below the required level, partly due to below inflation fares regulation in the Manchester metropolitan area. On top of that, costly franchise commitments needed to be implemented. Ongoing staff reductions coincided with declining operational performance and service cancellations led to public rebukes from Greater Manchester PTE. There was nowhere feasible to turn and despite contract changes and benign interpretations being agreed with OPRAF and subsequently the Strategic Rail Authority, losses continued to compound year on year.

Neil Atkins, formerly Commercial Director at Gatwick Express, who knew the original Great Western owners well from their time together at InterCity, joined North Western Trains in 1998 at around the time Great Western Holdings was bought out by FirstGroup. "Barely had I got my feet under the desk when it was announced they were acquiring all the shares in GWH and with that news, a one year nightmare began," he reminisced, reflecting on the way FirstGroup attempted to deal with the emerging financial and operational issues. For example, shortly after First took over, the franchise contract required NWT to introduce its first ever London services via a circuitous route from stations north of Manchester. "It left core routes in the conurbation short of drivers and cancellations were rife. In short we were in a mess," Neil recalled. "FirstGroup's actions made it far worse, sacking all the directors bar myself and one other, ridding the business overnight of hugely experienced talents like Keith Winder, Chris Kimberley and Peter Strachan. I would witness senior

FirstGroup executives saying cringeworthy things like 'from now on the train drivers will be treated the same way and with similar terms, conditions and pay to bus drivers'. The sad thing was they meant it."

During that time, Neil's responsibilities included managing the franchise agreement and the company's relationship with OPRAF. "One of the franchise commitments was that we had contracted to spend £7.2m on customer service improvements during the first three years of the franchise," he recalls. "A week before I left I was called by the then FirstGroup Chief Finance Officer and instructed to ring OPRAF to tell them that this commitment was being met later that year with the building of a new rolling stock maintenance depot at Chester. I tried to argue that this did not constitute a customer benefit in itself but I was told to shut up and do as I was told. I duly called my contact at OPRAF, apologised for what I was about to say, delivered the message and a week later I left the employment of FirstGroup."

This anecdote is interesting not least for what it says about the attitudes and approaches brought to railways in those early days by the bus companies. The rail and bus cultures were undoubtedly at odds and remained so for several years. The story also tells us about the keenness of the new Labour Government, through OPRAF, to keep things sweet with the franchise owners from the start. The acceptance of an initiative far removed from being a genuine investment in customer service improvement is evidence of that. It constituted removal of an investment obligation to assist the company's attempts to shore up its financial position. Subsequent contract changes included replacement of the commitment to operate new services to London, which were making heavy losses, with less onerous local timetable improvements. The result was far removed from the original franchise vision which was ambitious and entrepreneurial, if misguided commercially.

A defined way out of FirstGroup's North Western Trains predicament only arrived in March 2001 as part of plans for a wider franchise reorganisation in the north initiated by the Strategic Rail Authority which had taken over from OPRAF. It enabled FirstGroup to renegotiate its contract after paying a £38m fee to the SRA, taking the total pre-tax loss from three years of ownership to nearly £90m. While a hefty sum, the fee paid was cheap at the price. FirstGroup stated that the renegotiation would prevent "substantial [future] losses which were expected to be incurred until the end of the franchise in 2004". Instead, the deal would enable First to make a modest profit each year under a short term management contract with subsidy agreed annually and the SRA taking revenue risk. In the first year alone, NWT received £35m more in subsidy than scheduled under the original contract. In return, FirstGroup agreed to terminate the franchise early, if necessary, to suit the SRA's franchise reorganisation schedule, but that was never required.

Although NWT was haemorrhaging cash from the word go FirstGroup was able to not only sustain the franchise's losses but make a healthy overall profit from its rail interests due to the performance of its Great Western and Great Eastern businesses where patronage was growing well ahead of the bid plan expectations. Whether intentional or not the franchising authority's decision to award a number of contracts to a single owning group did provide cross cover for those elements that were never going to fly on their own. A wry smile may be justified at the realisation that the principal beneficiaries from the NWT saga were Great Western's BR managers and employee shareholders, who had sold GWH early.

MTL was in an altogether more perilous situation at Northern Spirit and Merseyrail. It appeared to me that its bidding tactic of front loading subsidy payments in the first year followed by huge falls was a recipe for a strong initial profit and then substantial losses; which is exactly what transpired. It was a situation that could only have been averted by wholly unlikely cost savings on both franchises along with dramatic revenue growth on the interurban Northern Spirit TransPennine services. Yet while the financial implications at Merseyrail looked painful, they were unlikely to be terminal for MTL due to the relatively small size of the franchise. Northern Spirit, however, posed an altogether different risk involving a very substantial fall in annual subsidy, from £223m to £146m over seven years. Considered in terms of revenue alone, the TOC would need to more than double its income. In terms of controllable costs, it represented an 88% reduction. My own estimate was that, at a considerable stretch, up to £49m in cost savings were potentially available, but that would still leave a need to increase revenue by 38%. The nature of the market and the requirements of the multiple Passenger Transport Executives in the franchise area meant these targets were virtually impossible. MTL had set itself on a collision course with reality.

It was a situation the company could ill afford. MTL was by some distance the smallest of the bus companies that had won rail franchises. Its other interests were largely confined to the former PTE bus operation in the Merseyside area which the management and employees had bought during privatisation and its bus business in London. The acquisition of the rail franchises meant MTL's turnover increased fivefold leaving the future of the business as a whole dependent on financial performance in its new industry. Its impending collapse did not take long to materialise. After an initial boost to MTL's finances from its rail franchises, the company posted an 83% fall in pre-tax profits to £3.7m for the year ending March 1999 as 'cliff edge' subsidy reductions began to bite. With further reductions of £24m scheduled for the coming year and another £15m the one after, MTL was already at a stage where, without a dramatic shift in gear at its TOCs, its venture into rail would wipe out its profits and plunge it deep into the red. Problems mounted rapidly with Northern Spirit losing an average of £1.5m per month during 1999. MTL was running out of cash fast and by the end of the year, banks that were providing temporary working capital facilities were threatening to pull the plug. MTL considered walking away from the contracts, but the penalties involved would have substantially reduced the remaining value left in the group as it sought a 'fire sale'. Its situation was sufficiently parlous, though, for the SRA to place my consulting company First Class Partnerships on standby to step in as the rail franchises' operator of last resort.

In the event, MTL's downfall was averted by a deal brokered between the SRA and a prospective buyer, Arriva. To make a sale feasible, the SRA agreed that Arriva would only operate the loss making franchises for a year, at which time they would be re-let. Effectively, the SRA appeared to waive MTL's liabilities to allow a takeover. Confirming the mire his company was in when the deal was announced in February 2000, Chief Executive Graham Roberts acknowledged that MTL "could not continue to rely on the support of the banking syndicate in the absence of a sale offer and without this support it is doubtful whether MTL could continue to trade". Arriva Chief Executive Bob Davies described the franchises as "not viable" but said that for a year his company would take the hit. The situation was factored into the sale price of £35m plus taking on MTL's £50m debt.

Euan Cameron, my erstwhile colleague at BR in the period of franchise preparation, who joined Arriva's main

Board in 2001, believes that the company had twin motivations in acquiring MTL. One was as a late entrant to a market the City expected it to be involved in, but the other (and possibly the main justification) was the enticing prospect of picking up MTL's profitable Merseyside bus operations which all the major transport groups had been eyeing for some time.

Despite MTL's dire straits, there were some winners. For the employee shareholders, the deal meant a special dividend of £13,000. It was their second in two years after the sale of MTL's London bus business along with a refinancing arrangement backed by Barclays had netted them a £48m windfall worth £20,000 each in 1998. In retrospect, that payment looks bizarre given the financial situation that would emerge. Even more incredibly, a final twist in the extraordinary saga of MTL's brief involvement in the rail industry was that after Arriva took over the franchises, it discovered that Northern Spirit had paid a £3m dividend payment to MTL towards the end of 1999. The new owner's legal team advised that the payment had been "unlawful" and Arriva successfully pursued its return.

Looking back in the context of the current polarised political debate on nationalisation versus privatisation and the emphasis on holding operators to their contract, it may seem remarkable that any Government, especially a Labour one, would bail a company out of increasingly embarrassing losses, as with FirstGroup at NWT. Even more remarkable in today's context is that the Blair Government was prepared to intervene to facilitate the takeover of MTL rather than let the company go bust and its franchises pass into the hands of an operator of last resort under the control of the public sector. However, these decisions, while controversial at the time, were less surprising than it may appear. The approach was in tune with a New Labour Government that had placed great store on establishing business-friendly credentials and these deals certainly demonstrated "friendship".

In the run up to the party's landslide victory in the 1997 election, Tony Blair had famously declared that the railways would remain "publicly controlled and publicly accountable". Some at the time thought this a reference to renationalisation but it became clear that it meant nothing of the sort. Instead the manifesto stated: "Some things the Conservatives got right. We will not change them. We have no desire to replace one set of dogmas with another." It also referred to a desire to "put public and private sector together in partnership to give us the infrastructure and transport we need". As if to exclude any return to BR it stated "our task will be to improve the situation as we find it, not as we wish it to be".

The Blair Government was elected on a manifesto committed to enhancing the role of rail using 'pro-business' policies to achieve its objectives. Overall strategic direction of the industry was to be overseen by a new rail authority set up to strengthen the privatised structure and promote growth, investment and service quality. The importance attached to this agenda was underlined by the appointment of Blair's deputy John Prescott to a brief that incorporated the railways. Despite having been a fierce critic of privatisation, and one who was inclined to rage at the train operators' performance in the early days of the new Government, politically within the New Labour project he was not strong enough to engineer renationalisation. He had also positioned himself as a crucial link between New Labour and the Party's traditions and would often talk about applying socialist approaches in a "modern setting".

Personally Prescott was totally committed to expanding the railways for the social and economic benefit of the nation and accepted the political reality as the price for pursuing his transport agenda. He sanctioned a policy devised by the SRA that put private sector operators at the heart of Labour's plans to fund a huge increase in railway investment. It meant there was a need not only to keep companies like FirstGroup on board, but to deepen the pool of financially strong players by encouraging new entrants like Arriva to enter the industry, while weeding out chaff. Apart from MTL, Prism and GB Railways were also seen as insufficiently strong financially to participate in the plans for a new era. Questions were even raised about the suitability of Stagecoach's financial credentials by SRA board members at a time when its ill-advised acquisition of Coach USA in North America was destroying its share price. The purchase was described privately as a "1bn bonfire" by one Stagecoach executive.

A second factor in encouraging MTL's sale rather than bankruptcy and transfer to the SRA's operator of last resort was the undesirability of a 're-nationalised' company running weak regional businesses on the back of franchise failures. Harking back to his roots, Prescott felt it would compare badly to the private sector London and long distance franchises that were growing strongly; which had inherited higher quality operations, and in some cases had investment plans underwritten in their franchise agreements. The wisdom of that position quickly become clear when Arriva ran into dire operational difficulties due to severe driver shortages that MTL had allowed to develop.

A third factor that assisted companies in negotiating bail outs was that to some extent operators had the Government over a barrel. After the Hatfield crash in October 2000, growth had stalled across the industry, adding to multiplying losses at the regional franchises. Outside the PTE areas, paring services right back to the minimum specified level – often the bare bones under the way franchises were let at privatisation – might have been an option. Another was surrendering franchise bonds and leaving the mess to the operator of last resort. Both of these courses would have been incendiary politically.

All of which meant that when the regional franchises started running into financial problems resulting from their unrealistic bids the Government determined not to hold their feet to the fire. Instead a decision was taken to provide cover for renegotiation and rescue under the guise of what became known as "franchise re-mapping", an exercise initiated by the SRA as part of its wider franchise reform agenda. My consulting company, First Class Partnerships, was engaged to do the work. Franchise boundaries were to be redrawn to reflect certain Government objectives. Plans to let new franchises with revised geography before existing contracts expired meant contract terms were to be adjusted to secure owners' 'co-operation'. It enabled the SRA to present the deals as helping to fulfil its objectives whilst at the same time bringing financial relief to train companies.

Whether by accident or design, the SRA's remapping agenda focused mostly on regional businesses making losses. MTL's franchises and NWT were central to the re-mapping agenda for the north enabling the SRA to pump funds into companies under financial stress or restructure them to facilitate a sale. It acted as a survival mechanism that minimised the financial losses some companies faced and avoided the political fallout that would have arisen from franchise failures. It also abetted the SRA's agenda to replace smaller owning groups with stronger players and new entrants by encouraging dialogue about the possible takeover of their businesses. The justifiable defence of the remapping policy was that its objectives included supporting Labour's political devolution agenda by aligning franchises more closely with regional political boundaries. So in the north, all Northern Spirit and North Western Trains metropolitan services were to form part of a new Northern franchise. It was also seen as a necessity to redraw the map following the creation of the Welsh Assembly, so plans included merging the Cardiff franchise with routes in Wales and West to form a new Wales and Borders business.

Prism's franchises were central to that issue, while its WAGN franchise was also slated for remapping to align with the future Thameslink infrastructure project.

This represented an opportunity for all concerned because by 2000 Prism, while still profitable, was in an increasingly difficult position. The Welsh franchises had achieved basket case status and after three years were racking up annual losses approaching £20m. The group was being kept afloat by its London businesses, however continuing to support the Welsh franchises was set to become more problematic. With subsidy at WAGN due to decline sharply in 2000/01, Prism was relying on exponential growth from increased Stansted Express services along with a patronage kick from new trains at LTS to continue turning a profit. While not necessarily unreasonable assumptions, it is fair to say that there was scepticism about Prism's prospects. The University of Leeds report stated that by 2000 Prism, along with MTL, was believed to be "close to bankruptcy". As a company that had no interests other than rail franchises, it would inevitably be in a poor place to cope with any financial stresses that arose.

For some time beforehand, Prism's founders had been seeking to sell the London businesses. At first, there were discussions with Sea Containers about a possible merger with GNER prompted by competition with WAGN on the East Coast Main Line and Prism's ambitions to encroach further onto GNER's territory with an open access application. It was followed by discussions with Arriva. However, after those talks collapsed, the SRA appears to have decided to intervene. Perceiving, rightly or wrongly, that Prism faced the possibility of going under, it scheduled the company for 'fast track' discussions on restructuring its business to make it attractive to a new owner. Euan Cameron, a Prism Board member before his move to Arriva, insists that contrary to much speculation at the time,

Prism's overall finances were "in fair shape" but recalls that "the SRA believed otherwise". He put this down to poor franchise monitoring where relatively inexperienced SRA staff were assigned to manage contracts and failed to understand the finances. Perhaps this coloured the Strategic Rail Authority's ability to reach the most beneficial deal for the taxpayer.

Prism rehearsed for the forthcoming negotiations by hiring Paul King, who had prepared BR's Welsh operations for privatisation, as a consultant to act in loco parentis of the SRA in simulated talks. As a prelude to the negotiations and to make sure it entered them in a position of strength Prism also played a game of brinkmanship threatening to refuse to release franchises required for remapping to suit the SRA's schedule. After a month of daily meetings, a deal was agreed in June 2000. With SRA chairman Alistair Morton at the opera, it was signed at two in the morning. The outcome was highly beneficial for Prism. The SRA would take back the Welsh franchises and the Great Northern portion of WAGN in April 2001 so that it could let new Welsh and Thameslink franchises that year. It meant Prism would have a smaller business but one that with the liabilities in Wales removed was making good profits with little risk. For that stability, Prism agreed to invest an additional £20.5m in LTS. It was a sum substantially below the losses that would have been racked up had the Welsh franchises run to their original completion date in 2004, even taking into account the hand back of its profitable Great Northern routes.

The restructuring arrangement gave Prism the platform it needed to sell the company, which had been its intention from the start. It did so for a very full price of £166m to National Express Group, just a month after concluding its deal with the Strategic Rail Authority. For the second time in quick succession, the remapping agenda had enabled the SRA to pave the way for a company it believed had uncertain prospects to exit the industry after it had cashed in when times were good. The sale benefited Prism's shareholders by a factor of 6.5 times the original price of their shareholdings. While their holdings had been diluted by rights issues, it still gave Chief Executive Giles Fearnley and Prism's other founders a return of several million pounds each. It would have been hard indeed to question Labour's claim to be business friendly.

The price paid was startling not only because it was difficult to see how National Express could recoup that sum but because it gave NEG as many as nine of the 25 franchises. Describing it as a "stonking deal" for Prism, Euan Cameron recalls that it took a discussion of less than two minutes for Prism's directors to accept it. Initially, NEG's approach had come from its Chief Executive Phil White who had been Giles Fearnley's boss in the finance department at South Yorkshire PTE before bus privatisation. It was apparent during discussions that White was keen on the additional "geography" that came with the Prism acquisition; a bit like acquiring the water and electricity companies on a Monopoly Board to add to a set of four London stations already owned. It was also a means for NEG to buy Prism's management team. The Hatfield crash, which directly impacted WAGN's route and had a devastating effect on patronage across the entire railway, occurred two days after the sale was completed in October 2000. Giles believes that "if Hatfield had occurred two days earlier, the deal would have been off".

An interesting aspect of the experience suffered by the owners of the regional franchises was highlighted in the University of Leeds Report which noted: "The problem faced by the regional TOCs was not inevitable and could have been averted at the franchise bidding stage by a more successful elimination of unrealistic bids." Even in retrospect, and not least in the light of my own report's findings at the time, it may seem bizarre that patently unrealistic bids were accepted by OPRAF during 1996 and 1997, as indeed they have been from time to time under successive Governments ever since. I knew all the key people who worked at OPRAF at that time and they were without exception intelligent and with sufficient understanding of railway economics and markets to know full well that there was a high risk of franchise failure and that such failure could come quickly.

In fact, OPRAF regarded it as an acceptable approach to take. According to Chris Stokes: "We did expect some of them to fail but [meanwhile the Government] gets a cheap railway for a few years." In particular, by the time the regional franchises were let towards the end Chris was well aware that "the market was getting over heated" with ever keener price competition. By then it had also become apparent that a number of contracts awarded early on had been won on generous terms. So OPRAF did not appear to have any qualms in accepting bids from companies offering unrealistic subsidy reductions later in the process when the heat was on. Another part of the reason why this was considered acceptable policy was that where owners held multiple franchises, a portfolio perspective[64] could enable loss making companies to survive so long as the financial situation was not terminal. Great Western is a good example of one such successful franchise that has remained as cover for loss making operations within the FirstGroup portfolio. Other factors may well have been at play too (perhaps political). The extreme subsidy reductions offered to win some franchises could be presented up front by politicians as a benefit brought to the table by the competitive dynamic of their privatisation policy.

Even if there were reservations within OPRAF and the Department of Transport about some of the more ambitious franchise awards, the whole process was so hard driven by the Treasury that doubts were overridden and the caveat emptor principle was applied. It is a tough political choice

---

[64]

to reject the best financial bid on the grounds that it is unrealistic or a lower bid offers better quality. Ask any civil servant who has worked in rail franchising and they will tell you the difficulty of making that recommendation and the rough ride Ministers could face in Parliament for it. Anyway why not accept challenging bids from a risk taking private sector? Why not indeed, especially when the record shows that others in that first tranche of franchising did survive and prosper on the basis of their initial strategies, particularly in markets where revenue growth was achieved, whether fortuitously or by design.

Among the long distance operators, where growing the market had most validity as a commercial strategy, a number of companies were enjoying much better fortunes. Reflecting the market potential, all bar GNER had franchise plans which contained commitments to order new rolling stock as a growth build, rather than fleet replacement as in London commuter operators' bids. However, only Anglia and Midland Mainline had been perceptive enough to base their plans on early introduction of new trains. To my mind, Midland Mainline was the best performer in the early days of privatisation, scaling up its ambitions from the start by increasing its order for new trains beyond the level contracted in its franchise agreement. After introducing its new timetable in 1998, it not only doubled the train frequency overall including to London from Derby, Nottingham and Leicester but quickly extended its service to new destinations. Its marketing and product development was a notable success too; for example a new offer in 1997 aimed at business travellers increased first class revenue by 40% through a whole journey package including car parking and travel on the London Underground along with on-board perks. It was the fastest growing TOC in the early days with passenger numbers 40% higher by the year 2000, a position it would retain for some time. It made healthy profits and although it had a relatively soft bid, deserved its success as there was clear risk involved in backing such a substantial increase in capacity.

Anglia recorded high growth on a par with Midland Mainline, through a similar plan to double service frequencies. It also made use of seed corn funding that was available from the SRA to expand its territory with innovative new services from the Great Eastern Main Line. While a cross-London route to Basingstoke was withdrawn after two years due to capacity constraints, a new Norwich-Cambridge service proved highly successful and remains an important link between the region's cities. However, unlike Midland Mainline it did not benefit financially from its development of the market due to the tough subsidy reduction it faced, struggling to break even from the start. It is fair to say that this was of the company's making due to its own bid commitments. Equally, it could be said that one of the ongoing perversities of the franchising system is that a company offering a well-managed service whose business plan is entrepreneurial and in tune with regional economic and social needs is often less well rewarded financially than poorly run, mundane operators.

In Virgin's case, subsidy reductions on its West Coast franchise were conservative prior to the scheduled big bang move into payments to the Government in 2002. It left the company with a fairly simple marketing task to turn a profit in those early years, but Virgin's commercial nous shone through with a flood of initiatives helping to grow passenger numbers 8% year on year prior to Hatfield. It proved highly lucrative with annual pre-tax profits as high as £50m at an almost eye watering profit margin of 14%. Things were going less well on CrossCountry however, where moderate growth was nowhere near the level required. Annual losses would have looked penal had it not been for West Coast's performance which kept Virgin Rail Group as a whole comfortably in profit. There was a suspicion that Virgin may have overbid for CrossCountry to ensure it secured the contract due to the benefits it would provide in co-ordinating services with West Coast, and its financial performance gave credence to these theories.

At the same time, Virgin's grand vision for service expansion on the West Coast Main Line was starting to unravel. By 1999, it had become clear that, as Chris Green put it to me, Railtrack effectively had "no plans for moving block signalling" on which the upgrade plan for the line and Virgin's business plan were based. This was despite Railtrack having formally signed up to deliver it little more than a year beforehand. Railtrack's unrealistic view of its ability to do so would require the route modernisation to be re-planned as a conventional project at many times the original cost, delaying service enhancements planned for 2002 for many years and preventing delivery of Virgin's full 140mph strategy. Repeated delays to introduction of the new Pendolinos would also hinder progress.

The only party that seemed to suffer no obvious financial consequences from the fall out was Virgin. Its franchise plan for the West Coast was bold and innovative, but its approach to risk management was shrewd and by no means cavalier; unsurprising perhaps given that the stakes were very high in respect of the new, untested rolling stock and promised new signalling, central to its bid. The revenue projections (undertaken by Steer Davies Gleave) were soundly based but Virgin needed a hedge against a failure to implement the rolling stock and infrastructure investment in time. According to Chris, who had joined Virgin's rail division as Chief Executive shortly after the contract with Railtrack was signed, its high calibre team had "outgunned" their opposite numbers during negotiations. As a result, when it emerged that Railtrack couldn't deliver the agreed upgrade to the agreed timescales, Virgin had a watertight contract that did not expose it commercially. In fact Railtrack was liable for substantial compensation. The rolling stock contract with Alstom also secured a high degree of protection because there was virtually no scope for contract variation from the manufacturer. The Virgin negotiators had included lawyer Tom Winsor who would go on to become Rail Regulator; and Richard Bowker who would succeed Alastair Morton as Chairman of the SRA.

Virgin had moved to de-risk its venture in other ways too. Initially, it planned to float Virgin Rail Group, which also included CrossCountry, on the stock market. However, in 1998, it chose to partner with Stagecoach which took a 49% stake in VRG for £158m by buying out Virgin's private equity partners. It enabled venture capitalists who had backed Virgin's move into rail to treble their initial investment.

On top of the long running delays to the infrastructure upgrade and late train deliveries, Virgin experienced significant teething problems introducing the new trains, not only on West Coast but CrossCountry too. In 2004 the SRA did consider removing Virgin from both franchises as a result. In my consulting role as an adviser to the SRA, I strongly argued the case for allowing Virgin to keep its contracts. My view was that replacing it with the authority's operator of last resort (also my consultancy) would have been unnecessarily disruptive of an essential rolling stock implementation process on a vital national route on which original upgrade plans had already had to be downscaled.

When the upgrade was completed, Virgin did go on to deliver a vastly improved high frequency service on the West Coast in 2009 and fulfilled its original projections of more than doubling passenger numbers. Franchise variations as a result of the disruption to its strategy, though, meant the huge premium payments to Government that Virgin's bid initially envisaged were never paid. In fact it received hefty subsidy, which it was able to negotiate through a series of short term contracts from 2002 following Railtrack's failure to deliver the route upgrade. There is no doubt which side came off on the right end of these negotiations with Government. Virgin West Coast remained a highly lucrative franchise to the current day until the DfT finally removed it from the chess board when the company, in conjunction with Stagecoach, submitted "non compliant" franchise bids, unwilling to take what it saw as unacceptably high risk for future pension liabilities. Virgin Trains had enjoyed a 22 year hegemony on the West Coast Main Line, and for much of that period had secured payments from the Government for operating the railway under management contracts.

By contrast, the ambitious plan for CrossCountry never really got close to achieving the huge growth in passenger numbers expected. The new high frequency timetable[65] implemented in September 2002 proved over ambitious and some routes needed to be pared back. Although it had looked an exciting and innovative franchise plan, in practice it had proved 'a dog of a contract'. In 2004 Virgin and the SRA would agree that it should be terminated early to allow a new franchise with a more practical service proposition to be let. At the time that decision was announced the franchise seemed on the face of it to have been a success in attracting new passengers. Numbers had grown 60%, second only to Midland Mainline among long distance TOCs but on closer inspection the word in the industry was that setting aside abstraction from other operators, growth amounted to just 13%. Furthermore subsidies were several times higher than planned due to a contract renegotiation as a result of the disruption caused by delays to the WCML upgrade. Taking into account the cost of the new fleet, the difficulty the new timetable had caused other operators; and overcrowding arising from deploying shorter trains, I wrote: "This must represent the worst value for money investment in railways since British Rail embarked on its marshalling yard modernisations in the late 1950s."

---

[65] Operation Princess

Commuter operators in the London and South East area were in a strong position from the start due to the burgeoning economy. They generally made the most of this good fortune, sweating the assets to increase services, although not without some significant overcrowding.

SWT with the softest of soft contracts had actually planned to cut services in its bid, as had a number of other operators that won franchises at the start of the franchising process. After an initial debacle of mass train cancellations caused by botched restructuring of driver numbers, it moved to capitalise on the high growth potential by introducing 300 more services per day into Waterloo and ordering 30 new train sets. An initial annual profit of £17m would more than double in short order. Interestingly, the requirement to reduce subsidy was sufficiently generous and the contract terms sufficiently loose that it opted not to introduce BR's planned driver only operation on its inner suburban services. This was one illustration of how little strategic direction had been given to the franchising process. It was a strong initiative that BR had implemented elsewhere on inner suburban lines south of the Thames and one that SWT might reasonably have been expected to complete as a means of increasing the railway's efficiency. However, the company had no interest in inviting industrial action which would only punch holes in its bottom line and saw no need to take it forward.

In fact it remains an irony that major train crew productivity initiatives were largely achieved under BR in the 1980s and not much by franchised operators since. Arriva, the one company that did take a strong line with unions in the early days of franchising incurred significant odium with little support from the SRA and ended up losing its franchises in the north when they were re-let, partly on account of its loss of reputation. Only when the Department for Transport more recently began to take an interest in driver only operation as part of franchise negotiation and award did it re-emerge as a priority. The union mood was significantly misread though, resulting in headline-making disruption and revenue loss, particularly at the Southern and Northern franchises.

In contrast to SWT, there were some commuter operators where my report forecast that achieving the growth required to stay profitable could be challenging. The highest revenue growth requirement was at Chiltern, but the TOC's strong business plan enabled it to stay in the black although not by much in some years. By 2000 it had delivered the infrastructure upgrade planned in its bid and ordered further trains in addition to the growth build it had committed to. As a result it was able to increase services and capacity more than any other commuter operator to cater for strong demand, much of which it generated through its own efforts. Like Anglia, it deserved a better financial result for its efforts amid generally strong profits being achieved by commuter operators that had done much less in comparison to develop services.

There is always an exception that is said to prove every rule and, in the case of London and the South East, that exception was Connex. It was replaced on the South Central franchise two years early in 2001, and had its contract for the South Eastern franchise terminated in 2003. The story of how this came about is worth telling.

Although revenue growth requirements were at the low end for the commuter operators, these were tough bids. The high density services meant there was a need for particularly strong railway management competence and at South Eastern, where major rolling stock replacement was planned, expert project management as well. It was only too apparent from an early stage that Connex lacked the experience to manage these important railways, had underestimated its task and that the bid accepted by OPRAF was not rigorously prepared.

Its bidding tactic was based on gaining an advantage through offering a large first year subsidy reduction followed by flatter relatively undemanding subsidy falls in later years. At South Eastern, this strategy outflanked the MBO team's bid which Dick Fearn, South Eastern Managing Director, described to me as a "continuum" of what the TOC had been achieving on an annual basis under BR. The management team thought this sensible as it gave time in the short term to plan how cost reductions might be achieved longer term. Having lost the competition it was frustrating for the them to discover that Connex "had no real plan" for achieving its commitments; yet the upfront subsidy reductions provided the French company's bid with a significant 'net present value' advantage over the MBO's when OPRAF assessed them. The acceptance of 'best price' bids was in keeping with a trend that has pretty much prevailed, albeit with greater scrutiny, ever since. The two franchise subsidy profiles meant Connex made large first year losses totalling £27m, which it said it had been expecting, but no doubt ramped up pressure on its businesses to make cost savings.

Initially Dick was asked to stay on at South Eastern and Connex offered him a significant 30% salary increase to do so but he recalls, "as the year unfolded I found that I wasn't really running anything other than day to day operations". Connex also had no clear rolling stock replacement strategy of its own despite this being the key requirement of the franchise and the reason for it being granted as a 15-year term. Instead it adopted that of the MBO team in the shape of a build of Class 375 units. Neither did Connex have any substantive cost reduction plans. Dick believes the bid as profiled was undeliverable in the timescales Connex set but there was a presumption that, being in the public sector, South Eastern would be carrying unnecessary costs which would offer low hanging fruit to be harvested by the new owners. Generally, BR had been run as a tight ship for years and the aspirations for cost reduction were not realised sowing the seeds for the contract's cancellation.

Connex may have relied on the former BR managers to run the railway but they were not running the business. According to Dick, someone from Paris was "planted to watch everything that was going on in finance" whilst Olivier Brousse, who was to take over as MD in the run up to the demise of the contract, initially "came in to look at the personnel side". Dick had to go to the French HQ every six weeks to be "given the Star Chamber treatment". Against this background in the autumn of 1997, less than a year after the franchise had been let, Dick was called for interview with Connex Chairman Colin Watson, who had gone through privatisation with National Power. He said: "Dick, you've done a splendid job but we think that you should take early retirement." Dick was 43 at the time. Watson continued: "I'm sure there will be other avenues for you to pursue. We can play this short (meaning 'clear your desk today'), or long (meaning 'leave within a fortnight')". Dick chose to bid a proper farewell to his staff.

After the initial heavy loss, things at Connex South Eastern failed to pick up in any meaningful way and profit margins remained wafer thin. It was recording the lowest passenger growth of any commuter train operator; was alone among commuter operators in having cut services; and was regularly at the bottom of the punctuality tables. Passenger discontent was rife.

Meanwhile Connex South Central was performing well only by comparison and had suffered an early blow when exercising an option in its contract to apply for a franchise extension from seven years to 15 in return for a fleet replacement programme. On the face of it, the proposals for an extended contract looked reasonably impressive compared to many of the initial bids OPRAF had accepted. As well as offering to procure £326m of new rolling stock, they included contributing funding to electrify the Ashford-

Hastings line and its Uckfield branch and eliminating subsidy by the end of the contract. However, OPRAF judged that the offer did not give sufficient value for money compared to a competitively-let franchise. It came at a time when Connex's operational performance was poor and John Prescott was warning operators with substandard performance that they would not be granted extensions, or in fact have any place in the industry. Subsequently, when the franchise was re-tendered under the Strategic Rail Authority's accelerated refranchising programme, Connex was beaten by Go-Ahead despite tabling proposals for greater investment in new infrastructure and agreed to relinquish its franchise nearly two years early in August 2001[66]. The underlying management problems at South Central were revealed when Go-Ahead took over and was so short of drivers that it had to institute an emergency timetable. Go-Ahead also claimed that it had inherited trains in a poor mechanical condition and that a new revenue protection scheme was generating an additional £2m per year. Olivier Brousse for Connex admitted that "we didn't hand over the best of train companies[67]".

The end was also nigh at South Eastern. The barely profitable business began making losses and then in December 2002 turned to the SRA and negotiated a bail out involving an extra £58m subsidy over the following year. The SRA justified the arrangement by saying that stability was needed for Connex to complete the franchise's rolling stock replacement programme, which itself was running behind schedule. As part of the deal, the franchise was to be terminated five years early in 2006 over which time it was reported that Connex was seeking a further £200m, indicative of the seriousness of South Eastern's financial problems. However, in June 2003 Connex was stripped of its contract, following an audit by accountants PWC which

---

[66] Go Ahead paid Connex £17m to compensate for lost profits.
[67] Reported in "Transit Magazine"

indicated that the company's financial controls were inadequate to justify a further input of public money. Connex was to hand control of the business over to the 'operator of last resort' within six months. This time, and unlike the West Coast situation, the obvious advantage of continuity during a fleet replacement programme would not save the franchise. Connex was too far gone. Richard Bowker, by now SRA Chairman, emphasised that the reason for termination was to protect taxpayers' money. "We have lost confidence in Connex's ability to be a competent financial manager," he said. The company had failed in the eyes of the SRA to implement a detailed action plan designed to improve the credibility of its financial custody of the franchise.

Bizarrely, given the issues exposed, and one can presume because the SRA did not wish Connex to walk out of South Eastern immediately, Connex was not disbarred from bidding for future franchises. Instead the SRA said it "would need to raise its game significantly". Effectively, however, it was the end. During negotiations for the new TransPennine franchise, FirstGroup's rail director Dean Finch got wind of information that Connex and First were the final two in contention. His response was to raise FirstGroup's price. When SRA negotiators asked him to reduce it, his response was said to be along the lines of: "So which one of you geniuses is going to tell the minister that Connex has won?" The franchise went to FirstGroup and proved very lucrative for the next 12 years.

When Connex withdrew from South Eastern in November 2003, the new Managing Director, Michael Holden, said: "Connex had a culture that was resigned to not having the ability to sort out some fundamental problems but I will be reinvigorating the management not to accept these problems and get back to the real nuts and bolts of running a railway." Recruiting more drivers was a key to improving performance. Following Connex's sacking, my

First Class Partnerships consultancy led a root and branch review of all South Eastern's activities whilst the French company was still running things, albeit under notice. The results were disturbing and the parallels with South Central plain to see. The TOC was poorly organised; had poor revenue, declining in real terms; poor budgetary control; and poor customer approval ratings that were the worst in class.

There were also serious impending operational and engineering issues (mostly associated with the rolling stock replacement and maintenance programme) risking performance in the immediate future. In my report to the SRA, I wrote that "failings stem from Connex's management approach and style" which principally exhibited a tendency to silo-style, command and control functional management with inadequate inter-functional team working and an organisational structure not well suited to the needs of the TOC management task. I also observed that there were still elements of Paris-based 'corporate' interest, for example "the finance, HR, marketing and new trains engineering functions not formally reporting via the TOC MD". To compound the problems, with the exception of Michael Holden, the top team was lacking in experience for an operation of its size and complexity. There had been five personnel changes in the key post of Operations Director in as many years and the company had been without a qualified Fleet Engineer in the top team during a period when new train replacement was a key priority. My main conclusions were that this was a big TOC needing much stronger governance and guidance to a relatively inexperienced, though potentially capable and enthusiastic, management team. Whilst the issues unearthed were perhaps not unique to South Eastern, it was the opinion of the review team that it was unusual to find so many problems all at the same time. We also warned that whilst the company was under SRA ownership it would have some serious and major tasks ahead in rectifying these issues, many of which would not be quick to solve. South Eastern remained under public sector control until 2006.

Looking back, the seeds of Connex's demise had been sewn from the start.

So the very early years of franchising were something of a mixed bag with strong growth achieved by some but with a number of high profile failures too. At least one owning group was saved from bankruptcy so it could be sold; one was sacked; Virgin's franchises were renegotiated due to the issues with the West Coast upgrade; and all the regional franchises were bailed out by a variety of means. National Express's regional TOCs did make it beyond Hatfield, but the writing appeared on the wall from the start for them too, particularly ScotRail. Conversely, in a number of cases, some companies made high profits while contributing relatively little, while some delivered high quality plans for low returns. There were few cases where you could say the balance was right.

Issues created by the fissures between track and train were also exposed very early on in the privatised industry's performance and not just by the Hatfield crash (which I will turn to in Chapter 8). Although an improvement in punctuality is often claimed in the very early days of privatisation, this was an illusion. The new integrated structure BR had introduced between 1991 and 1994 had had an immediate beneficial impact and during that time a combination of the new structure and performance management techniques led to punctuality improving for three years running in Network South East before the new privatisation structures were introduced. For a while afterwards the system had a momentum of its own as the same people and processes remained largely in place. By the end of 1998, however, it was clear that difficulties had arisen in managing the various new interfaces created between constituent elements of the system – train maintenance, crewing, planning, control, signalling and infrastructure. The impact was not necessarily apparent in the headline statistics which were similar to BR but in reality punctuality was worse than the official figures due to operators' ability to exclude void days, when service was particularly poor. An assessment I carried out at the end of 1998 showed that punctuality had declined markedly compared to the final days before BR was restructured for privatisation in 1994. The official figures for 1998 showed that performance was worse on 37 routes, and better on 28, but taking account of the void days the split was as high as 46 worse to 19 better. Sharply rising passenger complaints also indicated the true situation.

Even at this stage there was a chance to address the underlying faults in the industry structure put in place by the Conservative's ideologically-driven and hurried privatisation model. For a very short while the Strategic Rail Authority created a fleeting opportunity to bring management of track and train closer together and establish a much more ambitious and inventive model of privatisation. Sadly this never happened and I explain why in the next Chapter.

CHAPTER EIGHT

The death of privatisation?

The flaws in the privatisation structures were obscured for a while by the early success story of growth. As noted in the previous chapter, a number of franchises such as SWT, Thameslink and Virgin West Coast rapidly made what I would describe as supra-normal profits. Many others such as GNER recorded profit margins that, though not of the same scale, must have been a delight to their owners. This arose because patronage was booming way in excess of the level anticipated in their bids. One consequence was that a number of franchise plans were inadequate to cater for the surge in passenger numbers experienced. With the notable exceptions of Midland Mainline, Anglia and Chiltern few had plans for new rolling stock to absorb short term growth. Although they may have tried to sugar coat it, the resulting pressure on capacity caught many franchise owners napping.

Certainly the architects of privatisation in the civil service were surprised. GNER Chief Executive Christopher Garnett recalled that when the company's owner, Sea Containers, was being courted to participate in franchising, civil servants had mocked its view that strong growth could be achieved. This, he claimed, was why the franchise was limited to seven years with no provision for new trains. Yet it took little more than a year after franchising was completed before Sea Containers adopted a stance of using the situation to renegotiate its contract. Its bid had assumed an 18% rise in patronage over seven years but by 1998 its passenger numbers had more or less already reached that level. The company even warned that over half the people using its trains could be standing by the end of its franchise in 2003. Its plea was for the Labour Government to double its term to 15-years enabling it to expand the fleet with eight new tilting train sets alongside infrastructure investment from Railtrack. Sea Containers made clear that without a longer term deal, it was not prepared to take the risk of leasing additional trains to accommodate demand. It was a blunt challenge from a company in a strong position financially and which saw itself as holding a strong hand. Others were making similar noises, notably Thameslink which was quickly in serious breach of overcrowding limits as the boom on the route in the latter days of BR continued. However, a different stance was taken by Stagecoach at SWT which ordered 30 new trainsets, partly to position itself as a company the Government could do business with. It represented an interesting tactical contrast to Sea Containers.

In making calls for franchise renegotiation, companies were reading the Government's mood music and transport agenda. Despite his distaste for rail privatisation, John Prescott had accepted his inheritance pragmatically because he believed strongly in developing the role of rail. So he responded to operators by indicating he was prepared to renegotiate a limited number of existing franchises as longer term deals in return for investment in new rolling stock. This was confirmed as policy in his July 1998 integrated transport White Paper[68] which set out in detail the role of an expanded and higher quality railway as an engine for economic growth and social cohesion. However, no indications were provided at that stage on how the rail network might develop to achieve his objectives or which franchises might be renegotiated beyond 'those with poor punctuality need not apply'. That would be determined by a new Strategic Rail Authority which Sir Alastair Morton was appointed to lead the following year.

---

[68] "A New Deal for Transport"

Morton was Prescott's choice and an excellent one at that. He had been inspirational in his buccaneering approach to rescuing the Channel Tunnel infrastructure project and rapidly began developing a more radical agenda to fulfilling Prescott's ambitions for the railway than anyone had envisaged. Operators would be tasked with a key role in delivering Government's policy, not only by providing additional rolling stock but funding infrastructure as well. Railtrack was to be only one source of private sector finance for expanding the network. Speaking in March 1999, Morton said he strongly believed that cash flow for investment would be generated from rising passenger revenues and that TOCs must prepare to invest in the growth of the rail system alongside Railtrack. His statement that operators seeking longer franchises "must commit themselves to invest in service development" could not have been clearer. In a side-swipe at the infrastructure owner, he said that investment couldn't be slowed to "Railtrack's preferred pace". He added that the SRA would only fund new infrastructure when it was not viable for the private sector to do so. Recognising that new and enhanced infrastructure built before 2010 would not earn a return until 2015 or beyond, Morton envisaged that suitably designed public private partnership models would provide the answer. TOCs would be tasked with putting together alliances[69] comprising consortiums of City investors and international engineering conglomerates to fund railway upgrades, and in return long-term 20-year franchises would be awarded. While Morton anticipated that significant Government funding would be available to support infrastructure schemes, he stressed that the private sector would be expected to provide upfront funding in the majority of cases.

No time was to be wasted. Morton's aim was to replace all 18 short term franchises with the new long term deals by

---

[69] Special Purpose Companies, or Vehicles, known as SPCs or SPVs

the end of 2001 rather than waiting for existing contracts to expire in 2003 and 2004. Operators would be paid a fee to surrender their franchise early or, if loss making, pay a fee for early release from the contract. He made clear that high profit margin "sweetheart deals" on franchises let at the beginning of privatisation would not be repeated. Among the many new concepts Morton spoke of in setting out his vision was for the UK railway to develop as a market for world class railway infrastructure project management. As the companies closest to passengers, operators would have freedom to propose expansion of any schemes specified by Government, or entirely new projects. As the policy developed, he announced that in addition to increasing infrastructure capacity, operators' investment plans should be designed to meet a minimum punctuality target of 93.75%, well above the performance being delivered at the time, or historically.

As Morton announced the first batches of franchises to be re-let, operators began responding enthusiastically, exemplified early on by Go-Ahead setting up Special Purpose Companies (SPCs) to deliver infrastructure investment for its bids for South Central and Chiltern in the first tranche of new franchises the SRA planned to let. Its partners were the Royal Bank of Scotland and Bechtel[70], a very credible combination whose South Central bid included a £330m proposal for upgrading the Brighton Main Line. At the end of the franchise period the assets would revert to Railtrack, which might itself be considered as an infrastructure partner in the meantime. Connex's competing plans went further, seeking to create an entirely new main line route to London by upgrading and reopening the line from Lewes to Victoria via Uckfield. Meanwhile, construction company John Laing plc, which had become the majority shareholder at Chiltern, emphasised that its bid

---

[70] A global engineering and construction conglomerate established in the USA

to retain that franchise would involve providing financial backing for, and managing, a series of substantial infrastructure upgrades. Meanwhile Virgin announced plans for a 200mph section of new track in its bid for the East Coast Main Line.

To me this was genuine privatisation compared to the pallid version implemented by the Tories, even though its primary purpose was to meet Government objectives. In simple terms these were modal shift, supporting economic growth and social inclusion; and to be successful, bidders would need to pick up on these elements in their proposals to develop the network. Writing for *Transit Magazine* in summer 2000 I said: "Alastair Morton has set out a strategic view of a higher quality railway, operating increasingly on the basis of enhanced infrastructure funded by the private sector that will ensure a modal switch to rail with commercial benefits to train operators and social benefits to the country." Although the promotion of infrastructure investment by franchises would soon be abandoned, looking back I still see this as the moment Government policy changed fundamentally in setting out to encourage a resurgence of railway travel for economic and social reasons. This approach continued under subsequent Governments of every political complexion.

The innovative nature of what might have been possible through franchise-inspired infrastructure investment and operators' willingness to pursue it was evident in the next tranche of franchises the SRA put to market. Arriva proposed to invest in new rolling stock and services for the TransPennine franchise that would extend way beyond the existing network, to include for example, Glasgow, Peterborough, Stansted, Cardiff, Leicester and Nottingham, none of which appeared in the SRA's list of destinations for the franchise. First Group announced it would be bidding as a joint venture with French company GTI to form an alliance providing "complementary skills" which would enable the franchise to be upgraded and expanded. At the same time Virgin announced that its East Coast proposals would include services to London from regional centres not then served by direct trains to the capital, heralding what Grand Central would do later as an open access operator. Then, when the new Wales and Borders franchise was put out to tender, Mike Grant the SRA Chief Executive, stated "extra investment and better services will be the overriding criteria" in awarding the franchise. It was clearly recognised that private investment in both track and train was possible in situations where it would generate revenue and a commercial return.

The fact that companies were lining up to undertake such bids was indicative of a growing confidence, underpinned by Government's repeated commitment to an expansionist approach and public private partnerships. Credible new bidders from other business sectors started appearing on shortlists for new franchises, such as Group 4 and Serco. European state railways, the Dutch, French and Swiss, also started to bid heralding this sector's dominance of the market that would emerge over the next 20 years – a privatisation courtesy of other countries' state backed railways. Meanwhile, the SRA had been waiting for Prescott to back his White Paper vision with the public sector's contribution of hard cash, with Morton chiding him to 'show me the money'.

In July 2000, that arrived in the Government's 10-year plan for transport. A total of £29bn was committed with £10bn to support enhancement schemes including contributions to operators' franchise plans. It was an unprecedented commitment and one that the 10-year plan envisaged would be matched by the private sector contributing £34bn. Writing at the time I noted that in the initial round of privatisation, with few exceptions, vision had remained a buzzword on many a company white board but too often described something mundane rather than true business development. This was different, and in contrast to the days of BR, it had unequivocal backing from Government. "Many in the industry have said for years that commitment from Government was necessary to leverage more private investment and that is now precisely what is going to happen," I wrote in a magazine article at the time. "Sceptics thought that Alastair Morton would not get the money but he appears to have won the battle and in so doing has achieved the biggest single breakthrough for the national rail system for at least half a century." The stage seemed set for ways of testing the private sector's ability to bring commercial expertise and financial muscle to the railway; and of a more integrated approach to franchising and infrastructure management.

Unfortunately we shall never know how this would have developed because Morton's carefully considered approach was almost immediately torpedoed by the politicians' reaction to the Hatfield crash on 17th October 2000 when a GNER northbound express was derailed killing four passengers and injuring another 70. In the light of Railtrack's panicked response to what had been revealed by the condition of the track at Hatfield the whole railway was thrown into disarray. Speed restrictions were imposed throughout the network because, in the words of Robin Gisby[71], "nobody knew what was out there". Punctuality plummeted. Train companies experienced revenue meltdown. Railtrack faced compensation claims from operators while costs to restore the infrastructure soared. The 10-year plan money disappeared. As the consequences played out, it would end with the Government's decision to put Railtrack into administration a year later. In fact, the causes of the Hatfield crash, and with it the demise of privatisation itself, were inherent in Railtrack's approach from its inception.

---

[71] Robin Gisby held positions at the top of Railtrack and Network Rail continuously from 1997 to 2015

In considering the failure of Railtrack it is worth reflecting that the Conservatives' initial position was that the company would remain in the public sector following its separation from BR, and that potential privatisation was a longer term project. This was seen as acknowledging many of the concerns being expressed about the large project and safety risks inherent in managing the railway's infrastructure assets. However, the situation would soon be reversed at breakneck speed. To quote from a Parliamentary briefing memorandum: "When the original scheme for rail privatisation was unveiled in 1992 the idea of selling Railtrack to the private sector was scarcely mentioned. The priority was to transfer the train services to the private sector and only after that process was completed would Railtrack follow. At the time John MacGregor, then Transport Secretary, thought the step could be 10 years away." This was reinforced during the committee stage of the Railways Bill when Roger Freeman, the Railways Minister, declared "Railtrack will be in the public sector for the foreseeable future".

A year after the Railways Act was passed the Conservatives changed tack, driven by ideology and the prospect of the money that could be raised. In November 1994, MacGregor's successor Brian Mawinney announced that the Government intended to "privatise Railtrack within the lifetime of this Parliament". He told the House of Commons that floatation offered "the best future for Railtrack, for passengers and freight and for train operators. It will allow greater use of private sector skills in managing the network, improving Railtrack stations, delivering efficient track maintenance and encouraging investment in the upgrading of railway lines. It will provide even greater scope for private capital to be injected into better facilities". Sometimes the evangelical certainty of politicians is frightening, particularly so in this case where there was little understanding in Government of how Railtrack might fulfil these ambitions or be positioned to do so. This was cruelly exposed not only by Hatfield but by two other serious railway crashes that preceded it.

The creation of Railtrack began with the appointment of Sir Robert Horton to the British Railways Board in 1995. His role was to establish the infrastructure provider by separating the assets from BR. It was ironic coincidence that he had previously inhabited the same industrial sector as Bob Reid II, the BR Chairman. Some believe the choice was Machiavellian in seeking to create a tension at the top of the industry between the two former oil men. Reid had lost the political argument on the form privatisation should take and the appointment of an oil industry rival to head Railtrack was the personification of the key decision with which the BR Chairman disagreed. History has essentially vindicated the ex-BR man.

As well as being a nakedly political appointee who could be relied on to support the separation of track and train, Horton came with a reputation and an agenda. He had been forced out as Chairman of British Petroleum following a contretemps with the Non-Executive Directors and was handily available when rail privatisation emerged. He almost certainly saw Railtrack as a route to restoring his status. Others close to the politics of privatisation were appointed as reliable supporters of the privatised industry structure delineated by the Railways Act. They included the then youthful Archie Norman, Chairman and Chief Executive of ASDA at the time; someone who was soon to seek a career in Conservative politics as the MP for Tunbridge Wells which he represented from 1997 until 2005, ironically the high point of Labour's electoral success. Another Non-Executive Director close to the Tory Government was Sir Christopher Foster. During the privatisation process he had been a personal adviser to John MacGregor, who kicked off the separation of track and train. When Railtrack escaped BR's clutches in April 1994,

Horton's Board quickly sought to influence the Government to privatise. It took just 18 months from Mawinney's announcement to prepare the company for floatation in May 1996.

One of the key tasks in creating Railtrack was the selection of a management team which was populated by a mix of rail professionals and others from outside the industry, notably in the fields of finance and commercial activities. It was Bob Reid's preference for the Chief Executive to be Peter Watson, BR Board member for Engineering, who had himself come from a successful private sector background. Reid advocated the appointment because he considered that a technical understanding was critical to rail safety and performance. However, the move was vetoed by the Government and the role was offered to John Edmonds, a life time railwayman but someone who was renowned for his radical and often sceptical views on the role of engineers. At the same time the BRB Director responsible for Safety, David Rayner, was transferred to Railtrack.

Thus Edmonds, the architect of BR vertical integration, became the first Chief Executive of the newly separated infrastructure owner. The company then moved quickly to further separate the activities for which it was responsible. Whereas BR had integrated all of the various activities for operating and engineering a railway, Railtrack chose to contract out its maintenance and renewal activities to companies that were themselves created for sale to the private sector. More cash went to the Treasury as maintenance companies were sold with track renewals following a year later, in 1996.

Although, initially, some of Railtrack's newly appointed regional (zonal) chiefs were civil engineers by qualification, they didn't remain in those positions for long. One, Richard Middleton, was appointed Commercial Director and sat on the main Board, whilst another, the innovative York-based

Bob Clarke, was advised that if he wanted to continue as an engineer he should seek roles amongst Railtrack's suppliers. He joined Jarvis, the last contractor to be privatised, in June 1996. Robin Gisby, a future main Board Director of Network Rail, described the basic hostility that existed towards those with a railway background during those early years when he confirmed to me that not only was there antipathy towards railway people but "railwaymen were stupid". After all "why would you come to the railway if you could keep a low profile as a supplier and earn a lot more money?" Such attitudes were emblematic of how Railtrack structured itself to face the brave new world amongst the FTSE100 elite. It would become a company where skills in negotiating supply contracts were preferred over the management skills of delivery. It seems certain that this was motivated as much by a desire to reduce costs through competitive supply as it was by any other reason. A consequence was that engineering experience and knowledge were eroded at the interface between infrastructure controller and maintainer.

Neither did Railtrack benefit from its internal politics which at times seemed to border on the internecine. The Non-Executive Directors did not trust the top "railwaymen" they had inherited. In Chapter 3, I described how this was made clear to me when I was interviewed for a Board role in early 1997. "Do you think there are too many railwaymen on the Board of Railtrack", being followed immediately by the question: "Do you think the next Chief Executive should be a railwayman?" The first question indicated a suspicion and distrust of railway people whilst the second, with John Edmonds in post, indicated that they were already thinking about replacing him, and did so in short order. Yet the internal wrangling didn't stop there. The company's Commercial Director, the engaging and bright private sector import, Michael Howells, had recently been marched from the building under escort following an incident at a meeting when rivals for the top job pinned accusations on him concerning a recently negotiated freight contract. The knives were out. Who would be next? It was Edmonds, the railwayman. The way the entire company was being set up and run appeared to confirm in the minds of most senior railway managers that Railtrack was not a career of first choice. Bob Horton's reputation for bombastic arrogance, and John Edmonds's scepticism of engineers, had already influenced several good managers to opt for the world of franchising in preference to infrastructure during the creation of shadow organisations prior to privatisation. Neither did industrial unrest at the company in the form of a signallers' pay dispute in 1994 help to improve the siege mentality that seemed to pervade the organisation in its early days.

Around the time these unsavoury Boardroom manoeuvres were taking place and only a year after floatation, the company found itself in the headlines for all the wrong reasons. A collision between a High Speed Train and a freight train at Southall on 19th September 1997 resulted in the deaths of seven people. Perhaps unreasonably on that occasion, Railtrack bore the brunt of public criticism and so began the reputational damage which continued to be inflicted on the company as over the next two years further safety failings were exposed. On the same section of the Great Western Main Line, and only two years later, 31 people were killed in a collision between a local commuter train leaving Paddington and a long distance InterCity train arriving. The accident occurred at Ladbroke Grove on 5th October 1999. By the time of the first crash the Non-Executive Directors at Railtrack had got their way and John Edmonds had been replaced by Gerald Corbett, a friend of Archie Norman. So began a long history of successive Chief Executives of the infrastructure controller being appointed from outside the industry. Not only did they have no background in the industry they led but practically none had any previous chief executive experience either. Corbett himself has been described as someone with a breezy saloon bar manner but who, according to a senior director at the time, "was not really bothered about day to day railway activities". It was his first chief executive role and he "viewed Railtrack as something for the c.v. – a stepping stone to other things".

Despite this hauteur at the Board level, there seems to have been a presumption amongst those without any kind of railway background to inform their judgement that the professional expertise on which they relied existed at the operational levels from which they themselves were remote. They failed to see what others looking in could; that this engineering expertise had been ameliorated by the decisions they had taken whilst also slimming down the organisation by operating through a contractual matrix with suppliers. The regulatory environment also played its part in re-enforcing the company's own view about running a cost efficient railway. Under pressure from the Regulator to reduce costs the company was in the strange position that 85%[72] of its revenues were gleaned from track access contracts with train operators at a time when these charges were being regulated downwards in real terms. As a FTSE 100 company with shareholders and City investors to satisfy, the path to growing profits via this route was therefore very restricted. It may be considered surreal in these circumstances that the bulk of Railtrack's access charges were in effect being paid by the taxpayer via subsidies to train companies[73]. Yet this is what was called privatisation. The company's dependence on the taxpayer, of course, contained the seeds of its later destruction.

---

[72] Research Paper 96/54, 26 April 1996: House of Commons Library

[73] In the year ended 31 March 1995, the TOCs had total passenger receipts of £2,153 million and received total public sector financial support of £2,009 million. In the same year the TOCs paid £1,955 million to Railtrack for access to track and major stations.

Given this impediment, Railtrack seemed to focus on activities beyond the core railway as the way to promote shareholder interests. According to Robin Gisby the "mindset was for executing expansionist developments as a means of boosting the share price" so that, for example, taking on the Channel Tunnel Rail Link infrastructure was seen as more important than significant projects such as upgrading the West Coast Main Line[74]. When Edmonds was replaced as Chief Executive his successor, Corbett, gave little attention to the basic operation and appeared to be more focused on using Railtrack as a "springboard to international growth".

Whilst under siege from the media for its safety record and the industry's operational performance, Railtrack was also coming under fire from its own customers, the train companies, and from the Regulator. Dissatisfaction amongst train operators usually centred on the poor performance of the timetable but often Railtrack didn't seem to be on the same page. Euan Cameron, then running Thameslink, a Go-Ahead company, recalls a meeting with Corbett which Go-Ahead's Chief Executive had sought because of poor train service performance. He had great difficulty in securing a meeting in the first place and when the pair finally met, Corbett opened the discussion saying, "I don't know why we're having this meeting. You're too small a company to warrant much attention". Euan says Thameslink was never given anything other than second priority. A similar song is sung by others.

I didn't find Railtrack a hospitable supplier either. When I was trying to negotiate a track access agreement with its North East Zone on behalf of Hull Trains there was no interest shown towards a new, progressive open access company which was instead seen as an impediment to the major operator on the route (then GNER). All sorts of

---

[74] A project centred on the deployment of Moving Block Signalling designed to increase capacity.

spurious objections were raised to the prospect of operating one or two additional trains on the East Coast Main Line. It was frustrating that the then zonal director, a non-railwayman, clearly had no real knowledge or understanding of the operational railway claiming that there was no capacity for more trains. Once this had been disproved, he then insisted that there were no platforms available at Kings Cross. In fact they were being occupied by GNER trains for hours on end which could easily have been removed to sidings outside the station to release capacity. It took a change of director, in the shape of Robin Gisby, for Railtrack to see sense. Subsequently there was a substantial increase in the number of trains over the same infrastructure: well in excess of what Hull Trains alone had been seeking.

Meanwhile on the West Coast Main Line Railtrack had done rather the opposite and sold a lot of capacity for which Tom Winsor (the Rail Regulator) would hold it to account. Robin Gisby had by then become sponsor of the West Coast upgrade but its costs were escalating and questions were being asked about whether or not moving block signalling on which the upgrade depended could really work. It became apparent that Railtack was unable to cater for the track access rights that had been sold to all parties and, following a Regulatory Hearing, was compelled to buy its way out of rights held by some operators. In the end the signalling project was not delivered at all and by this time not only was Railtrack beginning to fall foul of the Regulator but the change of Government from Tory to Labour had altered the political light in which the company was viewed. Southall and Ladbroke Grove had begun to erode its credibility and "it was seen", Robin believes, "as a very Tory Board, one where profits and bonuses came before safety". It was with Railtrack's reputation for arrogance and incompetence pretty much at its zenith that its defining moment – the Hatfield crash – occurred in

October 2000. The cause was the failure of the track which had deteriorated over time without proper inspection. This was on the watch of the very infrastructure company whose privatisation the Tories had claimed would improve the country's railway assets.

One of the immediate consequences of the meltdown in the railway's operational performance and infrastructure cost control that followed Hatfield was that it scuppered any chance of the SRA achieving its ambitious timescale for letting new franchises, amid what Alastair Morton famously referred to as a "nervous breakdown" in the industry. Timetables were emasculated, journey times were extended, punctuality collapsed; and with it the revenues of the operators. Money was diverted in a hurry from rail development projects towards maintenance, renewals and safety. For a few months into 2001, Morton's programme of competitions for longer-term, investment-led franchises continued but with investor confidence in private financing for the railway falling and the new calls on public sector funding to keep the railway operating, it was apparent that its basis was being undermined. The Government suspended the letting of new franchise contracts while it worked out how it wanted to address a crisis in the industry, much to Morton's displeasure.

There was no disagreement about the seriousness of the consequences brought about by Railtrack's mismanagement. In June 2001, Morton set out the situation facing the railway in the aftermath of Hatfield and the implications of the Cullen Inquiry into the Ladbroke Grove crash[75]. Speaking at a conference in London, Morton said

---

[75] Lord Justice Cullen's report was published in 2001 and made significant criticisms of Railtrack. He said "there was a lamentable failure on the part of Railtrack to respond to recommendations of inquiries into two [previous] serious incidents" pointing out that in 1998 Railtrack had "dispensed with the services of a significant number of senior Great Western Zone personnel".

that the £29bn of Government funding allocated for the 10-year plan was "overcommitted without any noteworthy enhancement programme", and noted that Railtrack had withdrawn its own enhancement projects in the aftermath of Hatfield. He also voiced personal criticisms of the former Transport Minister, Lord Macdonald, singling him out as having put spin before substance, recalling a ferocious response to his own candid remarks to the transport select committee when he said that the Government's investment plan needed to be revised in the new circumstances. With his health deteriorating and Government support waning, it was not surprising that he used his speech to announce that he would not be seeking a further term when his initial period as SRA Chairman expired in two years. Stephen Byers, who had taken over from John Prescott as Secretary of State for Transport immediately after the June 2001 General Election, was quick to respond that a new Chairman would be "appointed as soon as possible". Later, writing in the *Spectator*, Morton criticised the Government's handling of the rail industry saying that the SRA "was not part of the Blair Project". Claiming that Prescott's support was ameliorated by Macdonald, he wrote that "niggling, fearful, untrained, short-term ministers and bureaucrats" were now in control of the railways. "I am not optimistic of the chances of the industry being reformed so that all players can work together more effectively", he wrote. Sadly he was right.

Meanwhile Railtrack bypassed the Rail Regulator and entered direct negotiations with the Government over the additional money it wanted. Incredibly, that did not prevent the company choosing to pay shareholders a dividend. It took stock market analysts in the City of London to see what the unfolding events truly meant. As early as February that year, Steven Bowen, an analyst at BNP Paribas, woke up an audience of rail professionals by stating that "dramatic action" from the Government and wider industry was needed to start restoring the City's confidence in Railtrack and create any prospect of the company resuming a role in funding investment projects. While that warning over the political environment the company operated in was largely brushed aside, it was hammered home shortly after the 2001 election when Christian Cowley and Phil Oakley, relatively junior analysts at ABN AMRO with a fresh pair of eyes, valued Railtrack's shares as worth between zero and 58p. Their note highlighted the political risks the company faced in attempting to persuade the Government to authorise "a huge transfer of wealth from the taxpayer" to a private company. It sent Railtrack shares tumbling below their flotation price of 380p and ejected Railtrack out of the FTSE 100. Two years previously, its shares had been trading at over £17.

If the signs were there that Railtrack was finished, it still came as a shock when the Government determined that it was not prepared to trust the company with the injection of the public funding it wanted in the aftermath of Hatfield, completing the chain of events that its set up, business strategies and the series of fatal crashes had triggered. On 8 October 2001, almost a year after Hatfield, the BBC reported that "Railtrack, the company that controls Britain's rail infrastructure, has been put into administration. The Government asked the High Court to take the action after it refused to put any more money into the struggling company. The order means Railtrack is now under the control of Government-appointed administrators, who will continue to run the railways." It spoke volumes for the people at the top of Railtrack that they appeared to blame the Government for the company's demise. Although this was literally true, it is surely obvious even to the most purblind that it was the company's approach to managing its own affairs that was to blame. It would not be the last time in the history of rail company failures that directors would seek to blame Government for the consequences of their own actions. A number of Railtrack shareholders subsequently pursued a court action against the Government but the judge, Mr Justice Lindsay, dismissed the action that had alleged "misfeasance in public office" and breach of the shareholders' human rights. On the contrary, he said that the Government had acted entirely properly and the idea that it should have funded Railtrack without limit and condition was a "hopeless proposition".

When the company re-emerged from a year's administration run by accountancy firm Ernst & Young it was under the ownership of a new not for profit organisation called Network Rail, the Government's preferred model. Byers had refused to countenance enquiries from potential private sector owners. Effectively the infrastructure and its development were now controlled and funded in their entirety by Whitehall. Under the dual leadership of John Armitt and Iain Coucher, and with a huge increase in Government funding, the company set about restoring the infrastructure to a more normal state. Armitt's engineering background and Coucher's centralising management style gradually got on top of the bad situation they had inherited and performance started to improve from the historical low point of the immediate Hatfield aftermath. One of the better moves was an early decision to abandon the contracting out of maintenance to private sector suppliers, something the vast majority of people with railway management experience believed to have been a flawed model from the start. The new management, keen to impress upon its workforce the wisdom of its approach, embarked on a charm offensive which it took to all corners of its new empire.

Robin Gisby tells an amusing story of being despatched to bring the glad tidings to the attention of Wiltshire's finest track staff. In late summer 2003, Coucher and Engineering Director Peter Henderson came into his office after a difficult Board discussion about maintenance. They wanted to accelerate bringing it in house. Robin had been running the Southern Zone for a few months following an earlier two year stint taking charge of the London North Eastern, Anglia and Eastern regions. He points out incidentally that "those three years made [him] the second most experienced Zone Director" in the company. He explained that when he went to York to pick up the reins following the Hatfield disaster in late 2000, he had never had a line management role in the rail industry. Even so two main Board Directors were asking his opinion. Balfour Beatty held the contract and Robin says that "without much discussion I proposed to bring it in house within three months. I didn't know how to do that but it was urgent and important. We got to work, made our plans and delivered". However, in his typically self-effacing style he went on to describe the reaction of the staff. A series of town hall meetings was arranged and he went down to Salisbury, coincidentally his home town, where he stood up in front of 70-plus staff who had mainly come in from their shift from up to 50 miles away and were in high visibility jackets. He recounts the following tale. "I bring you great news. You are all coming back to Network Rail," he said, whereupon a large track ganger in the second row stood up and replied: "I don't know who you are except you're another suit from London. Let me tell you what is going on here. Your lot are coming back to us. This is our railway not yours. We have been looking after it all these years while you sold us off to a bunch of motorway contractors. You're just an absentee landlord who has realised what is important. So get back on the train and go away and leave us to what we do best": or words to that effect. For the weekend of the change, Robin was worried about keeping tabs on the stock, tools and small plant used by the maintenance staff. In fact they took much of it home to "keep it away from those bastards at Balfours" and brought it back in on the Monday. The incident made him realise that they were "railwaymen not contractors". The anecdote, amusing as it is, is a perfect illustration of how Railtrack and its contractors were perceived by the very people on whom the industry relied to maintain the railway and keep it safe.

Network Rail would continue as a company limited by guarantee until it was reclassified as a central Government body by the Office of National Statistics in 2013. Whilst this was a far cry from the original privatisation template, Hatfield's impact on the concept of privatisation for train operating companies would be almost as great. Initially though a brief window of opportunity appeared to move in a more radical direction. During his resignation speech in June 2001 Alastair Morton had offered thoughts on how to get the industry back on track warning that "if we do not structure and fund things right from the outset we shall fail". The argument for change was that "the present structure, built around Railtrack, cannot deliver". Placing vertical integration back on the agenda he noted that there were contrasting views on its benefits but that these needed to be reviewed, questioning whether it was a good idea to "struggle on with an under-performing Railtrack".

At that moment there was a possibility of creating much closer integration between train operators and the infrastructure and a brief if impassioned debate took place on the future structure of the railway. Companies which had entered the industry during franchising had by now developed a greater understanding of the interface issues between track and train, an understanding that in many ways also reflected their complete mistrust of Railtrack, which was not only seen as remote but also incompetent. In July 2001, in response to Morton's comments, James Sherwood, Chairman of GNER's parent company Sea Containers, called for train companies to be handed control of track, signals and stations which he said were "cost centres" and not the "profit centres" viewed by Railtrack. Operators would make more cost effective decisions in what would have been a reversion to British Rail's vertical integration model but in the private and not the public sector.

A lobby also developed for franchising to move in the direction of joint contracts for managing the operation and maintenance of the infrastructure. I was briefly engaged by the SRA during the last months of Morton's tenure to test the water amongst owning groups for such an approach. I met Stagecoach chief executive Brian Souter to discuss a report he himself had commissioned to assess the pros and cons. It was clear he had become a convert. The company's vertical integration proposal devised by former BR Director Graham Eccles was billed *A railwayman's answer to the problems of Britain's Railways*. It highlighted how vertical integration could resolve lack of clarity over safety responsibilities, misaligned management objectives and Railtrack's weak management of relationships with maintenance contractors and train operators. Eccles had also given serious thought on how to overcome the various constraints and issues that had been caused by the industry's privatised structure, and were deterring some operators from supporting vertical integration. Chief among them was the risk caused by Railtrack's lack of knowledge on the condition of its assets and its lack of a comprehensive central asset register. Indeed the Regulator had lambasted Railtrack in this regard, though in part the problem had been caused by the privatisation structure itself. British Rail's data on each asset class had been kept locally in different areas of the country and stayed with the engineering companies created for sale to the private sector. Graham's proposal to overcome this key issue was that during an initial five-year pilot Stagecoach's South West Trains franchise would take over responsibility for managing infrastructure in the Wessex area, but Government would bear financial risk until Stagecoach had established the infrastructure's condition accurately. A successor body to

Railtrack would remain the asset owner to maintain compliance with EU directives for separation of track and train. The pilot would also test systems to ensure fair treatment of all operators under Stagecoach's operation of the infrastructure.

Presenting the ideas at a conference in December 2001, at which FirstGroup also produced a vertical integration proposal, Brian Souter said: "Responsibility for wheel and track should not have been split so dramatically at privatisation...There remains decades of expertise within the train operators' management teams, and Railtrack's administration allows those experts a last chance to get Britain's railways right." He argued that Stagecoach's proposal showed closer management of track and train was achievable and would be likely to improve maintenance and quality of service to passengers. He went on to say that it was not only practical at his company's SWT franchise but in other areas too. But it was not to be. At the same conference Richard Bowker, newly-appointed as Morton's successor at the SRA by Stephen Byers, made his first public comments and immediately dismissed vertical integration. Although Byers had agreed the matter should be considered, he was sceptical and Bowker's comments echoed the views of the Secretary of State. "We have a multi-user railway and not everybody shares the same view of vertical integration," Bowker said. He also appeared to have adopted the Byers line on funding by saying that the industry had first to deliver better value in order to "create a stronger bargaining hand" whilst at the same time reminding his audience that the current financial commitment from Government was something old BR "could only dream about". Indeed it could, yet given the same type of financial settlement, it would have been much more likely to have delivered the objectives the Government was seeking. Shortly afterwards, David Rowlands, the Government's Director General of Railways, advised

Railtrack's administrators that a break up to facilitate vertical integration was not going to happen. The decision was also taken to remove from the agenda any other form of TOC involvement in maintaining the infrastructure.

Byers himself was politically inclined towards public sector control of transport and, unfortunately for the new integration lobby, at that time there were justifiable reasons for viewing changes which gave operators a greater role as a political risk too far. The cause went back to Railtrack. If it couldn't be relied upon, why should other private sector businesses? Unsurprisingly the Secretary of State was concerned about achieving value for money if his growth plans were to be delivered, and in the aftermath of Hatfield and Railtrack's administration he was probably right to be so. Added to which the problems on the West Coast Main Line projects had extended from the cost and delivery of the infrastructure upgrade to the progress being made on introducing new trains, which had fallen behind schedule. Given the massive decline in operating performance post Hatfield it did not seem unreasonable either that Byers should proclaim an improvement in it as the most urgent priority for shorter term franchises. It was clear that the politicians had decided to assume greater control over an industry that had shown no signs of doing so for itself; and which was structurally incapable of doing so in its then form. It was, I wrote at the time, "desperately ironic that the privatised railways were in the grip of exactly the same political dependency that they had been experiencing for most of the past 60 years". Although his concerns were understandable, Byers' decisions did nothing to set the industry on a path towards addressing the underlying problems of railway financing and structure.

Shortly after ruling out vertical integration, the SRA announced its future franchising timetable and policy. The SRA itself, after consulting the industry, would determine infrastructure priorities where Government funding became available. It would soon intervene in the West Coast Main Line upgrade and ultimately did bring the project, whose costs at one point spiralled as high as £13bn, under control. Ultimately it was delivered for £8bn, albeit with some reductions in its scope. As far as franchising was concerned, Morton's approach based on operator-led joint venture investment was formally abandoned. With it went the concept, essential for such an approach to work, of longer term franchises. There was obviously a risk too that the three franchises where Morton had got as far as announcing a preferred bidder would not be let and that his major contribution to the industry would now be lost. Nevertheless it remained true that 20-year franchises incorporating Special Purpose Companies investing in enhanced infrastructure still offered a very promising way of securing the necessary investment and long term plans to cater for growing demand at optimum cost. Sadly in all cases but one it was abandoned.

It is worth recalling what had been planned for the three franchises in question. In the case of South Central Go-Ahead's 'winning bid' included upgrading the Brighton Main Line. In the case of SWT, Stagecoach's franchise retention proposal included commitments to increase capacity on inner suburban routes from an eight-car railway to 10-car by 2004, and redevelopment of Clapham Junction by 2007, plus a suite of schemes to improve the resilience of the railway. Depending on growth and feasibility, options that could then be considered included 16-car operation on longer distance services by 2006 along with further capacity increases on inner suburban services and converting viable routes for double deck trains. However, neither of these franchise awards was to survive the consequences of Hatfield. In Go-Ahead's case a 200-strong project team which had been formed with Bechtel to develop the proposal for upgrading the Brighton Main Line was stood down. According to Go-Ahead's statement, an inability to "contact specialists within Railtrack" compounded the difficulties taking forward the proposals, a shocking indictment of the infrastructure controller's lack of expertise at the time. The one Morton project that did get away was Chiltern which went on to expand capacity and transform the customer offer on the line through project managing the construction of new stations, new tracks, a new trains depot, new rolling stock, and ultimately, a brand new route to link London's Marylebone with Oxford. Chiltern became a role model of what could be achieved through integration. It could have been done elsewhere; probably everywhere.

It has become fashionable to criticise Morton's tenure of the SRA for an unrealistic approach to franchising which made it impossible to compare bids or award contracts. However, the evidence has shown that the former was possible, even if Morton himself acknowledged that the brand new concepts involved did mean progress was slower than he had hoped. Negotiating the detail of the contracts was certainly problematic, taking two years in Chiltern's case and proving impossible in the other two against the backdrop of Railtrack's spiralling costs, declining investor confidence and political scepticism post-Hatfield. One wonders if Morton's approach had been permitted to proceed we would still, nearly 20 years later, be waiting for all but one of the major schemes proposed in the 'winning' SWT and South Central bids to be delivered – the exception being the 10-car railway on suburban SWT services which was eventually introduced between 2014-17. However, time has shown that the vision of the Morton era has never been adequately replaced. Punctuality has fallen from the post privatisation high point in 2011 for seven years running, in part due to the strain on a railway that is insufficiently resilient to cope with demand. Infrastructure schemes of the sort proposed 20 years ago were, and are, badly needed, but so far most have either remained on the drawing board or only very recently been delivered.

When the re-franchising programme did resume in early 2002 following nearly a year's hiatus, it was in a radically different form under Richard Bowker. A surprise choice to head up the SRA, he nonetheless had a reputation as a visionary who had played a prominent role in the development of Virgin's bids. This gave many an expectation that new impetus might be injected into developing the role of the private sector and for a short while after he took office in December 2001, vestiges of the Morton era lingered. Influenced by Nick Newton, now the SRA's Commercial Director, the new franchising policy was to offer 15-year contracts as the basis for operators to take a longer term view and responsibility for developing timetables and responding to their markets. However, it was soon replaced by a policy of shorter term, highly controlled contracts. Keith Ludeman, then Chairman of the Association of Train Operating Companies, described the new approach as "suffused with micro-management" invoking a "dull nausea and disbelief that two parties could get into such an agreement".

There were other attacks on the concept of privatisation too. In 2002 Bowker took an impulsive decision to start removing competition in the expectation that it would improve performance. The absorption of the Anglia InterCity franchise by the Great Eastern commuter operation was the first stage of this policy. The new Greater Anglia franchise was not a notable success operationally, continuing to lag behind equivalent 'larger network' TOCs in the South East and I was shown evidence by the Regulator that the elimination of competition had diminished revenue growth from key stations.

So the die was cast and the industry was, once more, set on a course of centralised control of the infrastructure coupled with direction of the operating railway separated from it. It was in effect a publicly specified and procured railway with private sector companies fulfilling a purely contractual delivery role. This could not genuinely be called "privatisation". I'm not sure that this could even be described as a public-private partnership, which implies a greater private sector input to franchise specifications than was and is the case. It was at this point that the railway became "privatised" in name only. In every essential respect the industry entered a phase from which it has yet to emerge. Governments determine the objectives for rail. Governments provide most of the funding. Governments own the franchises except in the case of the devolved authorities in Scotland, Wales, and Merseyside, where a different form of public ownership continues. Governments specify major capital investments. Governments specify timetables and limit competition to the margins. The structures in place essentially encourage the monopoly provision of train services and guarantee it in infrastructure. Only the supply chain is private and the main impact of the private sector on the industry is through competing for contracts let by Government or quasi-governmental bodies.

The industry is not privatised. Perhaps it never has been.

CHAPTER NINE

It's Not Going Well: Let's Have a Review

The faults in the rail industry structure exposed by the traumas in the early years of privatisation and perpetuated by the decisions taken in their aftermath have remained a constant subject of debate and calls for reform ever since. The issues caused by the separation of track and train and centralised control have yet to be resolved, despite Ministers often appearing to support the need for sweeping reforms. At the time of writing, the Government has commissioned former BA Chairman Keith Williams to lead a review of the rail industry; yet by his own reckoning, his is the thirty-first review of one kind or another in the past 15 years. Much of the ground for his review covers matters that have been recognised in previous exercises.

In fact the need for a new direction was recognised by Government little more than a year after the creation of Network Rail when, in January 2004, Stephen Byers' successor as Secretary of State for Transport, Alistair Darling, announced a review of how to bring costs and performance under control. In a statement to Parliament, he said the Regulator had confirmed "the cost of upkeep of the railways is £1.5bn a year more than was thought necessary just three years ago", and that Network Rail had "a long way to go" to restore punctuality that had improved little since Hatfield. He warned there could be no further investment in the railway until it delivered value for money.

A year earlier, I had written a piece in *Transit* Magazine after Network Rail announced an anticipated loss of £1.8bn for 2002/03 due to the impact of Hatfield on its infrastructure costs, a situation that had a very negative effect on the Government's rail strategy by reducing the funds available for expansion. As a result, the SRA cut its passenger growth forecast to 25-35% by 2011, down from 50% in John Prescott's original 10-year plan. Under the headline "Structural change is the only way to cut costs" I noted how the devolved and integrated structures created in the latter days of British Rail had been successful in managing whole industry costs. I contrasted the business-led direction in which railway engineering was heading under BR with the fragmented structure post privatisation and the lack of customer focus in Railtrack. With some understatement, I argued that Hatfield and the response to it had shown that "the new industry framework delivered less well controlled management of the infrastructure" and that "the failure to manage contracts and major projects has made matters worse and is also symptomatic." The article continued: "Taking a helicopter view of railway costs now, there are no major new insights into why they have escalated. Industry structure is the prime cause. The solution to industry costs and quality is one and the same thing. It requires a new framework, the implementation of which is now the industry's most urgent task." In conclusion, I wrote: "We have recent experience of two models that work better than what we have now. One [Sectors and aligned Regions] casts Network Rail as an integrated but devolved supplier focused on the business needs of train operators; the other (OfQ) creates integrated train operators supplying one another. A combination of the two might be tried." Initially, Darling appeared to be heading towards a similar conclusion telling MPs: "There remains a further and very serious difficulty facing this industry - that is its structure and organisation. The way in which it was privatised has led to a fragmentation, excessive complication and dysfunctionality." His Minister Kim Howells even went as far as to say that he was "yet to see the logic of the decision to break the link between track and trains" and foresaw "some pretty big changes". My optimism rose, only to be dashed.

While Government statements had the effect of concentrating the industry on reform, it also set up a power struggle. Operators went into a huddle and most drew up or supported various vertical integration proposals. Network Rail responded by adopting a counter position that it should manage stations and run trains. Meanwhile Richard Bowker advocated merging the SRA's franchising and planning responsibilities with Network Rail to create a private sector National Rail organisation. A separate public sector Railways Agency would determine the industry's funding and what it should deliver. A merger was logical, reflecting the SRA's lack of influence over Network Rail and consequent difficulty in creating a coherent strategic plan. However, Darling had asked Bowker to advise on the industry's views and his submission split opinions and turned up the heat in the power games. Would the SRA be backed into Network Rail or vice-versa? What effect would it have on the commercial freedom of train operators already bridling against what they saw as the micromanagement of franchise contracts by the SRA? Was it appropriate for an infrastructure controller divorced from service delivery to lead industry planning? In the event, what mattered was the Department for Transport, and specifically Alastair Darling, who appeared to regard the proposals coming forward as providing the Government with insufficient influence over industry costs, adding to its disillusionment with the SRA and, it seemed, Richard Bowker personally.

Although all sides had been arguing for a move towards a more integrated railway, the final outcome was the worst of all worlds. It led to what the Government's independent transport advisor, David Begg, referred to as "an unholy alliance between Network Rail, the Department for Transport and some operators to get rid of the SRA", an outcome that in hindsight led to many of the issues the industry continues to face today. When a White Paper[76] was published in July 2004, the SRA was to be abolished and the widely tipped Railways Agency was dropped. Network Rail was to all intents and purposes positioned as the lead party in the industry responsible for timetabling, planning and operational performance. Vertical integration was sidelined in favour of a new concept called 'virtual integration' which would attempt, but in most respects fail, to align Network Rail and operators' priorities and regulatory incentives. The political manoeuvrings were reflected in Begg's recollection of why vertical integration was rejected. "Network Rail was frightened to death about the prospect of any part of its network transferring to train operators," he said, because, if conceded in one place, it could be adopted more widely. "The Department had to bow to that to retain Network Rail's backing for getting rid of the SRA."

A significant and early opportunity to put right the major structural weakness of the privatisation was lost as a result. In fact the outcome achieved the exact opposite of what was required in almost every respect. It created a structure that would not only remain dis-integrated but ensure the production element would carry more weight than the passenger-facing and commercial side. This was enshrined in a diagram in the White Paper showing the relationships that would be created. I wrote in *Transit* Magazine: "The chart in the White Paper that shows all the arrows coming down from the DfT via Network Rail and the TOCs eventually pointing at the customer is a magnificently Freudian Slip. Any marketing department of any small town college would have drawn the arrows the other way round." The apparent priorities were emphasised in plans to extend the SRA's policy of redrawing franchise boundaries, where possible, around Network Rail's production based regions

---

[76] The Future of Rail

rather than configuring them around the markets served by the operators.

The most misplaced aspect was the range of responsibilities the DfT would assume under the new structure which gave it direct control over every facet of the industry. Not only would the Government set the funding available for the railway and its objectives – clearly a sensible course – but its detailed strategy as well; how funding should be spent; and franchise requirements. It would also, in short order, start specifying and sponsoring major projects and, as it turned out, even branch out into rolling stock procurement. It gave Government a far greater role than it had ever had in the years when the railways were nationalised. My article continued: "Whilst the idea of civil servants directing the strategy is right, it is wrong that they should [direct its implementation]. The best role civil servants can fulfil is to determine policy, strategic direction and budgets whilst questioning and criticising what is put in front of them; but doing it requires an understanding of the operation and the market place. Strategy emerges from many elements, one of the most important being practical operational reality. A strategy that is disconnected from reality is as unhelpful as an operation that takes place without any reference to strategy. With the best will in the world it will not be possible for civil servants several places removed from the market and the operation to undertake this task."

Bowker resigned, branding the new structure "quasi renationalisation" – an ironic comment as it seemed to me more like a continuation of the direction he had taken at the SRA. Perhaps the most disappointing aspect of the White Paper though was what could have been if the Government had stuck to its originally stated intentions. Curiously the 2004 rail review did acknowledge the need for integrated structures and decisions to be taken closer to the market in announcing the ceding of certain powers over rail services to Scotland, Wales and London in line with New Labour's policies on political devolution. But these were to be the exceptions that proved the rule.

As part of this devolution agenda, the Government was also prepared to support the Merseyside Passenger Transport Executive's plans to explore a vertical integration pilot, against the wishes of Network Rail. The problem of its 'protectionism' was never far away. Earlier, in 2002, this was illustrated when Merseytravel gained unique powers to franchise rail services on its small, self-contained Liverpool city region network. Transport Minister John Spellar expressed surprise to Merseytravel negotiators that they had not made a play to gain control over the region's infrastructure too. Although this was on the PTE's agenda, its Director General Neil Scales reasoned that a more canny step by step approach would pay off, and that going for full vertical integration too early might jeopardise the transfer of franchising responsibilities. The 2004 rail review presented a chance to make the case and the PTE's hand had been strengthened by its award of the Merseyrail franchise to a joint venture of the Dutch State Railways and Serco, providing strong partners with significant experience of infrastructure operation, maintenance and renewal. Furthermore, the White Paper had stated that Network Rail should work with the PTE and the DfT to establish how the change could be made. With support from the Regulator, Merseytravel and its operators developed a business case setting out how local control of the infrastructure would improve train performance and responsiveness to the needs of the local network, as well as delivering cost savings.

Network Rail's response was simply to refuse to engage, with its combative Deputy Chief Executive Iain Coucher opposed to any precedent which could lead to a wider break-up. Scales recalls that Network Rail refused to provide information to help develop the business case and refused to engage in any meaningful discussion to the extent that Coucher banned the phrase "vertical integration" during meetings. Instead the proposal needed to be referred to as "full local decision making". When Network Rail rejected it, Darling acquiesced, seemingly content for the monopoly infrastructure provider to have the final say on a project whose business case seemed to tick the right boxes and which the Regulator was keen to proceed with as a means of benchmarking Network Rail's costs. Network Rail's stance was indicative of a culture of centralisation and protectionism that would endure and act as a block on integration and devolution under successive Chief Executives until the appointment of Andrew Haines in 2018. According to George Muir, who was Director General of the Association of Train Operating Companies at the time, the influence Network Rail was able to exert and its ability to block structural change was due to its position in the industry structure as a "de facto part of the civil service". It was seen as "a creation of Government and therefore could not be seen to fail" through exposure to competition.

Unwilling to test the potential of vertical integration trials to reduce taxpayer subsidy, the DfT had plans to use the franchising system to fulfil its objectives in other ways. Its desire for faster progress in restoring punctuality meant franchises were to be highly controlled. Advised by Network Rail, when specifying franchises, civil servants determined the service pattern, even individual train times and, to all intents and purposes, the rolling stock that would be used. Ironically, though, the policy was viewed primarily as a means of reducing subsidy – in effect to offset some of the inflated infrastructure costs caused by the inefficiency of the industry's structure. It was overseen by the DfT's Director General Rail Mike Mitchell, recruited from FirstGroup in early 2005 where he had been a main Board director. After joining BR as a management trainee, Mitchell had switched industries during bus privatisation, gaining a cost cutting reputation that had earned him the moniker 'Doctor Death'.

Value for passengers and developing services to fulfil a wider societal role came to have relatively little bearing on the way the DfT specified franchises at this time. Instead it was about raising or saving money. The same applied to the way franchises were awarded. The tightening of specifications meant there was minimal potential for bidders to distinguish themselves from one another other than in the premium payments or subsidy reductions they were prepared to offer. Adrian Shooter recalls franchise competitions where his company, Laing Rail, designed alternative timetables which in his opinion "offered significant economic benefits to Government and service quality benefits to passengers" but these "were not even evaluated" due to what he perceived to be the DfT's "not invented here mentality". At the same time, a buoyant economy and societal changes were driving rail use to new levels and European state-owned railways started bidding for UK franchises in force, creating an intensity of competition not seen before or since. Effectively Mitchell and DfT Procurement Director Jack Paine looked to soak bidders for premium payments to Government.

There were particular possibilities for the DfT to exploit competitions where an existing franchise operator's market position was vulnerable. The pressure was evident in Sea Containers' retention of its GNER franchise in early 2005. The manner of its victory shook the market with an offer to pay £1.3bn in premium payments over a 10-year contract. Chief Executive Christopher Garnett openly acknowledged that as GNER was Sea Containers' only franchise the situation had "concentrated the mind enormously" and "we had to win but win sensibly". Amid scepticism he insisted that the wider industry "didn't understand our bid because they didn't understand our revenue" on what was then the UK's premier route. He had a point. GNER had also seen a way to increase capacity through a local electrification scheme in Leeds that no one else had spotted – a last hurrah for operator-led infrastructure enhancement proposals before the squeeze on commercial freedom took hold.

Sea Containers' bid created a new expectation in the DfT of the money that could be extracted from operators, on paper at least. Something of a Faustian pact tacitly emerged. Companies offered Government highly optimistic, verging on undeliverable, premium payments to win franchises, which the DfT seemed happy to accept to massage its forecasts of Treasury funding needed to run the railway. However for the DfT to realise the promised riches, there was no room for any shocks whether external such as an economic downturn, or internal to the industry. The huge growth in passenger numbers that was occurring would need to continue unchecked; and it is fair to say that no one really understood the factors driving it. For operators, there were equally dark arts at play. The DfT's standard franchise contract included a new risk sharing arrangement, known as 'cap and collar'. It meant that if an operator failed to achieve the annual revenue forecasts in its bid, the Government would pay up to 80% of the shortfall, starting after year four of their contract. Ostensibly, cap and collar was introduced to protect operators from factors beyond their control and which they could not reasonably predict when bidding. However, its availability enabled bidders to ramp up the premium payments they were prepared to offer, safe in the knowledge that, so long as there were no disasters in the short term, they would be protected if their sums didn't add up. Companies used this protection to justify ambitious bids to shareholders. Effectively contracts were being won by 'gaming the system'.

This was illustrated in FirstGroup's retention of the Great Western franchise in 2006. The competition came at a time when First's only other franchise was the relatively small TransPennine business which it held in a joint venture with Keolis (a quasi-international arm of the French State Railways). The £1bn premium FirstGroup offered the Government over the 10-year Great Western contract was an extraordinary £0.5bn ahead of the field. For a while, the credibility of First's bid was the talk of the industry. It required annual revenue growth of over 10% per year, well in excess of the level rival bidders considered possible. However, FirstGroup had been careful to protect itself. Its negotiator Dean Finch had arranged a unique option to opt out of the last three years of the contract – a period when two thirds of the payments to the DfT were due. Immediately the contract was signed, Finch took the opportunity to arrange for cap and collar protection to kick in two years early if required in exchange for "technical changes" to the franchise contract asked for by the DfT.

National Express and Stagecoach were among companies having difficulty coming to terms with the environment as a further high premium bid was accepted for the Thameslink Great Northern franchise (also won by FirstGroup); and subsidy was slashed in Govia's winning bid at Southeastern, returning to the private sector after a two-year spell in public sector ownership after Connex's sacking. Brian Souter, Chief Executive of Stagecoach, commented that bidding in general was "frenzied" and indicated that he was prepared to wait for it to die down, adding: "If there are too many hungry pigs in the trough, let them eat first." He then got in on the act with a bid that was as outrageous as any to retain his company's only wholly-owned franchise, SWT, offering Government a £1.2bn premium. Like First's Great Western bid, it was over £0.5bn ahead of the field.

The bid fever that was taking place against a very positive economic background and an ongoing surge in rail travel reached a peak in 2007 in the competition for a new East Coast franchise that was necessary because, by then, GNER had collapsed. Unfortunately, it had not taken long for the company's plans to unravel. Its prospects had been hit early on by the impact of the July 2005 London bombings, higher fuel prices from a new electricity deal negotiated by Network Rail and, it claimed, forthcoming competition from open access operator Grand Central. By the end of 2006 losses were imminent and Sea Containers appeared unable to stand behind the business. It had emerged that the Bermudan company was in financial strife itself and in October 2006 filed for bankruptcy. The Government refused GNER's request to renegotiate the premium payments due, but Sea Containers' financial position meant a short term deal had to be agreed until the DfT could re-let the franchise. Although it was in a difficult position, my view was that the company's failure was self-inflicted and it should have been able to survive, even at the time GNER handed back the keys. I wrote then that what was required on this prestige service was a hard-nosed marketing and sales strategy to maximise revenue rather than the cheap and cheerful approach GNER adopted in the face of financial stress. I also felt Chris Garnett became irrationally obsessed about Grand Central which had only gained rights to operate on the route after a prolonged legal battle. I had personal experience of Chris's views on open access when expanding my Hull Trains business in the early 2000s. His emotional response was to portray open access competition as a 'smash and grab' raid on GNER's revenue. In fact Hull Trains had actually grown the market for both companies, but he was the 'man who wouldn't let it lie'. Despite this it was disappointing to see both Chris and Sea Containers leave. His was a business with a different brand development perspective to the rather homogenous bunch that dominate the UK train operating business to this day.

When the East Coast franchise was re-let, the winner was National Express Group. The award came at a time when the company was under pressure. Once the holder of nine franchises, its portfolio had eroded to three and it had built a debt mountain after an adventurous bus company acquisition in Spain. East Coast was seen in the City of London as a 'must win' to satisfy shareholders. The NEG Board sanctioned a bid offering £1.4bn in premium payments over seven years; it was higher than Sea Containers had previously offered for a 10-year contract. The prospect of maintaining the 10% annual revenue growth had David Franks, head of National Express's rail division, leaning back against a wall in despair and then laughter when asked about it privately with a glass of wine in his hand. The extent to which the market was overheating was more apparent when it emerged that NEG had not even offered the highest price. Arriva offered £150m more but was ruled out on the grounds that its operational plans were not deliverable. It had also hit problems in the East Midlands competition which Arriva was in pole position to win until its Board, at the eleventh hour, amended the timetabling and rolling stock plan devised by my FCP consultancy, rendering it impractical.

The party stopped abruptly when the Lehman Brothers Bank collapsed in September 2008, triggering the global financial crisis that was to last well into the next decade. First to feel the heat was the East Coast franchise which had started operating less than a year earlier. Revenue growth collapsed almost overnight as patronage fell and, equally critically, first class carriages emptied as passengers down traded to standard. There was not going to be a way back. In deep recessions, BR had found that the East Coast route was the first to feel the pinch and the hardest hit due to its dependence on business travellers buying premium fare tickets. The franchise was also vulnerable because cap and collar revenue support was not available for another three years during which time analysts forecast that National Express would have lost £300m. For a while it appeared Transport Secretary Lord Adonis was prepared to countenance a renegotiation. According to National

Express, a deal was close to being struck, only for the DfT to perform a swift about turn the day before the company was due to issue a statement on the future of the franchise in July 2009. Instead, the company was forced to announce that it expected to hand back the keys by the end of the year, paying exit penalties of £70m – cheap at the price. East Coast would be directly managed by the DfT's operator of last resort, a period of public sector operation that would last until 2015.

The pressures of the economic downturn created tensions as it became clear premium payments operators had promised would never be paid. While several franchises would make losses for a period, they were smaller or within touching distance of qualifying for revenue support so were not in the same terminal situation as East Coast. When cap and collar became available, it would reduce the premiums paid to the DfT by hundreds of millions of pounds per year across the franchises it had let, a situation that probably highlighted the commercial limitations of the civil servants who had overseen the deals. It also emerged that the department had bungled the negotiation of Stagecoach's SWT contract, with the result that cap and collar was available a year early at a cost to the Government close to another £100m. The DfT's attempts to resist the SWT obligation led to Brian Souter labelling the department "dysfunctional and deceitful". The matter was only resolved when Stagecoach took legal action.

All the while, the huge premiums the DfT had assumed it could extract from operators had not been accompanied by significant service investments. The priority of reducing the industry's bill to the taxpayer for running the railway meant passengers were squeezed too. There was a moratorium on new train orders at a time when rail patronage was growing at record levels, and operators had been encouraged to propose swingeing fare increases on off-peak tickets. The losses some operators were making had an impact too, in some cases cutting back on customer service initiatives and non-safety critical train maintenance. When cap and collar payments were made to operators they had a similar effect because the companies' revenue was largely guaranteed by Government, so there was less incentive to respond to market needs. At the same time, the DfT's grip on train operators and micromanagement of their contracts had prevented any genuine commercial innovation. Franchise contracts which the DfT and operators claimed in their publicity would position companies as modern customer-focused businesses were nothing of the sort. In reality, there was no way they could be. All the key aspects of business planning from fares to ticketing, train service plans and rolling stock allocation were in effect being controlled by civil servants with less commercial or railway experience than operators close to the market. The railway had barely started moving towards the retailing, customer service and branding innovations increasingly evident in genuinely privatised sectors. Neither were there any commercial visions or business plans of the sort that Virgin had proposed during the first round of franchising, or even comparable to those introduced by National Express at Midland Mainline and GB Railways at Anglia. The only genuine innovation in opening new markets was coming from a small number of open access operators which the DfT fought tooth and nail to prevent gaining a foothold. It is deeply ironic that new services to London developed by the open access companies were from less prosperous destinations such as Hull, Bradford, Sunderland and Wrexham. In this respect the one genuinely privatised sector of the industry was taking on more of a social role than the DfT's own franchising policy.

It was scarcely surprising that no new entrants with a record of entrepreneurship and innovation were attracted to bid for franchises during this time, or indeed since. Meanwhile state-owned European railways, comfortable in an environment of public sector control, arrived in force, including the Dutch, Danes, Swiss, Germans and French. Their interest was motivated by a fear of their domestic business being eroded – or senior management losing their jobs as the less charitable put it – under the European Union's plans for market liberalisation. They saw the UK as a learning experience for franchising in their own countries. Deutsche Bahn briefed that, ultimately, only five major European rail companies were likely to remain as the EU's policies played through. In the event, market liberalisation was much more controlled and slower to emerge than anticipated, but the situation offered an interesting perspective on their motivations. Go-Ahead Chief Executive Keith Ludeman was fond of characterising it as flag planting. "If the French have one the Germans have to have one. It really is just like that," he said at the time. He was in a position to know. Go-Ahead had recently won the Southeastern franchise in partnership with France's Keolis.

For some months, I contributed a series of articles in *Transit Magazine* setting out the consequences of the DfT's approach to franchising. One that summed it up was headlined "Privatised rail in public sector straitjacket" arguing that train operators were little more than fee-earners divorced of genuine responsibility for their market. I wrote: "What the private sector does best is not benefitting railways. In particular there is insufficient innovation and private investment and the distancing of train companies from being able to develop services to meet market needs is a massive defect in the system. In short the private companies are nothing more than suppliers to the public sector and it is this factor coupled with the huge subsidies going into the industry [principally via Network Rail] that makes for a massively inefficient model, not of privatisation but of nationalisation." In other articles I made much the same observations on the way Network Rail approached contracts with its suppliers.

The collapse of National Express East Coast would bring these matters to a head by creating something of a philosophical and existential debate within the industry over the role of the railway. It illustrated issues first raised by Northern Rail Managing Director Heidi Mottram when the DfT initiated a 'best value review' of her franchise back in 2005; in practice code for examining the potential for service cuts and huge fare rises. Ultimately Jim Steer's consultancy, SDG, which carried out the review, was seen as having "set out to do the industry a favour" in the way its report to Government highlighted the practical difficulties of making significant savings. Although putting a professional front on it in public, Heidi was seething at the DfT's portrayal of her company as a drain on the industry's finances. Privately, she was happy to confess that "it really winds me up", questioning the DfT's commitment to communities in the north and the social value of the railway. "You'd never believe it when politicians talk about railways, but subsidy is not a bad thing in itself," she continued. "Schools and hospitals are 100% subsidised because we need them, yes. The reason we get ourselves in such a mess with railways is because they are partly financed by taxpayers and partly by users, and the two funding streams get in eachother's way." Others in the industry expressed similar views on the Government's treatment of rail services. A particular concern was the DfT's approach to rolling stock allocation which had provided inadequate capacity on a number of franchises. One of its responses had been to encourage operators to consider pricing as a way of managing demand.

With the 2010 General Election little more than a year away, I arranged a series of seminars through my FCP consultancy to debate the way the industry was organised and how a Conservative Government might take a different tack. Many of the frustrations were summed up in a presentation from Chiltern Railways Chairman Adrian

Shooter. Arguing with obvious logic that civil servants should set objectives for the industry, leave delivery to the operators and stop playing at being "amateur railwaymen", he commented: "When we had the Strategic Rail Authority, we frequently cursed Richard Bowker and all his works, but now we have the DfT it is a lot worse. You would not believe the involvement, the detailed fiddling things Ministers personally have to sign off. It's an absolute nonsense." For his honesty, Adrian received a gagging letter from Chiltern's new owners, Deutsche Bahn, no doubt used to operating in an environment of servitude to Government in its own country. The DfT had raised Adrian's behaviour with Berlin.

Vertical integration and operators' relationships with Network Rail were other key issues debated at these seminars. Merseytravel had been far from a lone voice in continuing to press for integration trials. Stagecoach had raised the issue again in relation to SWT and FirstGroup Chief Executive Moir Lockhead lobbied hard for a change, calling for pilots at ScotRail and on Great Western. Alastair Darling had given it very short shrift telling operators who attended a meeting to discuss the matter in 2006: "There is no question of change," and words to the effect of "Why you're still going on about it I don't know." The Conservatives, who were widely fancied to win the upcoming election, were seen as potentially sympathetic to the industry's lobbying over the role of the private sector. Shadow Transport Secretary Theresa Villiers was one who attended alongside senior people from the train operating fraternity. So too did Robin Gisby, by now Network Rail's Managing Director Operations; a brave move given operator dissatisfaction with the company's centralised management style. During the seminar, the view was expressed forcefully that this approach rendered it incapable of responding efficiently to operators' needs or making good decisions on how to apply industry standards to local infrastructure projects.

Pressed on his company's opposition to vertical integration Robin came up with the argument that there were economies of scale to be had through a single network manager, particularly in the centralised ownership and distribution of expensive infrastructure renewals machinery. In response, it was pointed out that Network Rail could provide the equipment to vertically integrated TOCs in exactly the same way under a 'tenant-landlord' relationship. Basically, his argument was a red herring and in fairness Robin did at least claim that Network Rail would welcome a trial "to show we are more efficient than anyone else!" He also acknowledged that Network Rail's opposition had amounted to "competition is the way forward, as long as it doesn't apply to us". A consensus emerged at the conference that what really mattered was for Network Rail to devolve sufficient power from HQ so that its route managers could respond efficiently to the local infrastructure requirements and operators on their patch. Despite this widely supported view it was never really on Network Rail's agenda. An air of reluctant acceptance that integration was not going to happen any time soon was the dominant mood. Control would remain at the centre.

It is fair to say that other issues operators raised at this time, notably in relation to franchising, appeared to be taken on board by Government. Lord Adonis announced a major review in early 2010 shortly before Labour left office, which the Conservative-led Coalition would inherit when power was secured. Franchising would be curtailed for two years with short term extensions let while a new policy was framed, an indication of the severe shortcomings in the Labour Government's approach.

In the meantime, there were bigger fish to fry. In 2007, and before the global banking crisis, the Government had sanctioned a significant infrastructure investment programme for expanding the railway in Network Rail's 2009-14 funding period. *The Delivering a Sustainable Railway* White Paper recognised that something had to be done to accommodate the rising numbers of people travelling by rail and there had meanwhile been a degree of progress in reducing costs from the post-Hatfield high. The Government had also nailed its flag to the mast of reducing carbon emissions following the Stern Report on climate change. However, when it came in 2008, the banking crisis created a problem. By that time, Network Rail's funding for the period to 2014 had been fixed and it was soon clear that the premium payments the Government had expected to receive from franchises would be dramatically below the budgeted level. As the recession deepened the Treasury demanded significant cost savings from all Government departments.

So it was in the old age-old context of seeking better value for money at a time when Government finances were under pressure that the Treasury announced a major review of the rail industry in December 2009. Sir Roy McNulty, who had just retired as chairman of the Civil Aviation Authority (CAA), was appointed to lead it. His terms of reference included requirements to examine ways to reduce whole industry costs and find solutions to deliver value for money which took into account both costs and revenues. Early the next year I was asked by Sir Roy to serve on his advisory Board which received monthly recommendations and updates on the work of a team led by Ian Dobbs, formerly the Managing Director of vertically integrated Great Eastern in the latter days of BR. He had recently returned from Australia where he had headed up the Victoria State railways system, also vertically integrated. Other members of that Board were John Armitt (Chief Executive of Network Rail until 2007), Andrew Haines (a future Chief Executive of Network Rail but at that time Chief Executive of the CAA), Chris Bolt (a former Rail

Regulator), and David Rowlands (sadly now deceased but then the recently retired chief civil servant at the Department for Transport).

Initially civil servants were receptive to the review team's arguments which focused on the better value that could be delivered by integrating track and train. I was delighted at what appeared, at last, to be a genuine recognition in Government of the performance and financial benefits that could be expected from repairing the industry structure. I had articulated these in a paper (described as a 'thought piece') that I submitted to the review team in August 2010. In it I contended that "the railways had become more centralised than at any time in their history and that this had coincided with a massive increase in industry costs", going on to say that experience in BR had shown that devolution within the industry led to greater revenue growth, operating efficiency and customer satisfaction. I argued that during the commercialisation and integration of BR "experience had shown that devolved infrastructure management aligned with devolved train operations had delivered better value for money than production led structures". It was my strongly held view that "if suitable devolved structures were implemented as a result of the McNulty Review they would be likely to deliver substantial benefits to revenue, costs, customer satisfaction and efficiency" adding that "the lack of effective customer relations, devolution and empowerment within Network Rail offered the prospect of significant cost and quality improvements were these behaviours to be reversed". Coincidentally I felt that the creation of devolved structures for managing the infrastructure would provide mechanisms for comparing standards, quality and costs that didn't then exist, affording better regulation, potential competition within the provision of infrastructure services and consequent improvements both in standards and value for money.

Many of these points were argued strongly within the McNulty Board and not just by me. Recognising the constraints that had developed since 'privatisation', discussions did not focus solely on creating vertically integrated franchises. In some cases these were seen as practical to achieve quickly in more or less self-contained areas of the network, but not easily in all. One recommendation was to select certain areas for trials of "full vertical integration through a concession of infrastructure management and train operations combined" but in all parts of the network the core principle recommended was identical to the one established during BR's Sectorisation. Aligning track and train would provide clarity of the relationship between revenues and costs at "profit centre level". Industry "fragmentation" was described as one of the principal "barriers to efficiency". It was also argued that benefits derived from integration would include long term planning of track and train, the right commercial incentives for investment; and alignment of Network Rail geography with franchises (come back Sir Alistair Morton and John Prescott, all is forgiven!). Although there were several networks where it could have been done, initially a full vertical integration trial was proposed in Greater Anglia in addition to taking forward Merseyrail's proposals for which the PTE was still lobbying. However, Neil Scales's plans there were stymied once again, initially by the unions which held significant sway with Merseyside politicians and were opposed to the wider McNulty reforms in principle. They saw transferring responsibility for infrastructure from Network Rail to a franchise as an extension of privatisation, especially as the Conservative-led Coalition was now in power. Thoroughly disillusioned by the about turn from his local politicians, by the end of 2011 Neil had accepted a new job in Australia.

Received by the Conservative Secretary of State, Philip Hammond, in May 2011, the McNulty Study claimed that "rail costs should be at least 20-30% lower [than they were at the time]". It is worth pausing to reflect on that conclusion before moving on to discover that its recommendations were never really implemented anywhere and that McNulty went the way of several other rail reviews since privatisation. I've never understood why but perhaps in this case it was because the recommendations came to be seen as too difficult due to the political sensitivity of breaking up or privatising parts of Network Rail that the reforms could have implied but did not necessarily require. It was also overtaken by the West Coast Main Line franchising crisis in 2012. Nonetheless, there was heavy irony that having been the recipient of the report, Hammond would in 2016 become Chancellor of the Exchequer in which role he would preside over a policy of reducing public expenditure. Had he been more adept in his transport role, implementation of the McNulty Study would have helped him at The Treasury. It might also have avoided the perceived need for yet another review, underway as this book goes to publication. Under the leadership of Keith Williams ('McNulty mark 2'), this one is looking at the structure of the whole rail industry, including increasing integration between track and train, regional partnerships and improving value for money for passengers and taxpayers. If it sounds familiar that is because it is.

Devolution (as implied by the regional partnership in the Williams Review remit) was another key theme of the McNulty discussions, not just in terms of political accountability but of infrastructure management too. In 2005, I had written an article arguing that the command and control management style Network Rail adopted in its early days was no longer appropriate despite its success in starting to get a grip on Railtrack's legacy. Especially welcome at that time was Network Rail's recognition that its business planning approach must be route based, a vital requirement if it was to achieve buy-in from operators and act in the interests of regional stakeholders. However, I commented that this also meant Network Rail would need to exercise a more devolved management style as time progressed if it was to properly understand the needs and expectations of railway customers. This had been a consistent weakness within Railtrack and had remained so under Network Rail. I hoped at the time that this would improve but as highlighted in the seminars FCP arranged, it never got off the ground, and has yet to do so.

There was plenty of devolution talk, especially after Coucher left the company in 2010 at the behest of the chairman, Rick Haythornthwaite, with whom there were differences, not least on the importance of devolving authority to regional management. In February 2011, in came David Higgins, fresh from the Olympic Delivery Authority, immediately proclaiming the benefits of devolution, just as the McNulty Review was concluding. The time then seemed ripe for changes to be made in Network Rail's management approach and style and when Peter Wilkinson[77] came in on secondment from FCP to negotiate new alliance agreements between Network Rail and train operating companies the scene was set for a big step forward. Many held out the hope that Network Rail would once and for all begin to see itself as a supplier to its train operator customers.

It would be a generous to say that this happened. Yes, there was more bold talk of devolution and closer working relationships but in fact the company's self-preservation culture and reluctance at any stage to subordinate itself to the franchise operators or see them as anything other than transient occupiers of the infrastructure continued where Railtrack had left off. Retention of power in the centre remained a stumbling block. The failure of Network Rail's

---

[77] Managing Director First Class Partnerships 2001 to 2013; Franchising Director 2013 to 2014; Head of the Office of Rail Passenger Service at the Department for Transport from 2014.

'devolution programme' under Higgins was neatly summed up by Dave Ward on his retirement as Managing Director of the company's South East Route in 2015. He described the eagerly anticipated initiative as a personal "lowlight of the past five years", characterising it as a halfway house that failed to devolve any real control from the centre. "If you create a devolved route organisation but leave off so many things that the MD can't influence, change or directly set policy on, you are in quite a difficult position," he said. In some cases, it meant he had been unable to make the right decisions for his territory and customers, and was powerless to prevent wrong decisions emanating from the centre. "I should have known six months in when a document landed on my desk called the Devolution Handbook," he reflected recalling the ineffectiveness of the initiative. "They treated the change as process change; a standard change, not a business change, culture change or directional change."

The only initiative of note to emerge post McNulty was a 'deep alliance' between Network Rail and South West Trains which saw the two managed by a single team on the Wessex Route, headed by the train operator. Its creation in 2012 owed much to Stagecoach's longstanding belief in the benefits of greater integration and involved negotiating a contractual maze through legislation that remained fundamentally at odds with the concept. It took six months to develop a legally permissible structure. The preferred option of a formal joint venture to run track and train was impossible so separate legal responsibilities needed to be retained and formally overseen by a governance board. It meant integration was more limited than Stagecoach wanted. For example the company believed there would have been significant benefits from an integrated safety management system, but this was not permissible. So the experiment achieved less than it could have. However, it did illustrate many failings of the industry structure which improvements in punctuality had disguised at the time the

McNulty Review was commissioned, but became increasingly apparent subsequently as performance declined across the rail network under the pressure of ongoing increases in traffic and passenger numbers. Tim Shoveller, the alliance's MD, recalled that the closer relationship between infrastructure and train operation highlighted significant gaps in the industry's understanding of the underlying performance issues. "I just cannot believe how little we knew about our railway," he acknowledged at a Railway Study Association meeting. "There were people who knew everything about SWT and some people who knew absolutely everything about the route, but there was no one who understood what happens when you put the two side by side."

In particular, Tim said the alliance gave him a much greater knowledge of the very poor condition of the track which resulted in scheduling additional time for Network Rail to carry out maintenance and renewals. Possession planning for engineering activity was no longer a negotiation between separate parties with different priorities. A business choice was also made to carry out more work rather than taking efficiency benefits derived from the alliance structure as cost savings. Gaps in the companies' understanding about the pressures building on punctuality were also exposed, particularly the rise in small delays which were starting to have a significant knock-on impact on overall performance. Perhaps most significantly, solutions to plan schemes to increase capacity into Waterloo, which had been repeatedly seen as too difficult, were found. In this respect, Tim said the 'whole system visibility' the alliance provided had made the difference. He went on to say that the root cause of the pressures building on the SWT network was the industry's inability to deliver the investment in infrastructure resilience and upgrades identified 15 years previously in Stagecoach's bid for a long term franchise from the Morton era; or even to have a plan in place to do so. Presciently in the light of later performance issues South Western and other high density networks would face, he warned that the alliance had shown how his railway could be managed more effectively but knowledge needed rebuilding and pressures had intensified to a level where on its own the alliance would not be enough. Discretely, he raised the idea that as a profitable part of the railway a private ownership model could be investigated for the Wessex Route as a means of providing adequate long term financing for infrastructure requirements.

The deep alliance structure was disbanded in 2015 not because it was failing operationally but because of a lack of will to make it work, particularly after Mark Carne took over as Network Rail Chief Executive in 2014. It was reported that a key reason was Network Rail's failure to devolve sufficient power to its Wessex route. It also emerged that a priority from the alliance in Network Rail HQ was to receive a proportion of SWT's revenue, which the company wouldn't concede.

At the same time that the McNulty Review was taking place, the franchising review initiated by Lord Adonis was looking at how to harness the private sector more productively. Discussions focused on creating a system that struck a balance between offering value to passengers and funding for the Government. Plans included longer contracts, potentially up to 22 years if operators proposed appropriate investment in the service and infrastructure, and to provide stability for companies to put their mark on franchises. The approach was developed further by the Coalition Government when it took office in 2010 with an agenda to base contract awards on service quality, innovation and investment as well as price, and to relax prescriptive contract specifications significantly on appropriate franchises. Both principles were encapsulated by the Coalition's intention of allowing "the professionals who run our railways to apply innovation and enterprise". This was promising and suggested that the Coalition was prepared to act on a theme in the McNulty Review that Government needed to step back from its detailed role in managing the industry.

It didn't turn out that way. West Coast was the first franchise to be let under the new policy but key principles were nobbled within the Department for Transport before the competition got underway. Given that West Coast is an almost wholly commercial enterprise competing against airlines and car travel, and a huge revenue business to boot, this was not a welcome development. It is a franchise whose timetable quite simply should never be tightly specified, yet here were civil servants directing experienced commercial managers. Despite the circumstances FirstGroup, initially appointed the winning bidder in August 2012, had come up with some reasonable proposals. These included a package of small infrastructure schemes featuring several line speed projects which would have reduced journey times on the London-Glasgow route, among others. Astonishingly, the bid also involved a forecast that patronage would double to 60 million journeys per year over the 13-year franchise without, it seemed, commensurate investment; and committed to make £5.5bn in payments to the DfT over the life of the franchise. To many, it appeared there was no clear plan for how this would be achieved but it left the incumbent franchise holder, Virgin, trailing by £700m while the state-owned European companies competing, the Dutch and the French, found it too rich for their more conservative blood.

Astonishment would soon give way to farce when two months later Virgin successfully overturned the award, again showing its willingness to litigate, and sending the DfT into turmoil. It emerged that the civil servants had not understood how to evaluate aspects of the bids under the new policy and the systems in the department were chaotic. There were also suggestions of an institutional bias against Virgin which was widely regarded as having come off rather well in a series of one-to-one contract negotiations with the DfT – "stiffed them" as some put it. The lack of competence ran so deep that Transport Secretary Patrick McLoughlin cancelled the award to FirstGroup, suspended franchise procurement altogether and appointed Eurostar Chairman Richard Brown to review how it could be restarted. Meanwhile a review of the department's franchising capabilities by Centrica chief executive Sam Laidlaw, also a DfT Non-Executive Director, confirmed and embellished McLoughlin's initial views of his department's failings.

One striking finding related to the DfT's new policy on risk sharing. To deter the overbidding that had characterised the DfT's previous franchise awards a new arrangement had been introduced to replace the discredited cap and collar. The aim was to vary the premium payments operators offered in relation to fluctuations in GDP, protecting them against a major risk beyond their control but not against getting their sums wrong. A related change involved a requirement for franchise winners to provide a much higher financial guarantee to cover potential losses. In broad terms the DfT would base the guarantee required on financial risks in the bid. The system was being applied for the first time on West Coast, and Laidlaw found that the DfT had made a huge error in calculating the size of the guarantee it asked FirstGroup to provide. Instead of £190m it should have been £350m.

There was no disguising the anger in the industry. Quite apart from the DfT's inability to operate its own franchising system, several beneficial aims of the Coalition's policy had been blocked somewhere in the department. They included pledges from Ministers to give companies greater freedom to develop train service plans and an intention to place a significant weighting on benefits for passengers as well as price when awarding contracts. My friend and long-time business partner at FCP, Pete Wilkinson, summed it up along the lines of: "What this really tells us is all franchising is about is money, money, money, and that's the only way to win. You can have a bidder that offers nothing but a high payment and they'll win hands down against someone who's done something really innovative. Investment and innovation don't really count which tells me the system is broken in a pretty important way." At the time, Pete had been appointed to Richard Brown's review team. Things were so bad that initial estimates were that it could take 18 months for franchising to resume; in the event it restarted in six.

The embarrassment for the DfT didn't stop there. As part of his review, Richard Brown had recommended a further independent assessment into whether the DfT should retain its franchising responsibilities at all. It was led by Adam Jackson, brought in from the Department for Business and Skills. The review, which reported in December 2013, went further than Richard envisaged examining the organisation of all rail functions in the department. It was not a pretty picture. It showed that the DfT's approach to rolling stock procurement, specifying major projects and managing franchises was not sufficiently integrated in either strategy or delivery; neither within the department nor with the rest of the rail industry. As a first step Jackson set out a new integrated management structure for the DfT's rail team. His preference was for an arms-length Rail Delivery Authority with the specialist skills to co-ordinate all elements of the Government's rail activities. This would have been a good move but because no Parliamentary time would be available until after the 2015 General Election and despite Patrick McLoughlin accepting Jackson's recommendation, it never happened.

There were echoes in this of a debate that had occurred at the McNulty advisory Board. I recall an animated discussion about the desirability of creating an agency, at arm's length from Government, responsible for developing and overseeing the implementation of national rail strategy. There was near unanimity that this would be a sensible and progressive step forward. However, Sir Roy had been told by Philip Hammond that such an outcome, redolent of a return to the SRA, was politically unacceptable. Instead, Hammond insisted on a mechanism that could be portrayed as private sector industry leadership in the shape of what became the Rail Delivery Group, representative of franchise operators and Network Rail. It didn't seem to occur to anyone that not all operators have the same commercial company interests and that this might impede the sort of dynamic strategic leadership the industry needed. Anyway the concept of a strategic agency was not recommended.

Meanwhile, in the wake of the West Coast debacle, operators had dropped all reticence in calling for wholesale reforms to the franchising system. There was broad agreement that the Brown Review should ditch 'one size fits all' franchise contracts and replace them with arrangements appropriate for different types of business. Proposals focused on creating commercial models that would provide operators with a long term view of their markets, incentives to innovate and develop higher quality services for passengers, and add social value. So for long distance businesses like West Coast with substantial competition from airlines and motorways, the consensus was to give operators commercial freedom to develop the market, meet customer expectations and promote service quality in a competitive arena. Proposals included 30-year concessions to be sold for an upfront sum, rather than franchised, whilst another model would see more than one concession offered to further promote competition as a means of driving companies to develop their business. These options would have been accompanied by considerable freedom to vary service levels to match demand and economic conditions, and relaxed fares controls to enable reform of outdated pricing and retailing preserved in industry regulations. No revenue protection or risk sharing would be offered because in a genuine commercial environment operators shouldn't need it.

How National Express East Coast and its passengers could have benefited from such a regime which would have offered the company a long term view, the incentive to protect its reputation and the ability to take proportionate steps to combat the economic downturn that contributed to the failure of the business! Instead the company had responded to its inflexible regime and escalating premium payments to Government with futile cost cutting and by attempting to milk passengers. Its tactics included scrapping the much-loved restaurant service and introducing a hated charge for making seat reservations. You might as well have asked Ryanair to run it.

For London commuter routes ideas included franchises up to 15 years depending on investment offered. To ensure a financially stable business that could continue to invest in quality, while preventing excess profits in a predominantly captive market, premium payments to Government could be reset at appropriate intervals to reflect economic conditions. There were also suggestions that operators should be free to propose changes to fares regulation if they improved value for money to passengers. Elsewhere, on regional franchises greater specification by transport authorities was floated to incentivise local investment, with contracts attuned to local requirements. The emphasis of franchising on these networks would shift from cutting subsidy to developing the railway to meet local economic and social policies. In such cases contracts up to 10 years might be offered but with high levels of subsidy and local involvement inevitable, franchising powers and revenue risk might lie with the regional authority. Devolving direct control of regional services had also been raised but not implemented in 2009 in the previous bout of soul searching over the virtual absence of mature social policy objectives in the DfT's train operating contracts.

Devolution had already proved successful on Merseyside and in London. In 2006, the mayor, Ken Livingstone, had won powers to franchise the inner London Silverlink Metro services. They had been neglected before privatisation and continued to be so afterwards as National Express focused on developing the franchise's higher revenue commuter routes to Euston. The Cinderella nature of the metro routes changed dramatically with devolution. Transport for London's agenda was based squarely on modernising and expanding the railway and integrating it, not only with other modes, but with urban regeneration plans and business districts. The aim was to realise the potential of a run down, underused transport asset to support the economy and social opportunity and take pressure off the existing bus and Tube services. By any measure it has been a resounding success in managing and developing a city network[78] that serves a social and economic rather than commercial purpose. Needless to say Network Rail's protectionist culture saw it campaign hard against devolution, no doubt on the grounds that TfL had ambitions to determine infrastructure upgrades.

Despite the clear rationale for change, the Brown Review was something of a mixed bag. Essentially it was saying all the right things but not going far enough or with sufficient emphasis. An agenda to attract beefed up skills and judging franchise bids on quality weightings as well as price was clearly needed. However, a notable absence was true market distinction for long distance profitable franchises and where structural change was recommended it generally wasn't followed through. In reality, the one-size fits all system would remain.

In some ways, the lack of fundamental change was not surprising. A core part of the brief was to find a way for franchising to restart as soon as possible, which was

---

[78] Rebranded London Overground by TfL

achieved in March 2013 with Pete Wilkinson appointed as the DfT's Franchising Director, a very popular choice in the industry. I had several conversations with Pete before he took over and he was optimistic that it could be made to work. He was especially keen to stop the price war game franchising had been stuck in whereby exorbitant bids come in for precious little benefit for passengers. When the first franchises were let under the new system, he took things further requiring operators to set out how they planned to build management competence, keep pace with consumer trends and work more closely with communities to develop services. Closer working between track and train was another key objective, particularly with regard to infrastructure projects that were being implemented. Sadly, I think it is probably fair to say that under political and financial pressure from within Government, and letting franchises under a model and within a fragmented industry framework he probably doesn't believe in fully himself, things haven't worked out entirely as Pete would have preferred.

In a number of areas the Government failed to act. Devolution was a clear recommendation in the Brown review, but McLoughlin's successor, Chris Grayling, reversed an agreement to devolve significantly more services to Transport for London and in the English provincial regions six years after the Brown review, devolution is a halfway house at best. Neither has Brown's preference for a move towards smaller market based franchises happened. The Government also failed to heed recommendations on risk sharing and highly regulated short term contracts continue to be let and overseen centrally. You can tell that a procurement system to award contracts on a supposedly commercial basis isn't working if you keep adding to the specifications of what companies should seek to achieve. This is surely an acknowledgement that most urban and rural networks aren't commercial entities in the first place, while those that could be – particularly longer distance intercity services – are operating under a regime where companies don't have sufficient levers or incentives to understand and respond effectively to market needs themselves. Worst of all competition for contracts fell to its lowest level, a clear indication that the commercial basis of franchising is wrong.

The new policy of awarding contracts on quality and deliverability as well as price had mixed results too. While the DfT has specified higher service quality requirements, there was little emphasis on these factors in the way contracts were awarded under the new system, certainly in the initial batches, which cast quality and deliverability of companies bids as a tiebreaker when price was very close. Price remained the way to win, often with companies that needed to retain franchises seeming to bid against themselves.

The signs were there in National Express's retention of c2c in 2014, the first franchise awarded under the new system. By then it was the company's only remaining train operation and to retain it NEG offered the Department for Transport £1.1bn in premium payments, a sum that left rival bidders gobsmacked and briefing against both the company and the DfT. They had a point. The winning margin was over £300m, extraordinary given the size of the business; and as the temperature of the bidding war overheated again in the following years, NEG shrewdly exited the UK rail industry selling c2c to the Italian State Railway company Trenitalia for £72m. Trenitalia immediately started making losses following a downturn in rail travel. With payments to the DfT rising each year, and no risk sharing arrangements in place, it may well be that it remains loss making for the next decade. Having bought c2c to enter the UK market Trenitalia presumably considers itself to be in a position to grin and bear it rather than say "arrivederci".

On selling c2c in 2017, National Express Group chief executive Dean Finch said the extent to which the market had overheated meant he "saw no prospect of winning further franchises" on sensible terms. In a swipe at the DfT's policy he hammered home the message to analysts in the City of London stating that one of the reasons for the exit was that he wouldn't invest his personal money in a transport group involved in UK rail. Reflecting on the strong prospects companies were continuing to insist their franchises enjoyed at that time, despite the downturn in rail travel, he continued: "I earnestly hope no one of that view is managing my investments." Furthermore, he pointed out that NEG's substantial overseas interests meant the company had choices of where to play and other markets offered significantly better prospects with lower risks. It was not a position any of the other private sector UK transport groups enjoyed, perhaps explaining the bids several of them had entered into that appeared to be more generous to the taxpayer than to their own shareholders. For National Express it wasn't a painful exit. It was a triumphant one.

It is worth reflecting on why private sector companies involved in franchising have continued to take significant risks with their shareholders' money. Perhaps as Go-Ahead's former chief executive Keith Ludeman once frankly stated: "It's everyone's best chance to make a lot of money." Perhaps too the relatively small UK companies involved have not diversified significantly into new markets for the past decade and therefore depend on franchises for a substantial proportion of their earnings. They are huge contracts by any definition, probably the biggest the public sector lets outside major defence procurements. This creates a dependency and if a company's position is eroded by losing franchises, it builds pressure to win. Eventually a "must win" competition comes up. Keith was also honest enough to admit that the only certain thing about the revenue forecasts that underpin companies' bids is that they would be wrong one way or the other, most likely by a substantial amount creating the risk of a disastrous failure. Just as it is the best chance to make a lot of money, it is the best chance to lose a lot as well.

Under the structure of franchising that has prevailed since 1995 companies are essentially placing a bet. As passenger numbers and revenue have grown over the years it is an increasingly dangerous one, especially under the structure put in place after the Brown review. Not only did it fail to provide any effective risk sharing mechanisms in the event of a downturn in patronage, it put companies on the line for huge sums. Keen to avoid the political embarrassment of companies walking away from franchises, the Government insisted that they provide massive financial guarantees to cover potential losses. It hasn't been enough to stop one franchise going under with others looking on the verge of it. FirstGroup's winning bid for TransPennine in 2015 displayed all the old trends of a company overbidding for a contract it was desperate to win. The cost to FirstGroup so far is £100m. Stagecoach fared even worse losing over £200m when East Coast collapsed for the third time in 2018. Serial overbidding is another indication of flaws in the way contracts are structured that does no one any good and nothing for developing the long term value of the franchise.

Over the last three years the rail industry has been in an almost permanent state of review. We have had the Bowe Review on planning enhancement schemes, the Shaw Report on Network Rail, the Gibb Review on Southern, the Glaister Review of the failed timetables changes in May 2018, and some others too. It would not be a useful contribution to today's debate to go into a blow by blow account of these but there are many overlapping themes. These are reflected in the well-trailed issues the Williams Review is investigating such as an integrated, whole system approach to decision making, clarifying accountabilities and the need for customer-centric (market-focused in the language of Sectorisation) decision making.

One issue that does not seem to have been highlighted sufficiently strongly in any of these reviews is how the relationship between Network Rail and the operators should work. A point that struck me was made by Collette Bowe's review of the planning process for the behind schedule and over budget electrification schemes back in 2015. Straying deliberately outside her remit, she noted the importance of operator involvement in scheme development and delivery and recommended: "In enabling the department to make informed decisions about scheme development, Network Rail should be required to demonstrate that it has actively involved operators and the supply chain in the development of investment schemes including specifically in the planning of how they will be delivered." This is obviously correct, but I would go much further. At times there has been talk of Network Rail getting closer to its 'customers', the train operating companies, through organisational realignment. Currently a further attempt at creating a form of alliance is planned on the East Coast Main Line to the extent that the Secretary of State has said that the entire future structure of a new "partnership franchise" could be based around it. Thus far, however, no realignment has taken place that I can see to genuinely recognise the importance of the train operator as prime. This is despite some bold and welcome structural changes emanating from the desk of Andrew Haines at Network Rail.

Primacy of the operator is vitally important because it is the train company that exists to identify and meet the needs of its customers; the TOC best understands the market in which it operates. Looking at some of the issues that added risk and delay to the delivery of the electrification schemes that were the subject of Bowe's report, they include misaligned procurement of infrastructure and rolling stock, early cost estimates based on historic data; and funding allocation based on incomplete design work. It is tempting to speculate on how much better the outcomes might have been had electrification schemes been developed as part of business plans submitted by train operating companies with long term contracts and planning horizons; and whose bottom lines would have seen the benefit. Equally, when the Government cancelled parts of the Midland Mainline electrification, it sought to justify its decision in part on the basis that new bi-mode technology would fulfil the same benefits as full scale electrification. Putting aside whether this rationale was justified, how much more sensible it would have been for a train operating company to have made such a decision as part of an integrated trains and infrastructure investment case. Indeed open access operator Hull Trains has made exactly this decision in the light of its own attempts, frustrated by Network Rail, to electrify the route via Selby to Hull.

Giving train operators such space would, of course, require a radical change in Network Rail's culture to cast itself as a supplier to the train operators. The issue of its centralised management goes back to the company's formation and is now being addressed with some vigour by Andrew Haines. But up to now, the company has been able to resist all attempts at change, most recently following Nicola Shaw's report on the *Future Shape and Financing of Network Rail*. Nicola's principal recommendations included restructuring the company to devolve genuine authority to Network Rail's routes so they could operate as independent divisions; take on new responsibilities from HQ including planning enhancement projects; and work jointly with operators and communities to set and meet locally-agreed targets. Network Rail HQ would be recast as a support services unit to the routes. In effect this was an extension of the company's existing devolution plan with a suggestion that Chief Executive Mark Carne should get on with it. Like his predecessor as Network Rail Chief Executive, David Higgins, he appeared to support it but didn't make it happen. Incredibly when Andrew Haines took over he was appalled to find that there was a specific remit within the company to 'Kill Shaw', a revelation that, when I heard it, rendered me speechless.

Instead the ideas pursued following the Shaw Report through joint route supervisory boards, notably on the Western Route under the chairmanship of Dick Fearn, were no better than the virtual integration initiatives of the mid-2000s. Worthy and well intentioned, they were a poor substitute for institutional integration. As a former Chief Executive of vertically integrated Irish Railways I doubt whether Dick would have advocated the Great Western model to be applied in the Republic. As he pointed out in an interview published in 2008: "We're not arguing about contracts. Everyone points in the same direction". Dick was clearly an integrationist and one hopes that he continues to press the benefits sitting alongside Keith Williams on the latest review team.

Integration is once again firmly back on the agenda and there is a clear mood for change in the industry and among politicians. Chris Grayling, a Tory Secretary of State wants to see it; and the Labour Party is an advocate too. Network Rail's Chairman Peter Hendy supported track and train integration for the London Underground when in charge at TfL where his predecessors fought hard to try and fend off a public private partnership model that would have created a separation there and which subsequently collapsed under the weight of its own contractual complexities. The arrival of Andrew Haines as Chief Executive of Network Rail augurs especially well. His recently announced devolution proposals for the organisation herald a substantial movement in the direction of a close alignment with train operations at route level. At the same time they genuinely seek to place professional capability at the sharp end of running railways whilst restricting the power of central management to gate crash the party. Crucially his proposals are capable of being re-shaped without major dislocation to whatever structures emerge either from the Williams Review or from the political parties as they limber up for the next General Election.

What could possibly go wrong?

CHAPTER TEN

What Next?

When I started writing this book I was unaware that yet another review of railway industry structures was in the offing. Yet strangely and entirely by coincidence my concluding chapter was always going to be about that very subject. Indeed if you have got this far, it will have become very apparent that structure is a thread running through the whole narrative of the book.

Neither did I set out to write a book with the particular intention of influencing the outcome of railway policy. Rather my aim was to document what I have experienced and witnessed over a half century, a period long enough not just to describe an industry at a dramatic period in its history, but to also draw some conclusions. The book was to be a personal account of events whilst at the same time offering up opinions about what structures have worked and what have not. Along the way I have sought to test my opinions against those held by others who have been centrally involved in the development and management of the structures and organisations that the politicians have at various times determined.

As publication approaches the Rail Review commissioned by a Conservative Secretary of State is being undertaken at the very moment that the Labour Party is developing its proposals for taking the railways back into various forms of public ownership. It seems reasonable and timely in the circumstances to see this book as a contribution to the thinking of those who now seek to shape the industry in which I have worked for the whole of my life. I hope that the account of events and experiences that I provide adds ballast to my conclusions.

So where do we go from here? The first thing I would say is that the direction of travel should not be backwards. The way ahead must take account of the realities of the present and of the economic, social and environmental objectives that as a country we seek to meet in the future. Given that meeting future objectives in railways rarely relies on investments with less than a thirty year life, it is fair to say that this period represents the minimum timescale for defining the future. That means we need structures that encourage long term strategic thinking and investment.

Railways came into existence because of new technologies. They became both economic and demographic stimulators very quickly. It is no exaggeration to say that railways shaped the country as it exists today and that there is a symbiotic relationship between them, the economy and society. It is also the case that after a period of relative decline brought about by advances that gave a competitive edge to other forms of transport and distribution, the railways have returned centre stage and face a future every bit as exciting and influential as they did in the Nineteenth Century.

Whilst the 1997 privatisation of British Rail appeared to be an end in itself, not serving any clearly articulated strategic objective other than a change of ownership, it is surely remarkable that very soon afterwards the railways became more centrally directed than at any time before. It was Blair's Labour Government that set the new tone to achieve economic and social objectives and to back it with money and although Hatfield diverted much of its intended investment into unexpected areas, the money kept coming. Following the change of Government in 2010, it continued to come: so much so in fact that in public forums and industry lectures that I have given over the last decade I have questioned whether the railway industry is privatised at all. The transfer of Network Rail to the public sector and the more recent creation of public sector operations on the

East Coast Main Line simply provide reminders that the rail system is ultimately dependent on public money and is effectively one the shape and purpose of which is determined by Governments.

This is unlikely to change, however much Right leaning politicians may wish it were not so. With HS2 in the offing and already politically controversial; with Crossrail publicly funded though not yet completed; with environmental considerations even more to the fore than ever; and with Brexit prompting Government to consider its future industrial strategies for Britain, it is crystal clear that the strategic objectives for the railways will continue to be set by Governments and that these will need to be delivered by mechanisms and organisations that are fit for purpose. It is equally clear that these do not currently exist.

To me it is difficult to envisage that strategic development of the railway over the next thirty years can easily take place within a construct in which the private sector takes the lead: rather the reverse. Any ongoing private sector role is most likely to be in the role to deliver the specifications and objectives set by Governments. That is not to say that any private sector role has to be insignificant given that investment in the network and in trains could potentially be financed either directly or indirectly, in full or in part, privately. But at the end of the day it is Government that stands in readiness as backstop to failure and it is Government that will ultimately take the financial risk. Government will almost certainly continue to provide public funds in the form of asset investment and in subsidy if its strategic objectives are to be met.

Fifty years ago the railway was seen as a public utility. In the way of water and energy it remains a public utility; but one in which modern and increasingly innovative improvements to customer service have been introduced. It seems to me that the emphasis on customer service has been the biggest single improvement in the development of rail services that has taken place over the past quarter of a century during which passenger services have generally been franchised. In the early years of franchising this was especially clear and in my opinion might have overtaken the more traditional role of a railway serving the wider public interest had it not been for a change of political emphasis in the late Nineties. The extent to which parties of all colours have come to accept the role of Government in determining the strategic role of railways has been a stand-out feature of what has happened over the last quarter of a century. Public interest and public service aspects of service provision are now every bit as important as individual customer service, if not more so, than they have ever been before. Franchise specifications reflect that.

That this has happened under Governments of all colours is significant; and a harbinger of what can be expected (indeed what is necessary) in future. The Government's economic and environmental objectives will reinforce the trend to such public control. However, this will almost certainly take on a very different form in future than it has in the past because it is increasingly obvious that for the country to succeed economically and to do so more evenly and without risk to political schism, forms of regional and sub national government will need to be put in place. We have already witnessed this working successfully in Scotland, Wales and London, and recognition is now being made elsewhere of the necessity to create similar devolved structures in England. This political change will affect rail.

As it happens (let us call them) potential "regional" governmental structures fit very well indeed with the more integrated forms of railway operations that are manifestly required. It is surely now beyond doubt that the separation of the management of track from train has not served the country well. The impetus to create regional devolution politically brings with it the possibility of creating railway organisational devolution to fit. Handily there is significant coincidence of regional political and economic interest with the ways in which railways are best operated. Regional rail management units would be large enough to stand alone for the vast majority of all railway operational and infrastructure activity. Scotland is already well down that particular road and other regions, especially in England, are at least as big so as to be pretty much self sustaining. This would apply to a Northern Region covering the country between Cheshire, Humberside and the Scottish Border, for example. It would apply too to the East and West Midlands; and to the South West. Remember too that these railways are substantial in their own right. When I ran Network South East I liked to point out that the size and scope of the railway in a region that comprised nine self contained management companies, was equivalent to the whole of the Dutch Railway system. Last time I looked at that, not only was it doing rather well but it had also summoned up enough resource and energy to take on slices of the UK passenger franchise market as well.

It is to be hoped that the Williams Review provides the impetus necessary for railways to be aligned in ways that create synergy with the economic development areas that form the basis for much regionally focused activity in terms of industry, employment and housing. Whether regionally elected governments are created at the same time seems unlikely given the snail's pace at which our democracy seems to develop, but it would be entirely logical; and at some time in the not too distant future, highly probable that it will come about. The inhabitants of the English regions, especially those furthest from the capital, are unlikely to put up with the London-centric and over centralised form of Government we have. I write as one such inhabitant, and believe me this is a topic that has risen to the very top of the agenda in the North in much the same way that it did in Scotland in the 1980s. In fact the Scottish experience has thrown into sharp focus what is perceived to be the unfairness of resource distribution to the English Regions. Add to this the perception of London and the South East receiving very much more per capita transport funding than other parts of the country and the momentum towards regional government grows ever stronger. Perhaps the further damage being wrought to the country's politics by the Brexit debate may inspire faster moves to change the ways in which Britain is governed. Greater devolution could emerge as one of the outcomes.

So we come to money. Without doubt one of the major benefits of recent years has been Government's willingness to fund the railway to historically high levels of investment despite its sometimes questionable value for money. Coupled with it has been the implementation of forward funding frameworks that were denied British Rail. The adoption of the so-called SOFA mechanism[79] has been one of the more progressive and helpful measures to be introduced in recent years. The parallel introduction of what is known as the HLOS[80] has also served as a valuable tool in planning railway investment in order to meet social and economic objectives. The Scottish Government too produces its own HLOS and SOFA, and if this were to be replicated in the English Regions and in Wales it would be a major step forward. In short a commitment to continued public investment within financial control periods through both the HLOS and SOFA mechanisms is necessary for the future. If the funding horizon could be lengthened to at least seven years it would provide a massive boost to forward planning and the cost effective delivery of projects.

---

[79] Statement of Funds Available, or SOFA is a mechanism by which Government gives a three year forward commitment to the cash it is prepared to inject into the railway.

[80] High Level Output Statements which are used by Government in London and Edinburgh to articulate their delivery expectations in return for the money they invest.

Government won't find this easy. The Treasury can be expected to resist, and the mandarins there will find it especially difficult within a structure of devolved government in which regionally based transport authorities take responsibility for their own internal transport arrangements. But it must be done and if it is accompanied by the realisation that the current separation of track and train is wasting money, this could ameliorate the suspicions. Some comfort can surely be derived from the success of devolved structures in London, Scotland and Wales; more so probably by the incredibly effective Passenger Transport Authorities and Executives that have flourished since they were first mooted in 1968. They have brought a remarkable transformation to metropolitan areas and played a key role in regenerating deprived and neglected economies. They should provide confidence that bolder devolution would be likely to prove effective.

Various events described in this book demonstrate the frequent occasions since 1997 that the separation of track and train (and often too the separation within track; less so within train) has not only brought about financial shocks but both safety and performance disasters as well. A similarly inefficient form of separation of the parts also existed within British Rail prior to the development of sector management in the 1980s and this too I have described earlier in the narrative. So I have no hesitation whatsoever in stating that all of those railway activities that are essential to optimise performance in its various dimensions must be put into entities that direct, control and manage all the constituent parts.

Doing this regionally would work best but what of the strategic routes that are essential to bind the nation together? These will undoubtedly require focused management of their own within policy parameters set by the UK Government (working closely with the national governments of Wales and Scotland, as well as with the

English Regions) and this necessitates the recreation of an overarching strategic body (a slimmed down SRA if you like) to co-ordinate the rail strategies necessary to achieve the High Level Output Statements determined by Governments and regionally based transport authorities which, let it be stressed, are every bit as interested, if not more so, as central Government, in guaranteeing and enhancing links with other parts of the UK.

In addition there will remain a role for some network wide activities to be determined through the mechanism of national rail bodies, though probably not through the means of the same Strategic body. There is no case to dismantle the overarching safety review and monitoring mechanisms that already exist. Some operating and engineering standards too will need to be determined nationally, though others could be determined regionally, getting us away from an expensive "one size fits all" mentality. Many standards, especially in technical fields, are already determined by groups of professionally qualified managers meeting together to consider the evolution of best practice and this would not change. Indeed it needs to be encouraged.

None of this implies the need for the retention and certainly not the creation of large bureaucracies sitting atop the industry handing down the tablets like Moses to the Israelites. My own experience, as illustrated by some of the situations described earlier in this book, demonstrates the importance of clear accountability within devolved structures. When objectives are clear and when accountability is too, the railway works better than when these things are fudged, or contractualised; especially when the activities necessary to achieve them are managed by a myriad of companies, each with its own commercial interests and objectives. I have lost count of the number of times I have read Regulator or Industry reviews that talk about "perverse incentives". In fact the use of the word "incentive" in the context of trying to achieve a desired outcome (let us say a railway that runs on time) is by definition an admission that the system in place is unlikely to achieve the objective without an incentive to do so. This is indicative of a fundamentally flawed process and as I write this I find myself reflecting on how on earth it is that we have created a situation where financial incentive is seen as the essential ingredient in making things work better. It is surely a poor substitute for straightforward accountability that in a less fragmented structure would be the mechanism that drove improvement. It is fragmentation that has diluted accountability. It is the fudging of accountability that is at the heart of the industry's problems.

So what might new structures look like?

The "geography" is a matter of political choice. The North (including Merseyside), Midlands, Wales and Scotland might be said to define themselves. South of the Thames, either in the form of the Southern Railway of old, or as three self contained entities based on the current South Eastern, South Central and South Western franchise areas, these are all units substantial and resilient enough to flourish as integrated railways. East Anglia too is of a size to stand alone. Elsewhere the branch lines of the West of England, including the Cotswolds, would align most obviously with the Great Western Main Line operation, whilst Midland Main Line and local services around Nottingham and Derby, and in Lincolnshire, could follow a similar pattern.

This leaves us with the two Anglo Scottish routes, Cross Country services and few others. Given the pressures on capacity, West Coast could include all services into Euston and East Coast those operating into or via Kings Cross/St. Pancras low level. The West Coast configuration could include Chiltern as well, although there is an argument for this operation aligning with Great Western. It could go either way, depending on the choice made by politicians. Either choice would be valid. Within these large integrated entities there would remain scope for individual market or community based services to be separately managed. So Chiltern services would retain a separate train operations management. Neither would it make sense to manage the whole of the West Coast as a single railway when within it there are services focused on particular communities and markets. London commuting must be commercially defined and managed in London, for example. Manchester and Liverpool have their own needs too.

These larger regional entities provide a high degree of operational integrity combined with the potential capability to manage the vast majority of activities within their boundaries. Cutting the cake in this way would allow each entity to focus on building up its resources from within and would in particular provide the context in which staff and managers from all railway departments would re-learn what has been lost as a result of the separation and fragmentation that has been the hallmark of the last twenty years. It is a tragedy, and not the fault of the individuals themselves, that so many managers in the industry today have such limited career experiences that "they don't know what they don't know". This needs to change. It won't happen overnight but it will happen over time and my guess is that the period of time would be much shorter than some might imagine.

There is one model from the past that could be applied more or less immediately. The former BR model whereby infrastructure services were provided to train operating companies on a "supplier to customer" basis is one that has a lot to commend it as a means of making early progress towards a more integrated system. Indeed the re-organisation proposals offered up by Network Rail under CEO Andrew Haines provide the basis for just such an approach. The concept of devolved regional infrastructure bodies capable of being self sustaining for the vast majority of infrastructure activity could work well provided that route organisations exist within them that have the ability to determine resource activity and to focus on individual markets. What we most definitely do not need is a regional structure that adopts a big brother approach to the routes within it because these need themselves to be as closely aligned by essential function as practicable. In that sense a Network Rail Region providing certain functions (say project management or heavy engineering capability for example) would effectively be a "supplier" to a Network Rail route as a surrogate for the train operator.

The virtue of Haines' ideas is that they enable other options to develop in due course. In time truly "vertically integrated" models could evolve, whereby all train operations within a defined market are under the same management as the infrastructure activities that sustain them. In the meantime, the greatest benefit of all would be the development of a shared understanding of the dynamics of the interaction between a business and its various production elements. This was the clear benefit that arose when BR moved towards a similar alignment in the late 1980s and early 90s. It is what the industry has lost since 1994 and what it desperately needs to recover.

Fools rush in where angels fear to tread so I now come to the highly charged political issue of ownership. At this point in the narrative I adopt the role of "consultant" in the hope that I won't myself be seen as politically motivated. Whilst the exact boundaries of the integrated route based "companies" remain arguable at the margins, they nevertheless make sense under pretty much any form of ownership. So if asked as "a consultant" how these entities would work given different political choices, I would say that their geographical and organisational shape should not alter significantly in either scenario since they are large enough to be self reliant, including the management of major risk.

For those on the free market side of the political divide, franchising or the contracting out of train operations could remain as options (though franchising is increasingly seen as making a limited contribution in its currently highly prescribed form), whilst long term concessions for managing the infrastructure could be let at the same time. This has echoes of the Morton joint ventures promoted in the early 2000s. Outright sale would not be precluded either. Whether such structures, which would remain heavily reliant on government support (and therefore almost certainly subject to political interference), would be likely to attract private investors or public trust is an open question. I doubt it personally but long term concessions could provide such a framework for those looking for this type of outcome. Elsewhere, on the major intercity routes fans of the "free market" might prefer to promote the idea of companies in competition, something which the Rail Development Group has advocated in its submission to the Williams' Review. In such a case it would almost certainly be necessary to retain a separation of infrastructure management from the train operation, something that would appeal to "refusniks" at Network Rail. However, provided these are as closely aligned as possible in terms of the route geographies it is unlikely that anti-competitive factors would intrude. There is a common interest between competing companies in what they require the infrastructure to deliver.

The public sector model is easier to formulate, simply because all risk is self contained and ultimately lies with Government. Given that the infrastructure is to all intents and purposes publicly owned and controlled anyway, the model is already half way there. In this model the political and operational aspects of running railways would be much more closely aligned and in the provincial regions would be pretty much self-contained. Government would have to determine the mechanisms for cycling funding to them but could do so initially very much in the way that is currently done for London, Scotland and Wales, though I would hope for a bolder outcome that one day brings regional government back into the equation. Cash for the strategic "national" routes" would be funded via a rail authority of some kind; probably one that is not far removed from a slimmed down SRA. The same body would pull together and oversee the implementation of the rail transport policies determined by central and regional governments, thus removing from the Secretary of State, and the civil servants, the somewhat ludicrous responsibility of running the railway.

Within both models there remain options for raising finance (public and private) and for the involvement of private sector companies if that is a political choice. There is even a remaining role for an industry Regulator or Arbiter as protector of passenger interests and of freight, which could remain as presently structured, according to political preference.

Whichever option is chosen would be a substantial step forward from a railway where Westminster politicians are more central to determining outcomes than ever before in peacetime. Neither nationalised nor privatised but a hybrid, the limitations of which are now all too clear to see, the industry hardly even passes muster as a public-private partnership. Top priority is to move away from the overly centralised, unresponsive, slow moving, inefficient railway that "privatisation" has become; one that is more expensive to fund than it needs to be. If anything central control of the process has limited the role of the private sector and denied us the benefits of what the private sector might have been able to do. At the same time "industry knowledge" and the "corporate memory" have been so diluted that it is open to genuine doubt as to whether private sector companies yet have the knowledge and expertise necessary to take on what is required; not least in terms of the financial and reputational risk. Meanwhile Network Rail's performance like Railtrack's before it has been hampered by a lack of railway experience at the top of the company. This has become a serious drag on industry performance and must be reversed as soon as possible now that the people in charge there know what they are doing.

It is now beyond doubt that other than in defined, exceptional circumstances where Government wishes to promote competition, the separation of track and train management should not be allowed to continue other than as a stepping stone to a phased integration.

The record of the railways over the last half century provides ample evidence of what has worked and what manifestly has not. I hope that the personal account I have been able to give in these pages supplies that evidence. I hope that it will serve to stimulate the interest of those who, like me, care about this country's railways in the reforms that need to be made to put things right. I hope that the book provides strong pointers to those who have the fate of the industry in their hands. Well intentioned politicians mucked it up in the 1990s. Their successors have since acknowledged the failings on many occasions since but they have not as yet taken the bull by the horns to sort out what they know to be wrong.

We have reached a defining point and our politicians must not walk away from what needs to be done.

ABOUT THE AUTHOR

John Nelson has 50 years continuous experience of Britain's railways at the most senior levels. At the time of their privatisation he occupied the top job in BR's largest business, Network South East, overseeing its break up. With this completed he moved into the private sector establishing the First Class Partnerships management consultancy, quickly attaining global reach. He championed the start-up of "open access" train companies one of which, Hull Trains, has operated high speed services on the prestigious East Coast route for nearly 20 years. He has advised Government, The Rail Regulator, the Chief Executives of the former Strategic Rail Authority and many others in the UK and abroad, including a joint US Congressional transport committee. He was a member of the advisory Board established by Sir Roy McNulty to look into ways of providing better value for money from Britain's railways. He currently chairs transport consulting company Flash Forward and is a Director of "Passenger Transport" magazine. He has been a regular commentator, speaker and columnist since privatisation. Previous publications include "Britain's Privatised Passenger Railways 1998 – a practical assessment" of the bids made by those who acquired the first passenger franchises; and "Voters' Limits", a study of the history of Parliamentary constituencies in London, published in 2015.

Lightning Source UK Ltd.
Milton Keynes UK
UKHW011102111220
374897UK00005B/865